18-13-05

Writing for Her Life

Writing for Her Life
The Novelist Mildred Walker

RIPLEY HUGO

UNIVERSITY OF NEBRASKA PRESS
LINCOLN AND LONDON

Publication of this volume was assisted by
The Virginia Faulkner Fund, established in
memory of Virginia Faulkner, editor-in-
chief of the University of Nebraska Press.

An excerpt of this biography was
previously published as "Mildred Walker:
A Biography-Memoir" in *Cutbank 50*
(fall 1998), Missoula MT, 90–106.

The letters of Joseph Kinsey Howard
(outgoing correspondence, 1917–51) are
quoted in chapter 5 with the permission
of the Montana Historical Society Archives
(MC220, Box 1, Folder 2).

Permission to reprint materials from
the Mildred Walker Schemm collection
(#1393) has been given by the
American Heritage Center at the
University of Wyoming.

Library of Congress Cataloging-in-
Publication Data
Hugo, Ripley S.
Writing for her life : the novelist
Mildred Walker / Ripley Hugo.
p. cm.
Includes bibliographical
references and index.
ISBN 0-8032-2383-8 (cloth : alk. paper)
1. Walker, Mildred, 1905–98. 2. Women
and literature—Montana—History—
20th century. 3. Novelists, American—
20th century—Biography. 4. Montana
—In literature. I. Title.

PS3545.A524 Z68 2003
813'.52—dc21   2002029134
[B]

For my mother and father

Contents

Illustrations

Acknowledgments

In writing this memoir of the novelist Mildred Walker I had wonderful support from my family. George and Janet Schemm and my niece Elise Schemm gave me encouragement in my first thinking about the subject and, as I wrote, provided me with their clear memories of Mother as well as papers and journals that she had saved. I thank them for their steady confidence. I had help, too, from Christopher and Denize Schemm and their children. A special thanks goes to my nephew, Oliver Schemm.

Thanks, too, to Scott Elrod, M.D., who offered me valuable insights at crucial moments in my writing and often a perspective of humor that I was in danger of losing; and to Deirdre McNamer, who read the first draft of the completed manuscript with utmost care, understanding what I was attempting to bring about and pointing out major questions still to be considered; and to James and Lois Welch, loyal and nourishing friends who listened and considered my half-formed thoughts for the book through all the years it took me to finish.

Without the interested and helpful readings by Caroline Patterson and Rachel Stansberry, as each chapter was completed, I would have floundered more often than I did. And without the unflagging efforts of Mark Ratledge to teach me to be computer literate, I would have been lost. I am indebted, too, to Kim Andersen, who read the finished manuscript and offered her professional skills to search out numerous and obscure permissions. And to Kristi Hager, who applied her expertise to selecting and preparing the photographs.

When I think of the encouragement and support I had in evoking the novelist Mildred Walker, I want to thank all of my friends in the Missoula community who listened to me describe different aspects of my effort as we walked and talked—especially Dorrit Kara-sek, Lorraine Hill, and Geoff Carlson. Also, my friend at a greater distance, Sharon Bryan, for her sympathetic reading. And then my cheering section—my daughter, Melissa Hansen, and my grand-son, Derek Hansen.

I would also like to thank the staffs of the American Heritage Center at the University of Wyoming in Laramie, who gave me ac-cess to the Mildred Walker Collection; the Louis Jefferson Long Li-brary at Wells College, Aurora, New York, for materials from their archives; the Montana Historical Society in Helena, for their per-mission to use Joseph Kinsey Howard's letters; and the Missoula Public Library for obtaining copies of reviews and short stories from the 1930s and 1940s.

Introduction

I first became aware that my mother was a writer one hot summer afternoon when I was about eight years old. My brother and I, with neighborhood friends, careened around our backyard waging a water fight. To escape a stream of water from the garden hose, I scrambled up the side of the house to an unscreened window and leapt down into the cool darkness of the room. I landed with bare, wet, muddy feet on five clean piles of typewritten paper carefully stacked on the floor under the window. I heard my mother's agonized and furious exclamation. Horrified at what I had ruined, I saw too clearly the scattered pages stretching across the floor right to Mother's feet, her dark, cherry-stained desk with the typewriter looming behind her. Each familiar object in the room accused me. When I dared to look up at her face, I saw her large brown eyes staring at me in angry disbelief.

When people exclaim to me about the privilege of growing up with my mother, the writer, I think of how my brothers and I grew up more keenly aware of a mother who insisted in her role (in the 1930s, 1940s, and early 1950s) of a doctor's wife in a Montana town of about 25,000 people; a mother whose merriment or pleasure in shared moments seemed reserved for an occasion; a mother who insisted on decorum, performance of correctness in front of those outside the family; a mother who dressed and held herself exactly as other children's mothers we knew, giving afternoon teas, selling tickets for the Junior League, conducting dinner parties at which we could overhear her entertaining guests with vivid, humorous descriptions of our latest escapades. A mother who was not easy to live up to.

But it is my mother the novelist whom I have been asked to write about. The attempt to see her first as a writer and second as a mother has brought back many glimpses of her that I didn't know I had—glimpses that do not form any steady narrative. Those moments come back to me in a scatter of images, complete with colors, sounds, and emotions. I think they are still with me because I have clung to them as moments that taught me who she was and about the ways in which I could or could not interest her in my immediate desperations or delights.

One beautiful afternoon last spring, I listened from my upstairs window to my nephew Oliver singing as he worked in the backyard. It was a comforting sound that brought back to me snatches of a lullaby Mother used to sing to us. She crooned it when we were protesting going to sleep or when we were sick. It is the only song I remember her singing to us. By the end of that spring afternoon so many years later, humming the melody to myself, I had all the words back in my head:

> *Baby's boat's a silver moon,*
> *Sailing through the sky,*
> *Sailing o'er a sea of dreams*
> *While the clouds roll by.*
>
> *Sail, baby, sail*
> *Out across the sea.*
> *Only don't forget to sail*
> *Back again to me.*

I had remembered the last two lines first, and with them came the long ago comfort they'd given me: "Only don't forget to sail / Back again to me." I remembered how sharp my relief had been in the darkened room that, having set me sailing, Mother still wanted me back. It is the strongest memory I have of her nurturing us.

I must have been at least five or six years old. Did I care so sharply about the song's wish to have me "sail back" because I already felt that I was a disappointingly naughty little girl? Very likely! But I wonder now if it had had something to do with rarely seeing her during the day. When we clamored into her room where she worked at her desk, she would settle a crisis sternly, or tell us she was busy, then send us off to play. I could have been not only a naughty child but also a child jealous of whatever was more absorbing to her than my brother and I.

Whatever feeling of rejection we children may have harbored, it would have been brief. We thought that was the way mothers were, busy doing mysterious things of their own. Our days were mostly monitored by the different women who lived with us and took care of the household. In the evenings when my father was home, we were all together—until our too early bedtime. We often listened to my father tell stories by a fireplace made of odd-sized bricks that jutted in and out from each other. When we would ask for just one more story, and my father would finally agree, it was:

> *I'll tell you a story*
> *About Minny Morrie*
> *And now my story's begun.*
> *I'll tell you another*
> *About his brother*
> *And now my story is done.*

As we were hustled off, whining our disappointment, we didn't know what lucky children we were, but we felt very secure.

As I grew older, I worried about those women of our daytime lives who lived in a room in the basement of the house and were never invited to join our evenings. (It didn't occur to me that they may have craved their privacy by the time evening came.) But somehow I came to know that in Mother's mind people lived on different social levels. I didn't or couldn't articulate to Mother how that bothered me. These women were my friends in the kitchen, though, where I was sent to learn domesticity. Later, I understood that that was how Mother worked it out in order to write steadily.

By the time my brother George and I were six and seven years old, Mother planned special outings with us. Summers, when Mother took us to our family cabin for a few days, she would take us firmly in hand (at least I felt that resolve in her), sandwiches prepared, to hike up on a nearby ridge—an expedition. Because she was with us, I know that we were eager to go, hot and tired though we would finally be when we found a rock in the shade to munch our peanut butter and jellies. Mostly, though, I remember her admonitions "not to fuss" and "not to dawdle." What mother goes on adventures with her small children without admonitions? Presumably, we learned this way. But when I, in my mid-thirties, took my children on such hikes, I could still remember how I had resented those chidings—as if Mother were not one of us, not also curious about a beetle hiding under a stone.

Those afternoons, I felt Mother's interest in finishing these moments with children in order to get back to her writing. "Did you resent her for that?" a friend once asked me. No, because we understood that to be the relationship one had with a mother. When we had returned to the cabin, my brother and I would disappear to our own pursuits, but still we knew our outing had been something she wanted to do.

While we were children, we did not know her to have longings or questions about life. Our own attempts to ask questions about why summer didn't last or why someone died were dismissed, kindly but firmly, giving me, at least, the impression that it was our obligation to be happily engaged in our own activities. We never asked about her writing because copies of her newly published novels were never out on a table to look at, not until late into our high school years. By that time, I think, we had assumed that we were somehow not eligible to ask. It was a strangeness that has taken my brothers and me a lifetime to understand.

But we did know that she wrote books: at dinner parties Mother enjoyed telling stories on herself about being a writer. She told the story of being accosted at a cocktail party by a large woman with a large voice who was hard-of-hearing. "And you are a writer! I know about your books. How do you do it with a husband and three children?" Mother replied, paraphrasing Sir Walter Scott, "I just go about it using rump power." And the woman shrieked delightedly, "My dear, you do? On rum?" Then Mother would laugh and say, "I left her, and the whole room, probably, thinking I kept myself soused on rum in order to write." Her listeners loved the story and concluded, I think, that it said something about her readers in Great Falls, Montana—themselves included.

What I did resent for the first thirty-five years was not my writing mother but my social mother. Shopping trips with her were the worst, especially to Great Falls's only department store, the Paris. Her verbal scorn for the clerk who didn't carry the right brand of stockings made me burn with eleven-year-old hangdog shame. And I resented, with silent rebellion as I grew older, her put-down of people who were "not the right sort." They seemed perfectly good people to me. Her characterization of me in "ready-to-wear" affected me in a different way: "What do you have that my little girl could wear? She is no Shirley Temple." I had not yet acquired irony. I only felt sadly lacking when my gawky, tomboy self, wearing wire-rimmed glasses and walking slightly bent forward because I was growing tall, was seen as difficult to fit. Neither did I have any way of realizing that Mother was making her status felt.

Whenever I was with Mother in public places, I had a dim hurt feeling that she was ashamed of me for my looks and that I should try to stay in the background. I hung back and walked several paces behind her. Of course she was irritated, told me to "keep up," and seemed to move even faster ahead of me down the aisle. I knew Mother was a beautiful woman, probably five feet six inches, and gracefully erect with dark brown hair usually piled high on her head. Her hair set off her large brown eyes in a heart-shaped face, eyes that were radiant when she was happy and fierce when she was displeased. I felt it strange that she should have me for her daughter.

While I understood that I was "a difficult child" in my mother's eyes, I had no such feeling about that with my father. For him it wasn't my lack of moral fiber that caused me to set the dinner table incorrectly or to knock over a full glass of milk. When I, about eight years old, complained about the injustice of a curling iron, he took me for a good short haircut like my brother's. I only remember my mother's displeasure when she saw the haircut, but a good number of years later, she told me with wry amusement that he had left me on the front porch with a box of chocolates to atone for his deed. Unlike our mother, Dad was mirthful about social strictures, at least around my brothers and me.

In those years we children depended on Dad's sympathy for our enthusiasms, our disappointments, our projects, and even our misguided attachments. He, too, had dark brown hair but clear blue eyes that invited confidences. He stood about five feet eight inches, his bearing very erect but approachable—so approachable that we felt he listened to us with intensity. His serious response seemed healing and his humorous response a kind of guidance. Some years later, when I was nineteen and in college, he and I were down in our small horse pasture, digging out Burdock plants by the roots. Hot, sweating, and newly fallen out of love, I announced that I was never going to marry. I expected a mild protest. Instead, Dad said, "I'm sorry to hear that. Someone's going to miss a lot of fun." I hadn't thought of that. And surely, we saw him deeply and consistently in love with our mother in those years. They were having "a lot of fun."

In our earliest years, Dad would turn a well-appointed, sedate family dinner table into an uproarious fest with a well-timed plot. When, one after another, we three children would be in trouble— for elbows on the table, napkins on the floor, or slouching, Dad would surreptitiously fill his teaspoon with water and, still looking at Mother, flip it at one of my brothers. He met the giggles and hoots that followed with exaggerated innocence, ignoring Mother's outraged protests. The solemnity of a polite supper suddenly evaporated, to our great relief.

But I remember these contrasts between what my mother insisted upon and what my father deliciously undermined in our childhood as only the beginning. As we grew older, we clung to his examples rather than to Mother's of what was acceptable and what wasn't. From Mother we received edicts, and we rebelled against them, most of the time, silently. She felt it was her place to teach us manners, of course, but they often seemed arbitrary and sometimes unbearable.

Again the contrast: I never saw my father condescend to another human being or speak disparagingly of that person afterward. When I was very young, I remember listening to a steady respect in his voice as he spoke with a waitress or the elevator operator in his office building. Perhaps I registered on his manner so strongly because, as I grew older, I dreaded Mother's tone of voice, sometimes imperious, that put someone "in his place." Dad's was the more comfortable, more reasonable way to go about life, I remember thinking. And his way taught us things we might never have known. Once in a while, Dad took us, one at a time, to listen to the colorful Italian man who ran a barber shop in the basement across the street from Dad's office. Without much urging, the barber told about his earlier days living in New York City as he cut Dad's hair. When we met someone we were shocked by or shrank from, Dad calmly offered us explanations, sometimes commiserations for the person. With him we came to understand the complexities of life as opposed to what seemed the rigidly black-and-white pronouncements of my mother. But that was my social mother, not my writing mother.

During Mother's prolific years of writing, she had steady encouragement from Dad. He read a manuscript before it was sent off to her former teacher in Michigan and then to her editor at Harcourt, Brace and Company. The only times that I heard their voices raised in sustained argument with each other were in discussions about a character or scene, coming from behind their closed door. In the twenty-eight years of their marriage before my father's death, Mother published ten of her twelve adult novels.

In writing this family memoir of my mother, I have been keenly aware of the two lives that she had always led: the one, essential to her sense of well-being; the other, essential to the strength and excitement of her writing. She kept the dimensions of her life as a wife and mother separate from the more daring dimensions of her life as a writer. I have come to believe that she took few risks and asked few questions of her life as a doctor's wife because she could do that brilliantly and safely in her life as a writer. I think that dichotomy has a part in the strangeness my brothers and I felt—that we were not included in her writing life because we fulfilled a role in her nonwriting life. Picture her three adult, married children obtaining copies of her novels from secondhand bookstores when we could find them.

I couldn't have guessed how Mother's grandchildren would know her as a writer in the years to come. By 1973, when Mother was sixty-eight and living in retirement in Vermont, she had ten grandchildren. They came to know, as they grew older, that their grandmother wrote books, but she never spoke of her books to them. Of course, in her eyes, they were too young to be interested. Except that in 1971, she gave the manuscript of her thirteenth soon-to-be-published novel, a juvenile, to my ten-year-old son, Matthew, to read. She was pleased that he was absorbed in it.

Some twenty years later, in 1994, Mother's youngest grandson, Oliver, wrote about her while he was attending the University of Montana in Missoula to take a degree in art. To complete an assignment, he wrote a study of his grandmother—a person who did something to change the impression he had had of her. He begins when he is six years old. He and his seven-year-old brother are left in Vermont with their grandmother while their parents and older sisters are away for a time. Oliver describes vividly how dismayed they were by the days stretching ahead of them: " 'Hello, Gran,' we sang in unison. . . . She took us by her gnarled twisted hands. Blue veins played on her arms, tendons moved like bolts. Her age obscured her person. All we saw were the endless rules, dinners lasting for eternity, and early bedtimes that robbed us of our fun." On the following Sunday, "Gran" announced that they were going to church. When the little boys protested loudly, "her thinning hair shook and her rubbery face grew red." Instead of going to church then, she said, they were to sit in chairs all day until suppertime. "Gran was serious about punishment we could tell," Oliver continues. She had them sit on the back porch in "two hard straight-backed chairs." Oliver describes his only relief, as the hours went by, in his thoughts as he watched the water running below them until Gran returned to give them lunch. Afterward, she showed them a photo of herself when she was about their ages: "A cracked black-and-white photo, a small girl in a white frilly dress stared back at us. She didn't look much fun then either."

Gran sits "in a comfortable chair" to tell them a story. When she was seven, "a scruffy old man" told her the story of the river. Small "river people" came to the peaceful world of the area, started to kill the fish with sharp fish bones they found, went on to use these weapons to kill small field animals in quantities, and multiplied to live in every surrounding brook and river. Finally, the peaceful trees, rocks, remaining small creatures, and water consulted; they decided that water would flood the banks every spring and drive out the avaricious "river people." Then Oliver writes: "Believe me, we never crossed her after that. Gran had rules and we followed them. She didn't tell us a story like that again. It was as if it was a one-time gift she was giving us. A glimpse into her world I could never enter or try to understand, until I was much older."

I have had to retell the story in Oliver's essay because when he gave it to me to read, I marveled that Mother would tell such a fierce story. She had never told her own children such an imaginative story! Oliver only smiled at the time, letting it stand. But just last year I asked him if I could repeat it for this biography. After a short silence, he said, "You know, Gran never told that story. I made it up." I expressed my surprise, and he explained, "Well, I knew she wrote books and so I thought, when I was six, she SHOULD tell us a story." That notion seemed an enterprising solution that Mother's own children never attempted, not even Christopher, Oliver's father.

In recent years it's been important to Mother's granddaughters to read some of her novels. They liked those novels they read, but had never imagined the grandmother they'd grown up with would be interested in the particular characters of her novels. So that makes two generations of us wanting to have a sense of our mother and grandmother the writer. I expect that would have been a matter of indifference to Mother. It was a novel of hers, not her literary persona, that she wanted understood. Several times in her later years she expressed her displeasure that her grandchildren had not wanted to read, she was sure, or talk to her about her thirteenth published novel, *A Piece of the World,* a juvenile set in Vermont. But that was a parallel, I think, with my brothers and my early feelings. By the time Mother's younger grandchildren were interested in reading her novels, they felt themselves too old for a juvenile. Perhaps someday, especially when they visit Mother's Vermont home, their teenage children will be encouraged to read it.

When I first began this family memoir of Mildred Walker, I had some of her letters, stories, and my memories of her with which to work. But one day in 1993 when Mother was eighty-eight, I asked her if she still had a particular letter from the actress Eva Le Gallienne. She said no, she thought she might have sent it to an archive in Wyoming, perhaps in Laramie. None of us in the family knew that she had sent her papers to the American Heritage Center at the University of Wyoming in Laramie in 1971 and had continued to do so through 1981. With Mother's permission I requested the catalog listing of her work held by the Center. I discovered that she had given the Center a manuscript or galley proof version of each of her thirteen novels and a hardcover edition of each; her handwritten notebooks for most of the novels; and correspondence, original reviews, and news clippings. These holdings go back to 1934 when she published her first novel, *Fireweed.* But in 1993 Mother expressed no interest in discussing the collection.

Also included in the archival collection are translations of Mother's novels. The first ten of her novels are in Swedish editions. Her third novel, *Dr. Norton's Wife,* chosen for the 1934 Literary Guild Award, appears in Portuguese, Norwegian, and Danish as well as Swedish. Her sixth novel, *Winter Wheat,* chosen for the 1944 Literary Guild Award, is the most translated—into French, German, Portuguese, Arabic, Hindi, and Swedish. *The Quarry,* her seventh novel, is in Italian as well as Danish and Swedish, and *Medical Meeting,* her eighth, is in German and Swedish. Mother must have been pleased by the wide range of her readers that these translations attest to, but we never saw these editions as children nor, in her later years, ever saw them arranged on a bookshelf. My brother Christopher once caught sight of them stored in a closet.

By the mid-1980s, Mother's novels were no longer in print. But in 1991, Montana novelist James Welch recommended to the University of Nebraska Press that they consider reprinting Mother's novel *Winter Wheat.* It had become a Montana classic over the years, available in several paperback versions up to 1984. Its publication in 1992 with an introduction by Welch was well received and encouraged Nebraska Press to reprint all of her novels, the thirteenth and last in the fall of 2001.

In 1995, Nebraska editor Willis G. Regier asked me to consider writing this biography. After thinking about the material that was available to me, I thought I could set forth Mother's attitude toward writing. Doing research in Mother's holdings at the American Heritage Center a year later convinced me that I could.

But more resources became available after Mother's death at ninety-three in 1998. My brother George and his wife, Janet, opened boxes that Mother had left packed for a number of years. They found nine journals that she had written from 1955 to 1989. It is in the seventh of these journals that she records, "I am writing for my life now." Each of these journals contains her hopes and disillusionments about the writing of her last novels, quotations from writers who seem to speak to her own writing, and her sense of where her life is going. They also look back at moments in her earlier years. It is because of reading these journals, and all the earlier material she saved, that I am able to give an interpretation of her writing life.

All thirteen of Mother's novels are set in one of three locales: New England, the Midwest, and the Rocky Mountain West. Vermont, the source of all her childhood impressions, is the setting for four of her novels, but they were not her early novels; they were the seventh, ninth, eleventh, and thirteenth that she published. When Mother married in 1927, she went to live in Michigan for six years. Her written notes and lectures about her writing indicate that she gathered ideas for the Midwest novels during these years. They were her first, second, third, fourth, and eighth. Mother lived the next twenty-two years in Montana, the setting for her fifth, sixth, tenth, and twelfth novels. The first of the thirteen novels was published in 1934, and the last in 1972, a span of thirty-eight years. After 1972, Mother wrote another novel and a collection of short stories, both set in Vermont. These remain in manuscript.

I have arranged the chapters of the memoir to emphasize Mother's use of her three main settings for the novels—those places in which she lived for a period of time. After chapter 1 of Mother's early life in Vermont, chapter 2 discusses the writing of her four novels set in Vermont. Of necessity, this pattern precludes a chronological rendering. This book then continues with a chapter on her life in the Midwest and a chapter on her earliest novels set in the Midwest. And so with Montana. The arrangement has been essential to my understanding of how Mother wrote. But Mother should have the last word on the question of place. She insisted at various times that it was not her settings but her characters who lived in those settings that were most important to her. However, if her setting influenced a character's life, she pointed out, then the setting was strongly present. In that sense, she conceded, she wrote a Midwest, Montana, or Vermont novel.

This biography sets forth Mother's impressions of her own living in these settings, side by side with her characters who emerged in these settings. Its structure has been determined by knowing her daily life but only discovering her writing life. I hope she would approve of my letting her tell what seems to me a triumphant story, especially through excerpts from her journals.

The Novels

First published with Harcourt, Brace and Company:

First published with Atheneum Press:

Writing for Her Life

I
Childhood in Grafton, Vermont, 1906–1922

An early photograph shows Mother as a wiry, determined child of nine years with a very direct gaze, large brown eyes, her rich brown hair in ringlets, held back by a ribbon. I see her curled up at one end of a log swing in the barn loft of a modest, old Vermont house, writing with a pencil on a pad of paper. "I knew I was going to be a writer all of my life," she has told us. In Vermont, the barn and the woodshed are joined to the house, but even now the loft is a place to be separate from the bustlings in the house, a separation she made clear she had coveted as a child.

Perhaps I can imagine her there so vividly because I have known that loft since my own childhood. The long log swing is suspended above a raised platform of the floor, warmly lighted on sunny afternoons by a ten-foot-high small-paned window that brings the green leaves of trees inside, their shadows moving on the rafters and walls. In the darker corners of the loft there are still large chests, some filled with quilts and some with documents, letters, old family photographs.

An open staircase to the side of the loft leads down to the barn floor. Mother used to sit halfway down the stairs where she could look into the stall of the family's buggy horse, Tony, a sorrel gelding with a white blaze. She talked to him about important things from there, she said, and sometimes she went back up to the raised platform and addressed him in orations.

On the west side of the barn runs a branch of the Saxtons River, the sound of the water over large brown stones reaching up into the loft. The family calls it Brown Brook because it is shallow in summer and easy to wade. Across the brook, a hay meadow, and beyond it the road angling from the village crosses the larger branch of Saxtons River through a covered bridge. From there the road climbs slowly up through tall hardwood and fir trees and patches of cool green maidenhair fern. A low narrow window in the loft looks out to the covered bridge. On the east side of the barn lies the main road—in Mother's childhood and ours, a quiet road, lined on each side by tall, white shuttered houses and people occasionally walking by, sometimes waving to a greeting from the loft. Later, that road would have a part in Mother's four novels set in the village of Grafton.

Mother, her older sister, Margaret, and their parents first began to summer in Vermont in 1906, when Mother was one year old. Their home was in Philadelphia, where her father was a Baptist minister, but Mother was a fretful baby in the Philadelphia heat, and this determined her parents to travel to Vermont each summer. Both parents had family nearby. Her mother had grown up in the valley of Brookline, Vermont, just twenty miles from Grafton. And her father's father had been born on the Walker homestead along the Saxtons River one mile downstream from Grafton. Two of her father's uncles had homes along the dusty village main street where, by 1916, the Reverend Walker and his wife bought a permanent summer home: the modest Vermont house with the barn attached and the loft above, the house they had been renting for several years. It is the house to which Mother retired, and it is now a second home to my younger brother, Christopher, and his family.

I think Mother chose Vermont as her cultural background early in her life. From her stories it was clear that the three summer months of a year in Vermont were far more important to her than the nine months of each year in which she lived with her family in Philadelphia, then Scranton, Pennsylvania. Almost all of the stories she told us were of Grafton and its townspeople. It is true that we walked the roads and paths with her and looked out the windows of the Grafton house at people passing as we never did in Philadelphia. Perhaps she chose Vermont as her touchstone rather than Philadelphia because when the family was in Vermont, she knew her parents as part of its history. Many of their stories became hers. And equally important, I have come to think, she saw her parents in Vermont as more interesting than they were in the restricted world of parsonage boundaries and religious obligations.

The old Sidney Holmes house, which the Walkers bought in 1916, was sold fully furnished, complete with a valuable library. The family story goes that the house was bought with Grandmother Walker's wedding fees, those monies traditionally offered the minister by a grateful groom and duly passed on to the minister's wife. Always with awe, Mother told how her father found a first edition of Harriet Beecher Stowe's *Uncle Tom's Cabin* in the inherited library. Mother formed a lifelong interest in the Holmes family connections to an earlier Vermont, and during a summer visit to Grafton years later, she found letters of a correspondence in the library that would become an important part of her historical novel *The Quarry*.

Mother's stories made her childhood in the early 1900s vivid to us. Each summer the Walker family took passage from Philadelphia and sailed up the coast as far as Brattleboro, Vermont, then rode a train inland to Saxtons River, Vermont, where they stopped at a local stable, hitched Tony to their buggy, and drove the last twelve miles to Grafton. On one of their return trips by the same route, their ship sprang a leak in the night. Mother told us of their being awakened in the dark and advised to be ready to go down in the lifeboats. Her mother sat calmly before a mirror, piling her collection of jewelry on the top of her head in the coils of her hair, pinning it firmly, then covering it with her hat. Her father insisted that the family sit down to a breakfast of oatmeal and bow their heads for grace in the midst of the excitement of the other passengers crowding to the rail out on deck. "We were the only family eating breakfast in the dark dining room," Mother would remember in a tone of both dismay and respect. She was allowed to carry her pet rooster from the summer in a cardboard box, and she remembered a sailor who helped her down the rope ladder, being careful to keep the cardboard box from swinging out over the water.

Most of the photographs, too, like the stories, show Mother in Grafton. As a toddler she is usually with her protective sister, both dressed in white dresses with many petticoats, perhaps having just come from church services. There are photographs of large family picnics, a tablecloth on a long table spread with oval platters of fried chicken, gleaming ears of corn, heaping bowls of salad, tall white pitchers. Usually a croquet game is going on in the background. Later on, Mildred stands with a playmate, frowning into the summer sun. Once she is beside a cart hitched to a large shaggy dog.

Mother often said that her sister, seven years older, was proud of taking care of her, making up games to play and purposefully instructing her in how to behave. When they washed dishes out on the back summer porch overlooking the brook, Mother remembered, Margaret named the knives as fathers, the forks as mothers, and the spoons as children. We were told this matter-of-factly as if anyone could see the sense of it. And this same older sister made up games to keep Mother amused in church—folding a handkerchief into a small white mouse to run up her sleeve or under her wide belt or widening her eyes at something that wasn't there on Mother's Sunday dress. These antics made Mother smile whenever she described them to us.

She liked telling us of her rebellious moments, too. One summer evening her mother got out the pots and pans and her father brought in brimming baskets of peaches. The narrow kitchen was already hot from the wood stove. Mother said she did not want to help peel the sticky peaches. Her father looked at her sternly. "Well then, you cannot stay down here and have fun with us. You will have to spend the evening in your room." Mother wandered off upstairs to her room, feeling shut out, and listened to her sister laughing and talking with her mother and father as they worked away.

I've found an early essay of Mother's among her papers that describes an intimacy she has always felt for the Saxtons River running by the Walker house. The essay's title is "A Child Beside a Pool." It begins with the colors of stones that a child could see with her face down close to the clear water on a summer day. Then Mother characterizes the river from a grown woman's perspective:

> It is drawn always toward the sea and hurries to that end
> as a child hurries toward maturity. It runs with Time;

there is no beating it. First I was seven, then twelve, then seventeen, then twenty-seven . . . now thirty. The stream allows no hanging back; it is as clear as truth.

She notes that "it is here in this stream I first touched mysticism, was caught up from reality . . . for one long childhood moment." It is the summer her father built a dam across the stream at the corner of the icehouse so there was a pool to learn to swim in. "All the village came to see the dam," she writes, "and children came to swim there. . . . One day, the village minister asked permission to use our pool for a baptismal service."

On the next Sunday, people came in their carriages or walked along the dusty road. To watch the ceremony, Mother climbed up to a branch of a willow tree on the far side of the pool. The minister waded out to the middle of the pool and raised his hand to bless the pool. Mother writes that Mrs. Taylor's oldest son played "When We Gather at the River" while the people gathered, singing quietly. The first to be baptized was a girl named Hester Butterworth, who went under the water in a starched white dress and came up with the dress "limp and wrinkled around her, smiling gravely." "I sat in the tree," Mother writes, "a kind of prickly ecstasy in me that made my hands moist and my throat feel tight."

Next was "a farmer from out the valley, solemn and thin." Then another young girl: "She looked too frail to walk out bravely in the water, and I could see her bite her lip against the cold." Mother comes increasingly under the spell of the words of the minister and the singing of the people and the notes of the violin. She continues: "I felt the Holy Ghost I had always been vague about coming close to the water and the willows and the alder bushes. The whole stream was solemnized. I felt I would never dog-paddle there again or turn somersaults in the water. . . . A feeling of holiness moved in the stillness beside that pool." The essay ends by saying that a few weeks later heavy rains washed the dam away and that she never again found that feeling of mysticism in a brook. But she comments: "Perhaps a mystic is always a child looking into a deep pool. Perhaps that is why mysticism is hard to come by."

As they grew older, Mother came to feel that her sister had a much more interesting life than her own in the Grafton summers.

She would show us photos, pointing out our young aunt who had tight curly hair, merriment in her brown eyes, and a warm smile. Mother described her with the envy of a younger sister who felt herself to be "plain with straight brown hair" and "scrawny" by comparison. But photos don't bear that out; they show Mother as an equally pretty child, her expression perhaps a little pensive. One afternoon, Aunt Peg came home from the local swimming hole in tears because one of her friends had lifted her skirts so high in front of the young men that her ankles showed. Mother remembered her sister's shame. This would have been about 1916.

My brothers and I know two of the larger white houses with green shutters and generous porches for their importance to Mother's Grafton summers. One stands against the village green, the other at the fork of Main Street, both with wrought iron balconies above their main doors. On each of these balconies Mother and her sister and village friends had declaimed passages from *Romeo and Juliet* and *The Merchant of Venice*. Mother was pleased that several times she had taken Mercutio's role and that she had once been Romeo to her sister's Juliet. Not so many years ago, when she gestured to the balconies and retold the story for her grandchildren, we felt again her deep sense of belonging to the life of Vermont.

The story that equally thrilled and frightened us occurred on a summer day when Mother and her sister were still small. Their mother was driving them back home from a day's outing in the buggy. As they came along the dirt road nearing their house, the horse shied at some movement. In an instant he was a runaway. He veered off the road onto the wide green lawns of the large houses set back from the road, and Grandma Walker hauled back on the reins, commanding the little girls to get down on the floor of the buggy and hold on tight. She finally brought the horse down to a walk and guided him back to the barn while the neighbors watched from their porches. "We were terrified," Mother said, "but it was exciting!" As an afterthought, she commented, "Everyone said Mother was a good hand with a horse."

As Mother told these stories, I often sensed an attitude that accorded her mother the accomplishment of keeping house but not much more, not anything particularly admirable or instructive. Why? When I was older, she told me that her mother could always reduce the amount of ingredients called for in a recipe. Mother called it "making do." She suggested that this was commendable when the household was pinched for money but that she thought it otherwise without merit. Yes, it kept things going, but it was not an effort that Mother herself cared to make. It annoyed her that "shorting" recipe ingredients (1.5 cups sugar when 2 were required; 1/8 teaspoon nutmeg when 1/4 was called for) should be a matter of pride.

What Mother scorned was her mother's expressed wish to retire to Vermont and raise chickens. "Chickens!" Mother would say when she mentioned this. "How awful that would be." I did wonder about Mother's distaste because, after all, we later raised chickens when we lived in Montana. Still, they were not Mother's enterprise. We children cared for the chickens, and the woman who kept house for Mother prepared them for the freezer.

I knew my grandmother as someone who sewed "best" dresses for me and as someone who wrote me right back when I sent her a painstaking thank-you letter. Once, when my maternal grandparents visited us at our family cabin in Montana, Grandma took us into the thicket nearby to gather smooth stones and dig a hole to line a "dry well" for keeping vegetables cool. My brother and I were entranced. And when she whipped up scrambled eggs on the kerosene stove, she did it with a flourish I have never forgotten.

Why have I always remembered the little stories of Mother's, characterizing my Grandmother Walker? I wanted to know about her because I was only eight years old when she died. But whenever I recall them, I feel the implicit criticism in Mother's tone of voice. Now I imagine that Mother preferred not to think of herself as having a mother with such uninteresting ambitions as making do or raising chickens. Is it simply that she wanted her mother to be a different person than she was, as I, in my callow youth, wanted my mother to be, for other reasons?

Mother's stories about her father, in contrast, were always told with pride. Each vignette of him from her childhood emphasized how carefully, even exactingly, he coached her in important skills.

There was the day when Mother had proudly accompanied him in the family buggy to visit an old friend of his who lived at some distance from Grafton. Coming home, they were caught in a hailstorm, and they took shelter in a covered bridge. For the duration of the storm, her father taught Mother her multiples of eight. She always remembered the story happily, the snugness of sitting under the raised bonnet of the buggy. For Mother it was an example of his excellent influence on her, her approval that he never let an opportunity for instruction be wasted. (I remember thinking that might have been a waste of a good storm.)

She admired his resourcefulness, too, his "Yankee inventiveness." Rolling up his sleeves, he chopped enough stove wood for a week at a time, repaired leaks, and rebuilt stairs. He always approached tasks with exuberant energy, she said approvingly. We remember, from our childhood, his thunderous preaching once from the high pulpit of the Baptist church in Great Falls, Montana. The two arcs of his bushy white mustache moved up and down, quivering with vehemence, as his face turned from red to purple.

Mother used to tell us the story of her father's heroism. Walking down a Philadelphia street, he saw a department store on fire. Just as he drew closer, a man ran out with his clothes in flames. Grandfather tripped him and rolled him in his winter overcoat. As he bent over the man, glass from the large window above him blew outward from the heat of the fire and fell, slicing off the end of Grandfather's nose. "Without a thought," Mother would say grandly, "he found his nose and walked down the street to a nearby doctor's office to have it sewn back on." She explained that this was the reason his nose turned purple whenever he was "exercised."

Walks through the village with him were a pleasure to her. Whenever they stopped to visit with his friends or acquaintances, she was aware of his eloquence. He had faith in his ability to settle any dispute, she would say in the awed tone of a little girl. She told us when we were grown, almost inadvertently and with shy pride, that her father called her "Peter." He had wanted her to be a boy, she said matter-of-factly. He explained to her that Peter was his favorite name because Peter was one of the finest of the apostles as well as a fisherman. I sensed that being "Peter" assured her that she had a special role to fulfill for her father, perhaps of succeeding in a way that a girl would not be expected to, a way that set her apart from her sister. When I asked once how long Grandfather had called her Peter, she answered that it was until she went away to college, she thought.

Grandfather was a fine fisherman, bringing home a string of fish whenever he went off to the narrow, shallow streams of dark brown water that ran down the steep hills to join the branches of Saxtons River. Once, on a walk with Mother behind the Walker homestead, we were shown a smooth gray rock where Grandfather had surprised a mink with a large brown trout wriggling in its mouth. Tapped lightly on his head by the end of the fishing rod, the mink dropped the trout, and Grandfather caught it in his free hand. Mother always enjoyed telling of her father's fishing prowess, but she herself was not interested in trekking off to fish with him. Margaret was the one who followed him and learned to be as adept at fishing as he. Mother made it clear that what absorbed her most about her father was his intellectual life.

In her later years Mother said that her father was her greatest influence on her writing. It wasn't that he discussed her early novels with her; his influence went back to her earlier years when he inspired her to succeed in whatever she attempted. I imagine that her mother wanted that for her, too, but it may not have been with the same emphasis on ambition.

Perhaps Mother remembered those particular stories from her childhood because they helped her define her understanding of her parents. And perhaps the stories I have told my children about my parents stayed in my mind for the same reason. Stories I've told them about my father are certainly as different from those I've told about my mother as Mother's were. What I know now as an adult is that my stories remembered about my mother and father are not as much about them as they are about me—my reactions to them. And perhaps her stories about her parents worked in the same way.

Among Mother's saved letters I have found several from her father but none from her mother. It may be that these letters from her father, when she was twenty-nine, gave her a guidance that was important to her. One of the letters from her father was written April 2, 1934, two months after the publication of her first novel, *Fireweed:*

> *Of course you say that it is purely an accident and that it cannot happen again, but I can discover no good reason why it should not happen many times. Your success with* Fireweed *has given you a place of recognition, and consequently a favorable hearing for writing. You have not done the best that you are capable of. The years discipline and develop our mental powers, and brilliant as is the success which you have achieved, it would be foolish to conclude that there are not very much greater things for you ahead. Take time. Don't be in too much of a hurry. Do not whip yourself into writing when it is too labored. Brood over your mental children. Believe in yourself, and when the inspiration comes, surrender yourself, and expect that every effort will be better than the one that preceded it.*

The letter goes on to liken her writing to his writing of sermons in the sense that he has made "intellectual progress" over the years, and he feels that she will do the same.

The letter reminds me of the grandfather I knew when we were children. The winter when George was five and I was six, Mother took us to Philadelphia to live with my grandparents for four months. It must have been 1935. Dad was home in Montana studying for his Boards. Mother was working on her third novel, *Dr. Norton's Wife.* George and I were sent to kindergarten and first grade. In the evenings I was required to sit on "Gran-gran's" lap and read aloud to him. His disappointment was fathomless when I couldn't remember "the very important word" *please.* He was also the grandfather who made cautionary observations to us when he came to vacation with our family at the cabin in Montana. But he also taught George the art of fishing by letting my brother follow him doggedly along the Teton River near the cabin—starting at 5

A.M. His impression on Mother lasted her lifetime, and her late journals spoke of him as the prototype for her main character in her last adult novel.

I was startled to discover, when I first looked up their family histories, that Mother's parents had very similar backgrounds. It must not have been of interest to Mother to tell us. Her grandparents had died before she knew them, she said, but their small, gray photographs from the mid-1880s always hung in her bedroom. Mother's parents were descended from families who had emigrated to the Massachusetts Colony in the 1630s, on her father's side from Scotland and on her mother's side from England. The only mention Mother made of Grandma Walker's family background was that at one time she had been gathering the information necessary to qualify for membership in the Daughters of the American Revolution. It seemed to Mother a rather uninteresting pursuit.

Grandma Walker was born Harriet Merrifield in Newfane, Vermont, in 1865. Moments after Harriet's birth, Mother told us, the new mother asked the reason for the church bells tolling and was told that they rang for the death of President Lincoln. Harriet's father's people were descended from Merrifields who, after settling in the Massachusetts Colony, moved on to settle permanently by the mid-1700s in the Brookline Valley in Vermont. Harriet's grandfather, Oscar Merrifield, had been born in Newfane in 1837, into a well-established farming family. He had married Marcia Cudworth, born in 1839, from the nearby village of Putney, Vermont. Both their families were prosperous small farmers with good land holdings. Local people in Newfane still point out "Merrifield's Meadow" where they say young men were trained as soldiers for the revolutionary army. Oscar and Marcia Merrifield, Mother's maternal grandparents, joined the Baptist church, became involved in community affairs, and supported local schools.

Harriet Merrifield attended a round brick schoolhouse that still stands at a fork in the main road through the valley. The story told in the local historical museum's leaflet is that the first schoolmaster, a Scot, wanted the schoolhouse to be round rather than square with carefully spaced windows; in his earlier life he had been a highwayman, and he wished to see who was coming from all directions. The advantage for the children in the school was that there were no corners for the winter winds to shriek around, Mother remembered her mother saying.

Harriet Merrifield's description of her Grandfather Merrifield always made Mother shudder—a rather grim, upright man who ran his finger underneath the rim of each child's breakfast plate to see that there were no hidden pork rinds. But another story that Harriet told was of a more playful grandfather at his own family table. A suitor, favored by one of his daughters, had come to dinner. He was not the usual young minister coming to call, and the head of the table asked an unusual blessing:

> *Dear God of Love*
> *Look down from above*
> *And see how times have mended.*
> *We now have strawberry shortcake*
> *Where mush and milk were intended.*

Whenever Mother repeated this story, she seemed to enjoy the slyness of the comment—that the daughter had betrayed her preference for her caller by her choice of menu.

In 1880, Harriet's father moved his family west to Mendota, Illinois, to join his brothers in the Western Cottage Organ Company, which built melodeons and, later, pianos. (The Merrifield brothers had apparently been apprenticed earlier to the large melodeon and piano company located in Brattleboro, Vermont.) In the years following the Civil War, many families left for "the West" as economic conditions worsened in New England. (An old map reaching to the Mississippi River shows Illinois and other midwestern states as being settled by "Yankees.") According to Mother, those who moved west at that time showed "gumption." She mentioned more than once to us that those who stayed in New England had lacked gumption, a notion she would pursue in *The Quarry*.

Harriet Merrifield was fifteen when her family moved to Mendota. A year later, her mother died in childbirth, and Harriet took on the care of her five younger brothers and sisters. When her father married again four years later, Harriet was free to attend college. It was a matter of pride to Mother that her Grandfather Merrifield ensured that each of his children was given the opportunity to attend a college or to have means to start in a chosen line of work. At Dennison College in Ohio, Harriet studied to be a teacher and sang in the college choir. A young seminary student, Walter M. Walker, met Harriet at a choir performance and began courting her.

Although Walter Walker was born in 1862 in Wyoming, Illinois, and raised there, his father had been born on the Walker Homestead along the Saxtons River one mile downstream from Grafton. Samuel Walker, who settled the Walker Homestead in the early 1800s and built a large comfortable farmhouse that we children were taken to visit, was descended from the Walkers of the Old Plymouth Colony of Massachusetts. A record of the Plymouth Colony written in 1635 includes among its residents a widow Walker who had emigrated with her six sons from Glencoe, Scotland.

Walter's father, Orville, married a Sarah Milliken from a nearby village and, in 1852, moved west to Wyoming, Illinois. As Mother told us, her Grandfather Walker must have been the only one of that generation of Walker sons who had the gumption to move west. Two of her great-uncles built large New England houses in Grafton—along the same main street where Mother's parents would purchase their summer home in 1916.

Elgin, Illinois, became the permanent home for Walter Walker's parents where they were successful farmers. They were described in a family history as believing in community responsibility and becoming staunch supporters of the Baptist religion. Walter and one of his nine brothers went to a seminary school near Chicago, living in a boarding house run by his older sister. The sister devoted herself to making her brothers' education possible in this way. When Walter graduated from the seminary, he obtained a Baptist ministry in Illinois and kept in touch with Harriet Merrifield by letter.

After her graduation from college, her father had instructed Harriet to return to Vermont to keep house for her bachelor brother, who was running the Merrifield farm. But she also began teaching at nearby Leland and Gray Seminary in Townshend, Vermont. Her father had been a student at Leland and Gray and, while there, had delivered an oration on "The Advantage of Female Companionship." Her grandfather had helped found the seminary in 1834. But in 1890, Harriet left her obligations in Vermont to marry Walter Walker in Elgin.

There is a photograph of her newly married parents that delighted Mother. They stand on the deck of a ship about to depart for Europe. Her mother wears a stylish dress of the 1890s: thin stripes on a dark background, a long full skirt, and leg-of-mutton sleeves. She is smiling beneath a pertly brimmed hat. Mother's father wears a suit complete with vest and cravat and a traveling cap with the flaps tied up. One hand grasps the ship's railing and the other holds a large Bible. He looks directly at the camera, attesting to the importance of the event but unsmiling. "Aren't they handsome!" Mother would say to us.

Grandmother Walker was twenty-five when she married in 1890, but Mother was more than once wistful that she was not born until her mother was forty—"no longer a young woman," Mother said. Still, it was important to Mother that her father had honored his bride's wish not to bear children immediately. Their first child, Margaret, was born in 1898 in Elgin. At some time after that, her father took a parish in Philadelphia, where their second daughter, Mildred, was born in 1905.

Four of Mother's thirteen published novels take place in a village like Grafton. The roads she walked as a child, as a young woman visiting her family there, as a mother with children, and as a grandmother in retirement are present in each of these four novels. So are the main street with its tall houses, the Saxtons River, the covered bridge, the maidenhead fern, and the old cemetery.

In the late 1980s, when Mother left Vermont to live in Montana again because of her failing health, she transferred the Grafton house to my younger brother, Christopher. His family arranges to be there for most holidays and for family reunions. Mother's eldest granddaughter chose to be married in the Grafton Church in the spring of 1996. And Mother's youngest grandson presently lives in the Grafton house with his wife and daughters—two of Mother's four great-grandchildren. Perhaps because the house has been lived in for nearly one hundred years by Mother's family, older people in the village still call the Grafton house "the Walker Place."

2
The Vermont Novels

On those slow summer walks up Grafton's Main Street with Mother, when we were children, she would nod to a particular house and tell us who used to live there. Often the same person or family still occupied the house. She seemed in those moments almost to be speaking to herself, but I was aware of her voice rehearsing facts that had a particular significance for her. Main Street was still a dusty road, a little wider than the roads that led off it. I seem to remember skipping from one pool of shade to the next, pools cast by the maple trees that lined the road. Far ahead we could see the town bridge that crossed the Saxtons River. "And that's where the woolen mill used to be," she'd say. Usually our goal was the tiny post office or the general store with the sagging front porch. But once or twice a summer, we'd continue up the steepening dusty road to the church where my grandfather still preached at times or to the village park where we could roll down the small hillocks in the thick green grass. Neither my brothers nor I knew then that these people she described and the places she pointed out each summer would become part of her Vermont novels.

After our maternal grandparents died (I was eight, then nine, years old), we did not visit Vermont with Mother in the summers. But in 1943 or 1944, Mother went to Grafton with the intent to do research for her seventh novel. By then she was an accomplished novelist, having published six novels between 1934 and 1944. When she chose the Vermont she knew so well as a setting for her novels, she was in her early forties.

Both *The Quarry* and *The Southwest Corner* take their characters up and down the main street of a village very like Grafton, Vermont. In both, her characters travel across a small river like Saxtons River through a covered bridge, ascend and descend a fern-lined hill road resembling the road up Grafton's Kidder Hill. And in both, her main characters take their inspiration from villagers whose stories Mother grew up knowing and later telling to us. In both, the realities of place give way to the emotional realities of lives rooted in such a place.

Mother told me a few years ago that the source for all her novels was either an observation she made or a possibility that occurred to her. Grafton, once a stop on the Underground Railway, is still home to the descendants of one fugitive, a boy who chose to stay in Grafton rather than escape on through to Canada. In *The Quarry*, such a boy is taken on by a family up on the hill who runs a quarry, and he becomes the lifelong friend of the family's youngest son. "I just wondered," Mother remembered, "what a friendship between the black boy and a white boy of the village might be like for them as the years passed."

The Quarry spans the years from 1857 to 1914, from just before the Civil War to the beginning of the First World War, the years in which great economic changes come to the small villages of Vermont. The two boys grow from boys of nine and eleven to men of sixty-six and sixty-eight. And the events of their lives reflect the changes in their village and the surrounding countryside.

Mother's collection of papers and notebooks in the American Heritage Center at the University of Wyoming in Laramie includes the three-by-five-inch lined spiral notebooks that she had kept for most of her novels. In closely written longhand, in ink but often in pencil, she had entered facts, quotations, tentative names of characters as they were emerging in her story lines, queries and suppositions about how those characters might respond to other characters, and often a reminder to herself to have a character think or speak in a certain way.

The Quarry opens in 1857, when the village of Grafton had a peak population of fifteen hundred people. Its most flourishing industry was producing wool, and Windham County was said to have been raising ten thousand sheep in 1830. The grazing of so many sheep and a century of wood cutting had denuded the once forested hills surrounding Grafton. An old sepia photograph, printed on a postcard sold at the village post office, shows the bare hills. The photograph is dated 1904, but the sheep industry, with its woolen mills in each village along the Saxtons River, had bottomed out in the 1860s, so that in Mother's childhood the trees had begun to grow back. By the time she described this view to my brothers and me, those hills were thickly forested again. Mother's main character in *The Quarry*, Lyman Converse, worries in the early 1900s at the sight of small trees growing up in the corner of the hill pasture. It reminds him that the wilderness could come back.

The research entries in the notebooks for *The Quarry* are the most extensive that she gathered for any of her novels, taking up every historical aspect of the period covered. The notebooks record how she relived the period for herself, always in terms of those lives in the hill country of southern Vermont. Farm implements, planting and harvesting seasons, local and national politics, news from the Civil War battlefields and from the gold mining ventures out west, as well as what garments were being worn, what foods were being prepared, and how children were being reared—she took notes on each of the matters that affected the lives of her characters and those around them.

In her novel, the scenes in which Mother's characters move and think take place in a small village similar to Grafton called Painesville, in houses and fields like those she had absorbed in her childhood. In *The Quarry*'s opening paragraph, the boy Lyman lies in the bed he shares with his two older brothers in a room upstairs. He is nibbling on apples to keep himself awake and looking at the objects in the room:

> *An August moon painted a white streak across the gray shingles of the woodshed roof and the wide painted boards of the bedroom floor. The curled oak leaf in the rug, that was really a bright green, stood out a kind of whitish gray. The white pitcher on the washstand looked more like a guinea hen than ever and its white porcelain breast shone in the light.*

Each time I read this paragraph, I see Mother's childhood bedroom in the upstairs of the Grafton house, furnished with these same objects. The white pitcher is not set out anymore, but I remember it from my childhood visits and her saying to me that it had always seemed to her to be shaped like a guinea hen.

I don't know that Mother herself ever slid through the window and climbed barefoot out onto the woodshed roof and down the wooden lattice until she stood in a bed of tiger lilies, but I can see her in the nine-year-old Lyman who did, on his way to a secret meeting with the slave boy. I can see her particularly because the wooden lattice and the tiger lily bed are still there.

From this point on in the chapter, Lyman and the frightened slave boy, Easy, whom Lyman has stolen out in the moonlight to befriend and to share an apple with, begin the relationship that the novelist imagines for them. The details of the religious habits of the Converse family's breakfast, the Sunday morning rituals, the Abolitionist fervor in the church that is disappointed because Easy's story of being a slave is not as grim as the congregation had hoped—all are depictions based on Mother's careful research into the period as seen through young Lyman's understanding of an important moment in his life.

When I finally read *The Quarry* in my late thirties, I realized that this novelist's interest and insight into the feelings and thoughts of her characters had a depth I had never suspected possible of the woman who was my mother. The narrator of *The Quarry* was so perceptive of the feelings of the two boys that I envied them for a moment; I felt that as a mother she had never allowed my brothers and me to have the same complicated feelings.

Another part of Grafton's history was a flourishing soapstone quarry owned by a Grafton family for more than 150 years. By the time of Mother's childhood, the activity of the quarry up on Kidder Hill had ended. She spoke about it as a mysterious spot hidden in ferns and trees, the great pit of the quarry filled in with dark water. But from studying the records kept by this quarry and other working quarries in the area, she records in her small notebooks the sizes, weights, implements, and work activities that become part of the lives of her characters. From the time Lyman is in his early twenties, his life is circumscribed by the needs and challenges of conducting the business of the quarry, and Easy becomes a worker in the quarry. In the novel the Converse family's quarry and small farm, where Lyman and Easy first meet, is very near the actual abandoned Grafton quarry on the hill above the village.

Perhaps, though, it was equally Mother's memory of the letters she had discovered in the barn loft when she was sixteen that prompted her to begin writing *The Quarry* in 1945 or 1946. Thirty years after her fictional use of the letters, she described them in an article for the 1976 bicentennial edition of the *Grafton Gazette*:

> In 1868, the Goodrich quarry was inherited by Sophia Goodrich, but because she was living in Paris, a cousin, Sidney Holmes, who lived in Grafton . . . represented her interests in all the dealings . . . for the munificent sum of $50 a year. Some of the correspondence spanning the years 1876–1896 has survived: Sophia's letters in a spidery handwriting on yellowed notepaper; and carefully made copies of Holmes's letters to her, many of them meticulously written on brown wrapping paper.

Mother spoke of these letters several times in later years, each time suggesting that finding them there, wedged between two old volumes, had been great luck. And she added each time that the letters suggested to her more than a business relationship between the two correspondents.

In the novel Lyman inherits the quarry business in 1866 at his father's death. He is in love with his cousin Isabel, whom he is advised he should not marry because they are first cousins, and bitterly, he agrees, though he continues to long for her all the years that follow. When Isabel marries and goes to live in Paris, Lyman is able to correspond with her each time he sends a dividend check to her for the shares in the quarry that she has inherited from her father. She, in turn, writes back acknowledging her receipt of the dividends and describing moments of her life in Paris. Both write letters that betray their love for each other. Hers are letters that Lyman keeps hidden in his desk in the quarry office to read over whenever he is alone. Much of the appraisal he makes of what his life has become over the years takes place as he sits at his desk, looking out on Main Street.

Once, when I was probably in my forties, walking up Main Street with Mother, she pointed out a small white house with a broad window. The house was about midway up the street with a good view of all going by. She said it had been the Goodrich Quarry office. She did not say it had become in her mind the office where Lyman sat reading his letters from Isabel. And farther up the street, past the general store, Mother often lingered in front of a handsome big brick house, saying again that it had been where the village's senator to the Vermont legislature had lived. Lyman Converse lives in such a house, up the road from his quarry office. He is urged to run for a seat in the state senate, but he loses. His friends and supporters come by on the evening of his defeat to befriend him in a way that touches him as he stands on his front steps, saying good night and valuing his place in their loyalties.

Lyman's circumstances oblige him to "live always," as he muses bitterly to himself, within the perimeter of the village. As a young man he goes to Brown University, where he uses too much of his father's money in his discovery of the larger world. So influenced is he by his wealthy classmates that he invites Easy to visit him and, in front of his friends, treats Easy as his servant. He is guiltily aware of what he has done to his boyhood friend. Soon after, his father arrives to remove Lyman from the university and bring him back to the village. Burning with resentment but obliged to work in the quarry office until he has repaid his father, Lyman is forced by his father's sudden death to take over the quarry business in the village of Painesville.

In Mother's own family history, there was a "flamboyant" uncle named Fred (her mother's brother) who had been yanked from Brown University for incurring debt, specifically for equipping his college room with a piano. That situation Mother spoke about with awe and perhaps as a small triumph of self-expression. As I read and then reread *The Quarry,* I felt that Mother was exploring the nature of "those who stayed," rather than of those who struck out for the gold fields. Was this novel a reassessment of those who did not have the gumption to leave the certainties of village life for adventure and fortune? In Lyman's life, not leaving comes to torment him. Before Mother wrote *The Quarry,* she had absorbed much about the fortunes of New Englanders, in particular, those who had gone to the gold fields of Montana. By 1945 or 1946, she and my father had made their home in Montana for more than twelve years and become close friends with the journalist Joseph Kinsey Howard. Howard's nonfiction book, *Montana: High, Wide, and Handsome,* had been published in 1941. As a study of how much the development of the state of Montana had been shaped by easterners, it was investigative and descriptive, especially of what had gone on in the towns of Butte and Helena.

As the center of the Montana gold fields, Virginia City is portrayed in *The Quarry* through Lyman's eyes when he travels there to assist his older brother's young widow. Lyman's brother Dan had gone to Virginia City with his southern wife and infant daughter to seek his fortune, but also to get away from the small Vermont village of his family. Rough and raw though Virginia City looks to Lyman, it will become a place in his mind to which he might flee in order to escape the confines of Painesville. He will think of it more than once. And he will think of Paris where he could be near Isabel, even though she has married. Instead, he is living with his wife, Louisa, who was to have been the wife of his older brother, John. But John's death in the Civil War had left Louisa sad and alone in the village, and Lyman felt he should marry her.

The familiar pastures and roads, quarry workings and its success, moments with his two young sons, encounters with his friends, and the shifts of seasons comfort and delight Lyman Converse; they are also the bondage from which he cannot and will not free himself. "Something hunted," as his college professor defines the meaning of *quarry* when he hears that Lyman has gone into that business. It is no small part of the meaning of the novel's title. Lyman is hunting for something that eludes him. Perhaps the word *quarry,* in one of its meanings a prize to be found by a laborious search, does apply to Lyman: He wants his life to be something it isn't, but he has decided he cannot bring that about.

A *New York Herald Tribune* book review in 1947 characterized the novel as "the rich substance of the human drama of an individual, a family and a town" and "a mature story that probes the mainsprings of human conduct." Would Mother have welcomed this assessment? When we children were in our high school years, my father used to warn us that he was delivering a batch of reviews to Mother and that she might be disappointed. We later learned that she resented praise like the following from the *Chicago Tribune* because it ascribed "warmth" to the novel: "A serene and lovely novel of such deep-running warmth and integrity that it is almost an anachronism in these times of shallow writing" (March 1947). More than once in her later journals and in her remarks to us, Mother dismissed *warmth* as an adjective usually reserved for women novelists to suggest a less-than-literary achievement.

The Southwest Corner, the second novel with a Vermont setting, was published in 1951, four years after *The Quarry.* Mother was in her mid-forties when she wrote *The Southwest Corner.* Her protagonist was in her eighties. Mother's portrait of Marcia Elder facing how to remain in her family home on the hill farm in her old age had many readers. The playwright John Cecil Holm wrote a stage play based on the novel. The role of Marcia Elder appealed to the actress Eva Le Gallienne, who was at the height of her career, and the play was performed on Broadway in 1955. In a *New York Times* review (January 13), Brooks Atkinson praised the direction of George Schafer, saying the acting "is tender and perceptive . . . and some of it is very humorous." He adds, "Miss Le Gallienne, as the gallant old lady, gives the finest performance she has brought to New York for a long time. Without sentimentalizing the part, she gives it grace, wisdom and an undercurrent of anxiety."

In Mother's holdings at the American Heritage Center in Wyoming, I found the letter written to her by Le Gallienne. The actress thanked Mother for the role of Marcia Elder, saying how much it had meant to her to play it, and adding that Eleanor Roosevelt had written in praise of the play and attended it twice. Surely, Mother was impressed by these events. But she never betrayed any enthusiasm about them to us at the time. When Mother was in her eighties, she gave a copy of the novel to her physician, saying that she marveled she could have felt confident of knowing what was in her protagonist's mind when she, the writer, was only in her forties.

I think Mother knew these things from her deep affection for Marcia Elder's prototype, whom Mother had known since childhood. Mother always spoke of her as Aunt Helen Hamilton. For the recent University of Nebraska reprint of *The Southwest Corner* (1995), I was asked to help Mother write the introduction, and she began to tell it to me with the slow cadence of a childhood memory:

> *In the Vermont village where my family lived in the summers, I came to know Mrs. Hamilton, who lived across the road from us. One summer morning she came out of her house and called across to me:*
>
> *"Honey bug and molasses jug*
> *and sweet flagroot!"*
>
> *The funny words hung in the air. I was four going on five. I started across the road but she called to me, "Honey Bug, stay right where you are till the oxen go by." A pair of oxen came up the road with their slow walk. I stood on the horse block in front of our house and waited. When she said, "Come!" I ran across the road. It didn't occur to me not to mind her. And so our friendship began. (1)*

Later on in the introduction, Mother acknowledged, "My old friend from my childhood became Marcia Elder."

I learned more of Mother's admiration for Aunt Helen each time I came to Grafton for a visit. Again, the stories were always told without reference to the novel based on them. Aunt Helen had married in Grafton, setting up a small household until she and her new husband left to farm in Illinois. In that first year, Aunt Helen's husband was struck dead by lightning as he lay in bed beside her. She returned to Grafton to live in the house across the road from the Walkers. The neighbors who had bought furniture from her on her departure quietly returned the pieces they had bought. My Grandmother Walker must have told Mother this story, because Mother always repeated it with the gravity an adult uses to address a child.

After Mother died, I discovered a bound collection of five essays about Grafton in a trunk with her personal papers. She had changed the villagers' names, but each was familiar to me from knowing them or being told their stories. The narrator in each essay is a young woman who describes the village from the point of view of long familiarity. There is no date for this collection, and no title page, but there are hints the narrator uses throughout the collection that suggest Mother may have written it during a summer when she was back from college. Penciled in at the beginning of a sentence, she has written, "And being 20." The whole sentence reads: "And being 20, I wondered, most of all, how love flourished in those prim houses with the narrow doors."

The title for the first essay is "Time in Vermont . . ." Its first paragraph reads:

> *Time runs slowly in Vermont; more slowly than the brook outside the door, or the wind in the tall elm tree above the roof, or even than the pendulum behind the painted window of the kitchen clock. Those born there, who live and die to that slow time, are unaware of the odd tempo of their lives, but I have been away and just come back.*

In this essay the narrator takes an evening walk up the main street and thinks "of all the lives inside of every house I passed (or how they endured where no life was)." There is Great-aunt Amy (called Bessie in the essay), who was the seventy-year-old postmistress when we were children and whose whispery voice intrigued my four-year-old son one summer afternoon. In Mother's essay, Bessie knows the secret hiding places of the maidenhair fern. The narrator observes, when Bessie appears in the twilight, "I forgot that she was hump-backed she crossed the brook so swiftly, with a nod at me, and disappeared into the woods as fleet as any deer." And farther up Main Street, "in the neat, green-shuttered house with the barn that seems to climb the hill," is Aunt Helen (called Mrs. Meldon in the essay). "She has queer words for a woman born in these narrow valleys; she calls cats, kittens, and all the village children 'honey-bug and molasses jug and sweet flagroot.'" And when lightning storms come, she "goes upstairs and pulls the shades and shuts the door and hides her head in her feather bed." Mrs. Meldon's husband, the narrator explains, was killed by a lightning bolt as he lay in bed beside her. In *The Southwest Corner,* Marcia Elder will remember the same lightning story when she is in her eighties and how she came back to the hill farm, "empty-armed."

In Mother's childhood Aunt Helen cared for a retarded younger brother who played in a sand box beside the house. Mother was often invited to join him there when she was very young. Once a week, Aunt Helen rode sidesaddle to Bellows Falls, Vermont, to tune the organ reeds being manufactured there. It was a ride of about fifteen miles each way. But most prized by Mother were the summer afternoon walks with Aunt Helen: "Always up the hill back of her house, and sometimes we had a picnic." There must have been much more that Mother told me about Aunt Helen, but these things I remember most, perhaps because they were always said with such quiet admiration for a woman I would never know. Why was it that Mother didn't tell me *The Southwest Corner* was based on Aunt Helen's stories about her life until I asked her about it at least twenty years later? She may have decided I wouldn't be interested. But I think, instead, she had decided from the first of her career that her children were outside her writing life. Or as the novelist Deirdre McNamer suggested, Mother may have thought of her novels as "separate from 'lived' life and thus not worth talking about."

Lately, I have found several photographs of Aunt Helen. In each she is always outside her doorway, dressed in a long skirt with shoe button boots. She stands very erect, turned sideways to the camera with a humorous half-smile on her face. A later photo shows her standing with two canes beside the long soapstone step into her house. While Mother and I talked about Aunt Helen for the reprint of *The Southwest Corner* in 1995, she told me that shortly after its original 1951 publication, a neighbor had read the novel to Aunt Helen, who was then living in a Vermont retirement home. "I was told that Aunt Helen had liked the novel," Mother said thoughtfully. "I hope so."

The title of this novel comes from a common term in the deeds of early Vermont farmsteads. Built on the southwest or southeast corner of these farmhouses was always a room or a set of small rooms with an entrance separate from the main house so that the aging parents could move in once a child of theirs had taken over the farm and moved into the main house with children. Later, Vermonters called it a form of "old age insurance."

Among Mother's papers is a copy of a deed from my father's side of the family dated 1806 in Bridgewater, Vermont, giving land and farm from a Samuel Ripley to his son, Joseph Ripley, "excepting and reserving to my use during my natural life, the Room in the southeast part of the dwelling House now on said premises." But Mother first learned about such a deed, she says, when her father told her of seeing one kept in his family. And Grandmother Walker remembered visiting her grandparents on the side of the family homestead as a child and being reminded to knock on the separate door. Aunt Helen had grown up in an old three-story brick house on Kidder Hill with its southwest corner. After describing the appearance of such a hill homestead in a brief prologue to *The Southwest Corner*, Mother continues:

> There is another door, set in the soft red brick, to the left
> of the parlor windows and partly obscured by a tangle of
> smoke bush and lilacs, that is identical with the main
> door except for its narrow width. It, too, has a fan above
> it, like a halo, an old iron door pull, a large keyhole and
> heavy white wood panels. Beyond this door are two more
> windows, one of them cut off at the corner to fit under the
> roof, which slopes sharply down to the height of one story.
> This low sweep of the roof seems to make the brick house
> part of the hill that rises behind it. *(10)*

For the reprint in 1995, over forty years later, Mother says about Aunt Helen, or Mrs. Hamilton, as she preferred to name her formally:

> When I returned to the village with my children for a visit
> after a number of years, I found my friend much older.
> She now lived in the southwest corner of her old house,
> and took her meals with her daughter's family, who occu-
> pied the main house. I remember that she gave me a small
> birthday gift. *(2)*

In Mother's childhood the road up Kidder Hill led to the Good-ridge Quarry but also to a good number of eighteenth- and early nineteenth-century farmhouses that were still occupied. Near the top of Kidder Hill the house that belonged to Aunt Helen's family had become the village poor farm. When Mother was a girl, Aunt Helen had told her that it was a place she hoped never to have to go to. Mother shuddered with the memory of Aunt Helen's dread when she told me, so many years later. Such an end never happened to Aunt Helen nor to *The Southwest Corner*'s Marcia Elder, who contrives to remain in her home at the age of eighty-three. As the smartly dressed innkeeper explains to the narrator in the novel's prologue, "That's Marcia Elder who sold me this house, all but *The Southwest Corner*" (10).

In the last chapter, Marcia Elder gets back to Ryder Village from the stuffy house in town where she had felt so lonely for her hill farm. It is a triumphant drive in a Model-T with the handyman, Orville Greenstead, and the prospective innkeeper. Marcia urges Orville on through the snow, out of the village, through the covered bridge, and up the hill road deep in snow. During summer and winter visits to Mother in the Grafton house where she had retired in her sixties, my brothers and I and our children have climbed the Kidder Hill road with her. Each spot important to her since her childhood she would point out again, always with the same emphasis. As she grew older, she had us stop at each level place in the road, about the length of a horse and buggy, "for a breather," just as Marcia Elder commanded Orville to do as the old Model-T struggled up through the snow.

Soon after the publication of *The Southwest Corner* in 1951, Mother had a "delicious story," as she called it, to tell on the rare occasions when she spoke with friends or admirers about one of her novels. She would acknowledge their praise for *The Southwest Corner* but go on to say that one woman had written saying the novel disappointed her: No mention was made of what happened to "Tim the cat" when Marcia Elder moved down into town for the winter. Mother told the story in such a way that her listeners delightedly disparaged the complaint. "I don't know how I could have overlooked the cat, do you?" was Mother's rueful but smiling comment.

The back page of the dust jacket for *The Quarry,* on its publication in 1949, has "A Note About Mildred Walker." It is a sprightly retelling of biographical highlights that Mother must have supplied to the publicist, and it shows how she saw herself in those years in which she wrote her first two novels set in Vermont. These two sentences in particular are interesting to me:

> *She started off her literary career at the age of seven with a eulogy to the Seasons, and continued it during childhood summers in Vermont, where her father's people had lived for several generations. At Wells College in New York, she thought her [writing] future was assured when she received a $50 prize for an essay, but she became less confident after her graduation when the best job she could get was in marking Puerto Rican nightgowns and selling bargains on the aisle at Wanamaker's Philadelphia store.*

When I first read this note, I wondered if she had consciously omitted that her mother's people had also lived "for several generations" in Vermont. She had told us as children that Grandmother Walker's family home had been in Brookline, Vermont, twenty miles from Grafton, but nothing about the generations of Merrifields. In some way, I think, she omitted them because her mother's ways of thinking were not as important to her as her father's. She absorbed all her father's admonitions as essential to "amounting to something," and she thought of him as her intellectual parent. Her mother's remarks, though sometimes dear to Mother, almost always reflected a woman enmeshed in matters of running a household. In a similar way, when she humorously notes her employment in Philadelphia, she has no interest in mentioning that she took a job there because Philadelphia had been her family's permanent home where she had grown up, except for those Vermont summers. Her reason must have been that she had never felt any affection for Philadelphia. We children mostly heard her express dismay about the family circumstances of living there, about moving from one "poorly appointed" parsonage to another.

After those sentences, there are arch references to her marriage "to a young doctor" which "reduced her temporarily to writing articles and ads in contests." A few sentences later, there is reference to the fifteen years in which she "produced" six novels and to her domestic life in which "in the same period, Miss Walker has had three children, and presided over her husband's career as a specialist in Internal Medicine." *Presided* is an interesting choice of words because it suggests she somehow directed my father in his work. I wonder at the amount of influence she felt she had, but the important point in her self-description is that she felt she did.

In 1960, Mother published a third Vermont novel, *The Body of a Young Man*. This eleventh novel was dedicated to "FRS," her doctor husband. As the writer Sharon Bryan describes it in her introduction to the 1997 reprint, this novel, "nominated for a National Book Award when it was first published in 1960, is a beautifully wrought meditation on the meaning, limits, demands, and failures of friendship—especially on what happens when a long-standing relationship is tested and found wanting" (viii).

I want to describe here the changes in Mother's life out of which *The Body of a Young Man* came. Her husband, a hardworking physician all his professional life, became ill at the age of fifty-four partly due to inherited hypertension. During his illness, Mother turned to two old friends, a physician and his wife with whom my parents had remained in touch since medical school in Ann Arbor, Michigan. Mother hoped that these friends would provide both medical and emotional support. The physician persuaded my father to come to his VA hospital in California for treatment.

During the six months of this stay, the friendship became strained because the friend was convinced that he could change my father's attitude and therefore his physical condition. Not smoking anymore was the big issue when my husband and I went to visit them. I saw the toll it took on my father, and I resented the friend because it was carried out with a bluff, hearty, nearly bullying self-confidence. And I had never known my father to be impressed by self-righteousness in matters of health. Six months later, to my father's great relief, my parents returned home to Montana. It seemed to me, at the time, that Mother felt she had betrayed her husband by counting on a friendship that belonged to a time thirty years earlier. She would say much later that her impulse had been a mistake, that it had cost my father a lot of energy. But she would never mention that *The Body of a Young Man* had pursued that realization.

My father died a year later in May 1955, when he was almost fifty-six years old. *The Body of a Young Man* is the most autobiographical of Mother's twelve novels. Published five years after my father's death, in 1960, it is a love story in a deep sense: a woman wants to help her husband regain the peace of mind she feels he has lost. In the course of the novel, the wife gains an understanding of her husband that reassures her—but not without a silent apology for having questioned him.

Mother's choice of a Vermont setting for the novel reflects another major change in her life at this time. In the first month after my father's death, she decided to move back east. Her older sister deeded her part of the Grafton house to Mother, and Mother sold our home in Montana. In three months' time the sale took place and she had the entire household packed for her permanent move to Vermont.

The ache of our leaving the old ranch house on the bank of the Missouri River was numbed by how rapidly we carried out Mother's decisions and by her hourly bitterness that she had lost her husband. One old friend who helped her pack my father's medical books said to her finally, "You know that this loss has happened to many women before you." Mother repeated their exchange to me, still bitter and proud of her reply: "Not what I have lost!" Even at the time, and all these years since, I have felt that she considered my father's death a kind of shame, a defeat: her life should be triumphant, she felt, not compromised by incurable illness or irreversible loss. By moving right ahead, she would overcome it—what she called her "situation." She may have felt further that she would know better how to do this when she had returned to Vermont.

My brother Christopher, seventeen that spring, was the only one of us to whom Mother turned for emotional support. And the burden it was for him showed in his young face. He had ridden the train back home with her after the funeral in Michigan where my father's brothers had prevailed upon Mother to have the burial.

Christopher said that on that trip Mother went through every detail of how she would move from the Montana home and how she would remodel the Grafton house when she arrived there.

Although my brother George and my husband and I were there in Montana, too, packing and finding homes for our horses, I think Mother felt closer to Christopher than to the rest of us. We were six and eight years older than Christopher and had lived away from home longer. Mother made it clear that George and I were not helpful in thinking she might regret selling the house so soon. Christopher must have known her better than we did, sensing how important this decisive change was to her.

I remember our last night in the house. The moving van had taken off down the road with everything, it seemed, we had grown up with. At the end of the long August day, very tired, we lay down on the floors of our own rooms to sleep. The next morning in the early light I lay listening to each familiar sound of the narrow river valley and wondered what Mother was thinking. She had made a lovely comfortable home along this river for all of us. But it had become a place she loathed—without my father.

When Mother discussed her decision to leave Montana after twenty-two years, she said emphatically that she did not want to stay without her husband and be known in town as "the widow." As soon as she was moved into the Grafton house, she rented a small house in Aurora, New York, where she had been hired to teach as a professor of literature at her alma mater, Wells College. The main emphasis of the English Department curriculum during her first teaching year, 1955, she said to me morosely, seemed to be "on works about death." But she was principally engaged by the college to teach creative writing, and she read widely in novelists whose work she admired, especially Henry James and Virginia Woolf on the techniques of writing.

The title of *The Body of a Young Man* is from a passage that Mother quoted from Woolf's *To the Lighthouse.* Mother uses the quotation as an epigraph for the novel:

> *[H]is affection ... had in no way diminished but there*
> *like the body of a young man laid up in peat for a cen-*
> *tury, with the red fresh on his lips, was his friendship, in*

its acuteness and its reality laid up across the bay among the sandhills. (To The Lighthouse [New York: Harcourt, Brace, 1927], 35)

On a page torn from a notebook kept sometime between 1955 and 1959, Mother writes, "I won't keep quoting. This is my journal. But just this to think of." The quotation is again from Virginia Woolf, an entry which seems to me of singular importance to her writing of *The Body of a Young Man:*

> *I must eliminate all waste, deadness, superfluity, to give the moment whole, whatever it includes. Say that the moment is a combination of thought, sensation, the voice of the sea. Waste, deadness, come from the inclusion of things that don't belong to the moment, this appalling narrative business of the realist getting on from lunch to dinner; it is false, unreal, merely conventional.*

Following the Woolf quote is an exercise for Mother's creative writing class: "A mother with her children at six stages, beginning with pt. of allegiance with them [against] her mother to pt. of their allegiance with their children [against] her. Try it for an exercise and suggest eliminating the 'narrative business of the realist.'" I think that in *The Body of a Young Man* Mother was using these techniques she encouraged her writing students to try. Mother consciously used writing techniques in this eleventh novel that she hadn't used with such concentration in the earlier novels. Sharon Bryan's perceptive introduction to the 1997 reprint of *The Body of a Young Man* describes Mother's commitment to a particular technique:

> *By keeping what dramatic events do occur mostly offstage, . . . the author keeps our attention where she wants it: not on the events themselves, but on her characters' responses to those events. . . . This is a novel so beautifully quiet we can hear tiny shifts in the relationship of the characters to themselves, each other, and the world. Reading it is like looking into a clear mountain stream and seeing not only the rocks and leaves, but the shadow of the water itself, as the wind ripples it. (x–xi)*

Mother seemed to have a personal need to clarify those "tiny shifts in the relationship of the characters to themselves" that compelled her to write this novel.

The novel is eerily autobiographical. The mannerisms, the play of speech between the husband and wife, repeat those of my parents. The novel's main point of view in the third person is that of the wife, Phyllis, who has brought about this summer visit to New England. The novel opens as, driving from their home in Illinois, they are nearing the small Vermont village where Phyllis's husband, James, spent summers. The moment is so similar to my rides with my parents that I could be driving in the car with them. Phyllis and James and their young son, Harp, are clowning in the same ways that my father and my brothers used to do, teasing about the driving, about what their hosts will be like, about being face to face with a skunk. And Phyllis thinks to herself that her decision had been a good one: "Simply the coming here to see Josh and Lucy had lifted James's spirits."

The village, one James has known well, is strange to Phyllis, who notes the differences from Illinois as James and Harp make a stop in the village store. They pass "an old brick house" that James says he used to think of buying, and I see the very house just up the hill from the village, the one where Mother had told me my father had thought he would like to retire someday. She told me, then, that she had never thought much of retiring, that it would be boring. I know I remembered that moment so well, that house, as I read the novel because it was only five years after my father's death and I wished sharply that he could have had that chance to retire.

Most startling of all are James and Phyllis's thoughts when they observe their Vermont surroundings or think about conversations with their friends. These exchanges are familiar to me as being those of my own parents when we were with them—especially their careful attempts to persuade one of us children to think this way or that. I remember imagining the thoughts that must have prompted my parents' remarks and finding them in Phyllis and James's remarks to their son.

In the novel, James has been teaching physics in a high school for a number of years. One of his best students, one whom he had coached for a college scholarship, had jumped off a bridge into a river and drowned just before he took his exams. Twice, in the second half of the novel, Phyllis lets herself remember the article in their hometown newspaper: "Body of a Young Man Found Drowned." It is her husband's guilt, his depression, that has caused Phyllis to appeal to James's old friends to talk him out of this depression. In the first week, after a supper party, the two wives, walking toward the guest cottage, overhear their husbands argue about why James feels such guilt. The argument has turned into a harangue, as Josh demands to know why James blames himself for his student's death. And James answers him:

> *"I was just using him, without knowing it, to build up my own self-esteem. Once, when he seemed tired of working so steadily, I told him he . . . he couldn't let me down. Now do you see why I feel responsible for his death?"*
>
> *The question hung motionless in the July night. Phyllis covered her face with her hands and sat down on the edge of the stone steps.*
>
> *"Jim, for Christ's sake, you're a damn neurotic over this. Of course, I don't see any such thing. You're simply letting this thing get away from you." Jim's voice was so quiet and colorless that Lucy winced.*
>
> *"No, I don't think so, but I have to face it." (36–37)*

Josh accuses Jim of hugging "this guilt complex you've dreamed up" and says, "You've got to forget about it." Lucy thinks, "Josh was too vehement, too impatient." And when Lucy tries in a whisper to comfort Phyllis in the dark, Phyllis replies, "Don't you see, he doesn't listen to what Josh says. Josh can't reach him either" (37).

Throughout the novel it is the wives who interpret in their thinking the way things are going between the two men. The two wives speak to their husbands or to each other out of these thoughts. When Lucy is working on her loom and Josh is whittling on one of her empty spools, he says to her, dejectedly,

> *"Jim's such a tender fellow, you know, that boy's death's just torn him apart."*

> *She turned on the bench so she could see him. Josh's*
> *face was grave. He was looking down and the strong line*
> *of his profile was cut against the open doorway. Josh was*
> *another, she thought. So devoted to Jim he could be torn*
> *apart, too. (43)*

Both women are protective of their husbands' feelings as the novel progresses. Their thoughts about those moments that widen the differences between their husbands foreshadow the outcome. Lucy sees Phyllis as odd and a little uncomfortable. And Phyllis, though she keeps the conversation going, is wondering what Lucy and Josh say to each other about James. About the sharp retort that James made to a remark of Josh's the night before.

Phyllis goes on a walk that leads to the old cemetery, so old the headstones are thin upright stones of slate with inscriptions in cursive. She flees after she reads an inscription for "William, drowned 1841, Age 18," wondering if he had committed suicide. When Lucy comes to take her to the old quarry for a swim with their husbands and children, Phyllis tells about finding the cemetery, and Lucy says she likes to go there. "Peace always comes dropping slow," she says. Phyllis replies:

> *"But I think I prefer to go to a place that is free from old*
> *living, absolutely clear of joy or grief or anyone's hopes or*
> *fears."*
> *"No," Lucy said slowly. "There's a kind of strength in*
> *a pattern made of other lives."*
> *What were they really saying to each other, Phyllis*
> *wondered. Somehow they were explaining deep differences*
> *in themselves, without quite understanding them. They*
> *hadn't said as much before. (49)*

At the quarry, both families swimming, Phyllis is fearful when James stays under the dark water for what she thinks is too long, but her dread vanishes when he comes up. She begins a playful banter with him, he responds, and she begins to understand that his way of looking at things is something she loves about him, a way that is different from that of his old friend.

The sites in this Vermont setting are familiar to me from *The Quarry* and *The Southwest Corner*. The quarry is there, the hill road, the covered bridge, and the weather that depresses or exhilarates. But the principal characters in *The Body of a Young Man* are summer people, not natives to village life. Summer people like those Marcia Elder observed from her southwest corner as they passed.

Now, in the 1960s, as in her childhood, Mother again had become a summer resident. Her principal friends in the village were summer residents, coming from academic and artistic endeavors, from business careers, or from family attachments to the village. (My brothers and I would be introduced to them when we came to visit her.) Her interest had shifted from the lives in the village to exploring an experience that was her own—and the Vermont setting, so familiar to her, must have seemed the right one into which to introduce her main character, Phyllis, an outsider. Phyllis's concerns, fears, and anxieties, born of a love for her husband, were familiar to Mother, too.

The relentless way that the plot of *The Body of a Young Man* evolves works for me as a reader apart from my recognition that it is informed by Mildred Walker's personal questions. But I find Phyllis's silent commentary on her reactions to the others and to herself distinctly recognizable as Mother's. And although the incidents, especially those that involve the three fictional children, are conceivable in any summer's events and essential to the plot, they startle me. I cannot see them as I should from the perspective of a reader. They are described exactly as they occurred, chiefly in my youngest brother's family years. I exclaim mutinously to myself that these moments have not even been transformed by the novelist's imagination! Calmer, I acknowledge to myself that I may have no justification in making this demand of the novelist. Is it simply because I am one of her children that I make this demand? If so, I have not yet become readerly enough to resolve this question. My own dilemma put aside, I can reiterate that *The Body of a Young Man* is unusual in Mother's body of work because it draws in so many ways upon her personal experience. And I wonder, at times, if that has to do with her returning to the Vermont setting where the surrounding details have always belonged to her life.

By 1960, Kidder Hill had become so thickly grown that old-timers in Grafton mentioned it as "the wilderness returning." The differing views of the two husbands in *The Body of a Young Man* are emphasized by two different trails they take down "the mountain" after an argument: James loses his way in the density of the trees for part of his descent but then finds his way. My brother Christopher lived at the Grafton house with Mother during the summers of his college years. He worked for a local contractor and came to know the people of the village. He also explored the country on long walks. Once he walked what seemed a trail from the top of Kidder Hill and told Mother that the disappearance of the trail had caused him to bushwhack down and come out on the far side of the hill. Mother said that trail had long been a kind of cart road for oxen but that she thought it had been overgrown since her childhood. I wondered if her son's adventure had reminded her of that trail. Mother discussed the scenes in the novel with him often that summer, perhaps as she had once done with Dad.

In 1959, Mother came through Minneapolis where my husband and I lived, both of us teaching at the University of Minnesota. She asked me to read a scene from her manuscript of this novel and to tell her if I thought her depiction of the friend, Josh, was too harsh. In 1959 this was still a rare request from her. When I told her that I thought her characterization of the man was justified, that his dialogue portrayed him as a contemptible verbal bully, she became incensed. "Look here," she retorted. "*All* of my characters are noble!" I was completely taken aback, and I wondered at her using the word *noble*. She was through with the conversation, however.

Early in *The Body of a Young Man,* thinking of how her husband's preoccupation with his failure seems to have separated them, Phyllis remembers:

> *Everything good had begun with James; everything gay and silly and sure. The night they had danced at the amusement park, a stranger had looked at them and smiled, and James had told her that everyone who looked at her loved her. She had laughed at the absurdity of it. People had never much looked at her at all, but when he said it, she almost believed it for a moment. (46)*

Twenty-six years after the novel was published, Mother made an entry in her journal, noting that the day was the anniversary of my father's death, May 16:

> *The day Ferd died. But no man was ever more alive in the hearts of his children and wife. As George once said, "His paths were all clean." [She quotes three lines from Robert Bly's "Silence in Snowy Fields" that she calls "joyous" and continues.] Right to go from writing of the day Ferd died to a mood of joy, for Ferd led me into a world of joy— loving and living with him was joy that I couldn't have known without him.*

Mother's sense of her life being wonderfully changed by the man she had married is very like Phyllis's silent outcry about her husband, James.

Perhaps Mother's closeness to Dad, and her sense that she needed old friends to help him get well, was not what led her to see Phyllis's well-intentioned impulse as a form of betrayal. But maybe it turned out to be in her imagination. In later years, after the publication of *The Body of a Young Man,* Mother referred more than once to the mistake she had made in submitting Dad to what she had hoped would be a restorative influence. I think she wanted to confront Dad's illness, believing that by some means she could make it go away. In her fictional worlds, human recognition circumvented total despair—or death.

In 1972 Mother published her fourth novel with a Vermont setting. A juvenile, it was taken by Margaret McElderry at Atheneum Press. While Mother was writing it, she called it "The Rock" and later "The Erratic Boulder." But McElderry persuaded Mother to change the title to *A Piece of the World.* Mother asked the Vermont artist Christine Price to do the illustrations and was pleased with the look of the novel when it was published.

At the heart of the children's story is the mystery of the great boulder left on a Vermont hillside by the glaciers. In Mother's childhood such a boulder was visible from the surrounding fields. Two hundred years of cutting timber and grazing sheep had bared the hillsides. A postcard dated 1904 shows the boulder completely exposed and calls it "Serpentine Rock." By the late 1930s when Mother took us to see Serpentine Rock, young pines had grown almost to its top. By the late 1960s and early 1970s when we took our children to see it, the boulder and the trail leading to it were completely hidden. Whenever Mother was with us on this walk, she became silent, conspiratorial, and somehow proprietary. Each time, the walk and the discovery of it were a ritual for her that the juvenile novel captured.

The walk all of us took over the years from the village of Grafton into the hills is the same walk that the girl, Calder, in *A Piece of the World* takes when she discovers the boulder for herself. Mother never spoke of why she chose to tell Serpentine Rock's story through a young girl's eyes. But in this story she is able to describe the village life of which, in her retirement, she had become a part. And it is the mystery of the Rock's presence as a story idea that she mentions in her journal of those years—a mystery that belonged to Mother's own childhood.

In the novel two children, around twelve years old, delight in the hidden presence of Serpentine Rock. Calder is visiting her grandmother for the summer in Vermont, and the boy, Walt Bolles, is local. Together they join Mr. Cooley, a retired geology professor, in trying to protect the Rock from being promoted as a tourist attraction. But they can't prevail against the determination of the Development Society, which finds a benefactor to pay for the expense of bringing the Rock down onto the village common.

The Rock has to be dynamited into four parts in order to be moved, a violence that appalls the two children. Only Mr. Cooley's encouragement that it will be interesting to see the inside of the Rock eases their fears. When the Rock has been split, they see the deep green, dark green, color that is serpentine—covered for centuries by exterior weathering. That inner mystery is hidden when the Rock's four parts have been cemented together on the common. In the story's last scene, Calder slips out of the house in the dark, undetected by the grownups talking on the porch, and climbs to the top of the Rock. When she returns to the house, she has kept a chip of green serpentine with her. As long as I can remember, Mother has kept a chunk of serpentine on her desk.

It always hits me with a lurch to think that Serpentine Rock might now be sitting on the Grafton commons, visible to every passerby to the village. It isn't, of course. That was Mother's imagination of an ominous event that would shake her young heroine's faith in what should be. But I still hear Mother saying with awe that when the stage coach road stopped being used up Chester Hill in the mid-1800s, the village, house by house, was moved down into the valley along Saxtons River to take advantage of a thriving woolen mill. The house belonging to our grandparents had been one of those. I wonder, now, if that fact was in Mother's mind when she imagined the removal of Serpentine Rock in *A Piece of the World*. My son, who loved the mysterious hidden presence of the Rock in the thickly grown woods surrounding it, must have been shaken and perhaps greatly relieved that it had never happened "in real life" when he read the manuscript at age ten.

3
College and Early Years of Marriage in Michigan, 1923–1933

Philadelphia and its suburbs where Mother was born in 1905, and where she lived nine months of the year until she left for college, was never a place that lived in her imagination. Her stories made it a place of events in her childhood that concerned her family and, as she grew older, a place of remembered personal irritations. But as a novelist, interviewed in 1948, when she had published seven novels, she would speak of her father's parsonage as a good place for an incipient novelist to grow up. The *Wilson Library Bulletin* quotes Mother as remembering, "We did not live by bread alone but by faith and humor, and the spoken and written words were vital and thrilling" (excerpt from an interview by Miriam Allen de Ford).

Grandfather Walker "supplied parishes" (a Baptist Church term Mother used) in a number of locations in Philadelphia and in outlying areas like Scranton and Germantown. This meant making the family home in parsonages—partly furnished houses set aside for the resident minister and his family. The Walker family moved often during Mother's high school years. "Four different high schools in four years!" she would exclaim indignantly. It was clear that she disliked the frequent moves and the parsonages. Only once did they live in what she described as a "well-appointed" parsonage: "carved moldings; tall, mullioned windows; a spacious kitchen; and a foyer with glass panels on either side of the front door." In Mother's married life, she would see to it that the houses she lived in were remodeled to include a foyer.

Equally distasteful to Mother was her sense that the family had to scrimp in these parsonage surroundings. She spoke of scrimping in a tone that was mildly scornful. In her notes for *The Quarry*, Mother quotes the Vermont saying, "Cutting the pattern to fit the

cloth," a form of scrimping. For Mother there were more important accomplishments.

Mother's descriptions of Grandfather never associated him
with unimportant accomplishments, only ones she considered to
be of value, even thrilling, as a youngster. She always kept a small
leather trunk full of his sermons, and over the years she brought
them out one by one to show us how beautifully he wrote in longhand. She held the folded separated packets open, suggesting that
each had much of value, and said she often took them out of the
trunk to read over. In Mother's last historical novel, *If a Lion Could
Talk,* the main character is a young minister who writes eloquent
sermons.

The moments she enjoyed most in her Philadelphia girlhood
were with her father. He took her along to his church on the days
when he wrote his sermons, allowing her to sit on the floor of his
office where she pretended to write sermons, too. Being allowed to
roam through the church while her father wrote was the favorite
story of her childhood, I think. She described herself as standing in the high Baptist pulpit, giving sermons to the empty pews.
This would be the reason, perhaps, why it seemed natural to "be
saved" on the evening of evangelist Billy Sunday's coming to their
church. Whenever she told us the story, she used the same words
with the same emphasis: "I was just seven years old when he came.
Billy Sunday called for those who were saved to come forward, so I
stood in the congregation and went with the rest. I remember that
Billy Sunday took me on his knee and Father, beside the pulpit
with him, looked proud."

I understand how Mother, as a child in Philadelphia, might
have chosen between her father and her mother. A minister dealt
in words, in lofty aspirations, in the eloquent performance of giving a sermon. (My brother George and I once heard him preach so
thunderously against sin that we shrank in our pew.) A housewife,
however fashionable and merrily bustling about her tasks, must
have seemed without aspirations to a daughter eager to excel in all
she undertook. But did it seem that way to Mother in those summer months in Vermont? Probably, because a mother who once
taught and knew how to handle a horse did not interest Mother in

the way that a father did whose eloquence announced his presence wherever his daughter accompanied him and whose fishing was spectacular.

A letter from her father that Mother saved was written to her when he remained at his church in Scranton and she was with her mother in Vermont. She was five years old in 1910. He addresses her as "My dear Mildred" and begins: "I received the picture which you sent me and how very glad [I am] you are well enough to draw it. I have been so sorry to have you sick away from home where I could not help take care of you. . . . I have missed you so much at home, and I have been so lonesome without my little girl to come into my study to see me." Grandfather closes the letter saying, "I have put the picture which you sent me up on my desk where I can see it and it reminds me of my little Sunbeam, whom I hope very soon to see. With ever so much love, Papa." All of Mother's stories about her early years in Philadelphia suggested to me that her devotion to the church had more to do with idolizing her father than with being dedicated to religion. By her college years, she had tired of the Baptist Church, the Sunday school classes she was obliged to teach when she returned during vacations, and the attendance at the three services required each Sunday—morning, midday, and evening.

In her high school years, Mother had admired the lifestyle of a classmate whose father was a Presbyterian minister. There was no scrimping necessary in the Presbyterian parsonage because the congregation was wealthy and the minister's family did not have to move frequently. More than once Mother described how happy she always was to enter her friend's house: stained glass windows in the foyer; the rich colors and designs of oriental rugs; tasteful and appropriate furniture. "It set a standard for me, an atmosphere that I wanted to achieve," she explained. She had resolved early in her life, I felt, to surround herself with belongings that appealed to her but that also suggested a certain level of status.

Attending college as a freshman in 1922 gave Mother the first of many opportunities to move her life in a different direction than that of her parents. In those years some colleges waived tuition for ministers' children. Wells College for women in Aurora, New

York, was one of these, and my grandparents chose it for their two daughters. Since Mother's sister, Margaret, had gone to Wells seven years earlier, Mother anticipated her own turn impatiently and said she took on all that was offered from the first moment she arrived. It was at Wells among young women "of means," as she put it, and an atmosphere of high aspirations to learning that Mother saw the success she wanted. "But I wrote home to Mother and Father every day so they would know how grateful I was to be at Wells," she told me.

She knew her determination to succeed was ensured by her enthusiasm for college. Part of that certainty, I think, was a private vow never to be dismayed. She found no difficulty in mastering her classes. She came to revere one of her professors, the poet Robert P. Tristram Coffin, who encouraged her in her writing. At some point, her years at Wells convinced her she would write the great American novel. "A lot of us thought that," she told me wryly, though American literature was not read in classes at Wells in the 1920s nor for quite a few years afterward.

Mother's stories about her college years suggested to my brothers and me how colorful she must have been. She told us of her dismay with a capacious, thick flannel bathrobe that her mother had made especially for her to take to college. The flannel was a gray background with a red and black pseudo-Indian design, edged in thick black braid. Mother said she kept it packed away except for dramatic skits. I see it as I'm writing, hanging on a peg against the log wall of our family cabin. It has been hanging in the cabin since I was a child. Even now, when I wear it, I imagine I am performing.

Mother convulsed us with her story about being so tired of college food, hungry for something tastier, that she entered an eating contest held at the local inn. Aurora was a small college town then and still is. So the event interested many of the students. The student who could eat a full breakfast and twenty-five pancakes at one sitting would not have to pay for her meal. Losing contestants must pay. Mother told us she had no choice but to win. Afterward, she was physically miserable but triumphant that she had won until she heard the dean of women's Sunday sermon the next morning on one of the seven deadly sins—gluttony.

I was an instructor at Cornell in the late 1950s, thirty miles from Aurora. My great find was meeting, by chance, a man who had been a janitor at Wells when Mother was a student. He remembered her as a lively young woman, so energetic that she parked a cart outside classroom buildings to sell hot dogs between classes. Her fellow students had named her "Pep" and sung to her:

> *It's not the pep of the pepper pot,*
> *or the pop of the popcorn popper.*
> *It's just old-fashioned P-E-P*
> *that's what we call Pep Walker!*

My brothers and I sang the chant to her at appropriate moments, but warily! She would glare playfully at us, but I do know that she liked being thought of as "peppy." She considered it a social attribute, I thought, in my glum adolescence. I often heard her use the word to describe someone favorably.

Mother kept in touch with four or five of her classmates through the years, and several of them visited our home in Montana. They dressed as she did in casual but expensive clothes—"well pulled together," Mother would point out to me, suggesting I learn the art. At Wells College, Mother seemed to have acquired the style, the flair, "the look," and the personality that she wanted for herself. And the success, too. She graduated magna cum laude and earned a Phi Beta Kappa Key. "Father was my greatest influence in being a success at what I did," she told me. "He expected me to be successful."

What may have been Mother's first publication was an essay written in her senior year called "Gargoyles." Submitting the essay to a competition open to college students, she won both fifty dollars and publication. She and Wells College were delighted until the essay was read by the townspeople of Aurora. Many townspeople were employees of the college and saw themselves in the essay: Not only were they described by their duties at the college but their real names were used and their limited lives were described. Mother saw them as the guardians of the college in this opening paragraph:

*The college is not of gothic architecture, and yet there are gargoyles about its corners. They are homely gray old faces with a humorous smile or a vacant patience; Haw-kins, the pointed face that needs only a pointed beard to make him a replica of some old French master, old Mary whose childlike eyes peer out of the face of an old, old woman, funny and eerie faces when the gray winds blow, starved and blanched in the cruel sun. Never, any place in the world, have I seen so many queer old people come from nobody knows where, or remembers, which is the same thing. (*Wells College Chronicle *30 [June 1926])*

Those employees so depicted were outraged enough to hire a law-yer who sued Mother and the college. Mother did not seem to re-member much about the outcome but knew that the college had to pay in the settlement.

Four years after her graduation, while living in Ann Arbor, Michigan, she received a query from the publishers Liveright & Co., asking if she might have a manuscript they could read. Appar-ently that letter mentioned they were writing at the suggestion of Samuel Hopkins Adams. A letter to Mother from Adams, dated Au-gust 28, 1932, explains his interest:

I remember quite clearly your essay which so disturbed the authorities at Wells. Your surmise is correct, concerning the lawsuit. Counsel for the college—who chanced to be my golf partners—knowing that I had had much experi-ence with libel suits, asked me to read your article and ad-vise them as to the danger inherent in it. I told them that your indiscretion was equaled only by the promising qual-ity of the writing. Which interested them not at all! Sub-sequently I suggested to Liveright & Co., my publishers, that you might be worth looking up.

In response to Liveright's query, Mother said, she hurried to finish the novel she had been writing, "God's Elect," but the manuscript was turned down. "It was one of those autobiographical first novels that one has to write," Mother said airily, her way of dismissing subject.

I found a clue to what that novel concerned in a talk she gave to Wells College students in 1940, fourteen years after her graduation, a year after her third novel had been a Literary Guild Selection. In the talk, printed in a Wells publication, she poses the question: "Why is it so difficult to write a novel about college?" She then describes her own experience:

> *I tried it once. I wrote a novel . . . that died at birth. A large part of it had to do with college. Inevitably, the college was a small one, with a red tower that overlooked a lake. The girl in my story was amazingly like myself. It came back to me as fast as I sent it out. One kindly editor bothered to write me a criticism. He said that the college part was the weakest section, the part that came the most feebly to life. (And that was the part not imagined!)*

She answers her question by acknowledging that "life is there in college . . . but [only] in moments" not always adding up to give " 'that judgment on life' that Edith Wharton calls the 'vital irradiation' necessary to any novel."

Mother was still in college when she met my father. In the summer of her junior year, her first summer not spent in Vermont, she took a counselor's position at a camp for girls in Rhinelander, Wisconsin, called Bryn Afon. A photograph showed her in fashionable knickers, her dark chestnut hair pinned up at the back of her head. She is a lovely young woman of twenty, her expression eager and confident.

Mother told us she was sitting under a tree reading Bede's *Ecclesiastes*, when she saw the young camp doctor reading down by the dock. "He was the only young man at the camp who read," she said, "so I set my cap for him." We saw the romance of the scene. The doctor's name was Ferd Schemm. He was twenty-six, beginning the last year of his residency at the University of Michigan Medical School in surgery. "He was reading *The Life of Sir William Osler,* a book his mother had just sent him," Mother said approvingly. He seems to have courted Mother the rest of the summer with moonlit canoe rides on the lake, good talk, and picnics. A photo shows him in a white shirt, sleeves rolled up above his elbows, tan shorts, brown hair, smoking a pipe.

Mother observed him at work in his profession, too, as he encountered a situation that was of deep sadness to him. A young woman counselor was brought into his infirmary in distress. He diagnosed her illness as appendicitis and drove her immediately to the nearest hospital. He returned to the camp, relieved, but learned in the morning that the operation had not taken place and that the young woman had died in the night. My father was bitter because the death could have been avoided and he felt she had died because his diagnosis as a resident was not credited.

Hearing the pain Mother felt for the young doctor in her retelling of the moment, I thought her growing affection for him must have deepened and her awareness of the complications of life must have been expanded. In this situation no amount of learning, good sense, or determination had prevented the tragedy. That was not her view of the world at this point in her life; her father had taught her that most obstacles could be overcome if one tried hard enough.

My parents' summer romance did not end after they returned to their respective work. My father wrote several letters or notes a week, responding in his letters to the remarks Mother had made in her letters. We have found his letters written in 1926 when Mother was finishing at Wells College. Mother told us of a weekend at Wells for which she and her roommate invited their "young men." The two students booked a single room with a double bed and realized too late that this greatly amused their guests. She said ruefully that the weekend was not too successful.

My father's letters continued that year, often mentioning that he had been on duty for such a long stretch that he was almost too weary to write. One letter begins:

> Dearest Mildred—
> I've been sitting here in a dog-tired state for numerous precious minutes—too lethargic to write—just enjoying thinking about ya. When I finally came over to quarters

after the weekend duty, I had the joy of taking my shoes
off for the first time in two days—really appreciated a
good shower and change and now before I turn in—just
a wee chat.

The letter ends trying to arrange a phone call when she would be at home so he could enjoy "the thrill of your darlin' voice!" Other letters that Mother sometimes showed me from that year are two to three full pages, handwritten, full of stories of people Dad had been working with, glimpses of humorous moments with his patients, and hopes that he would have a note from her soon. In all of Mother's anecdotes about their courtship over the years since my father's death, I sensed that her happiness at being loved became a new and widening dimension side by side with her strong ambitions to succeed in her work.

By the summer of 1926 Mother had graduated and begun to work in the John Wanamaker Store in Philadelphia. My father had completed his residency in general surgery and taken a position as contract surgeon in the lumber town of Big Bay, Michigan, in the Upper Peninsula. His letters change to an urgent, insistent argument that they should marry and she should join him. Her letters, Mother said, explained that she liked her work and that she was being promoted from aisle walking to writing advertisements. She was now allowed to wear a hat and white gloves, and she liked that. Letters back to her wished for a description of her hat and a hope that soon she might think of things she could like even better.

Soon Dad's letters were addressed to "Rib"—as in Eve's creation from Adam's rib. We guessed that Dad was protesting that he needed his rib. We children never heard him call her Mildred, always "Rib." Her letters began to address Dad as "Bizy," although we always heard her say "Ferd."

Mother has said that during that year, she came to like seeing herself in print, as a step on her way up, and was flattered by the attentions of her department head. But she visited Dad at his mother's home in Ann Arbor, and Dad visited her at her parents' home, at that time in Scranton. Still with deep pleasure just a few years ago, Mother remembered how "fitting, tasteful" the atmosphere was in the Ann Arbor home and still, with chagrin, how much a contrast her own parents' home in Scranton must have seemed to my father. In a postscript to his letter, he seemed to be making a protest to her expressed feeling. He wrote: "But the Scranton spree was fun."

Sometime that summer Dad sent Mother a salt cellar shaped like a small yellow dog (the souvenir sort), explaining that she'd have to come to Big Bay to live in order to have the matching pepper cellar. (The road from Big Bay to Marquette followed the Yellow Dog River.) I remember the two yellow dogs on our kitchen shelf when I was a child. The surviving salt cellar now sits in my spice cabinet.

By the summer of 1927 Dad had won. They would be married in October, but Mother first exacted certain stipulations. She wanted to continue writing; he agreed as if that were understood. Further, she would not do the washing. He agreed again. These were the examples she gave, but there must have been others having to do with her concept of an ideal marriage. One provision always described with a special intensity, and my father's response to it, seemed to make her proud of them both. She said she told him that he was not to let the marriage, or his love for her, relax his professional interest in his work. In answer, he quoted Ben Jonson's lines: "I could not love thee half so well / loved I not honor more." Her love of him for his way of looking at the life they would have together must have clinched the engagement. "His answer was of the greatest importance to me," she said with a tone of solemnity and a lift of her chin.

I am apt to repeat, perhaps too often, that Mother retold these stories about herself more than once over the years. I think she was reaffirming who she was, and had been, more often than entertaining or informing us. By contrast, my own stories that I have retold too often to my husband, my children, my nieces and nephews, even, I'm afraid, to my close friends, come from an impulse to impart, well, remarkable or soulful events. I have simply forgotten that I have already told them. No excuse. But these repeated stories of Mother's, so often descriptions of how she conducted her life, seemed to come from a determination to define who she was for herself as well as for us. Some were told with downright rectitude.

Mildred Merrifield Walker and Ferdinand Ripley Schemm were married in October 1927 in Scranton. Mother wished they had been married in Philadelphia because Scranton seemed a less important place to her. And she remained embarrassed into her late eighties about the event because she felt her parents' social circumstances were socially below those of the Schemms. Mother and Dad drove to Montreal for their wedding trip and then west to Michigan. The doctor's house in Big Bay was a narrow two-story clapboard, side-by-side with others down the street. The infirmary and the hospital were in just such a house a little farther down the same street. Mother said with amusement that much earlier in its life the building had been the town's ice cream parlor.

The little house was well furnished when Mother arrived with my father because Grandmother Schemm had, as Mother said, "seen to it." Grandmother had sent up from Ann Arbor some of her special belongings to transform the house from her bachelor son's surroundings. She had made curtains for it that Mother remembered made the house seem warm and comfortable. A cherry drop-leaf table and ladder-back rocker, furniture that we children grew up with, gave Mother a feeling that the inside if not the outside of the house had a distinguished air. From the beginning, I think, Grandmother Schemm was an important person in my mother's new life; she represented a way of living Mother craved, and Mother wanted to be at ease in that world. Later, Grandmother's family would become the basis for Mother's fourth novel, *The Brewers' Big Horses.*

My father's maternal and paternal grandparents had been residents of Saginaw, Michigan, since the 1860s. His paternal grandparents were farmers who emigrated from Bavaria in 1853 for political and economic reasons. They farmed first in Warren, Michigan, and then established the Schemm Brewery—known for its fine beers—in Saginaw in the 1860s. Although closed by Prohibition, the wrought iron title of the brewery, supported by sturdy brick walls, still stood in the 1970s when my brothers and I visited Saginaw. She never said so, but it must have fascinated Mother to have this connection with a brewery; in her Baptist family no one thought of taking a drink, even a social drink.

Born in 1819, my great-grandfather was thirty-four years old when he and his wife arrived in the States. Once the brewery was a success and he had three daughters, he built a large brick house on a quiet Saginaw street. Its dark, brick squareness was unlike the three-story white houses of Saginaw's first townspeople. Grandfather Schemm was born in the brick house in 1862, the only son in the family. He became a doctor, studying first at Jefferson Medical School in Philadelphia and then at Göttingen University in Germany. His given name was George Christopher, after whom my parents named my two brothers.

Not long after Grandfather Schemm set up his practice in Saginaw, he met my grandmother, Maude Ripley, who was born in 1870. She worked in the local newspaper office, a first for a young woman in Saginaw and against her parents' wishes. Also a first for a woman, she rode a unicycle about town: It was a glimpse of her as a young woman that we children cherished. My grandfather walked everywhere with his St. Bernard and used to send the dog up the steep staircase of the newspaper office when he called for my grandmother during their courtship.

Maude Ripley's family, English and Scots, had come from New England to Saginaw and, unlike the German Schemms, lived on what was considered "the right side of the tracks." Great-grandfather Ripley had come in the time of the wealthy lumber barons, perhaps as an investor. Mother said his work was never described by Grandmother, and Mother referred to him as "a gentleman who was not always well-off." He had married Emma Ashley, who was Dutch on her mother's side and a well-read woman. Her beautiful small volumes of poems and novels, leather-bound sets, had a place of honor on my parents' bookshelves. According to Mother, the Ripleys were not happy about their daughter marrying the son of a brewer even though he had become a doctor. Nor were the Schemms pleased with their son's marriage, at first, because they had hoped he would marry a German girl from that community.

When my grandparents married in 1898, they lived in a handsome three-story house that my grandfather had built for them. (When my uncle, Ripley Schemm, showed us the same house years later with great affection, he explained that one front side of the house had been his father's clinic where the children were never allowed entrance.) Three sons were born to them in the next five years, my father in 1899, and his two younger brothers in 1901 and 1903.

The lasting sorrow in the young family was that Grandfather Schemm became ill with pernicious anemia, which at that time was incurable. He was treated at Johns Hopkins Hospital in Baltimore by Dr. William Osler, the famous diagnostician who was later knighted for his work. My grandmother stayed with her husband at the hospital for months at a time, reading aloud to him. Grandmother had a studio photograph taken of their three young sons for her husband, but when he saw it, he told her that they looked like they needed their mother with them. Mother told us these details with a kind of reverence, especially for my grandmother's courage and sorrow, but also as a family story to be carefully remembered. She never told us that Grandmother's loss had been the basis for the sorrow of the heroine in *The Brewers' Big Horses*.

My father was only five years old when his father died in 1904 at the age of forty-two. But he told me that he had two vignettes of his father in his memory and cherished them. One was of his father lying on a couch with his three little boys climbing on him, and Grandmother taking the boys away, telling them that their father was tired. Another was of sitting on his father's lap and being shown a watch. My father's greatest regret about his life was that he had not had a father to grow up with. After my grandfather's death, Dr. Osler sent my grandmother a signed copy of *The Life of Sir William Osler,* saying that if one of her sons grew up to become a doctor, he might like to have a copy. That is the book that Dad was reading when Mother first saw him in Wisconsin.

When her husband died, Grandmother was just thirty years old. She told Mother that she regularly invited her brothers and male friends to the house so that her sons knew that atmosphere of laughter, talk, and drink, and especially the aroma of pipes and cigars. One incredible story that delighted my brothers and me described an evening when guests were seated around the table downstairs in the dining room. From their playroom upstairs where the three little boys could be as rowdy as they chose, one of them sailed a football over the banister ("A mistake, Mama, a mistake!"). It landed, the story went, on end in the opening of the tall coffee pot from which Grandma was pouring. That coffee pot, a tall Turkish design in whorls of dark metal, complete with a sugar and creamer and tray of the same design, always stood on the sideboard in my parents' dining room. We children regarded it as a noble object.

At times Grandmother's sisters lived in their house and thought the boys seriously rowdy. Dad used to repeat a chant that he and his brothers delighted to hurl at a red-haired aunt out an upstairs window: "Here comes Aunt Carrie, the red raspberry!" My father and his brothers each told us of Grandmother arranging with their gardener ("because a lady couldn't be seen in the street at that hour") a 4:00 A.M. trek to watch the circus animals being unloaded and paraded when the circus came to town, "the elephants waving their wide ears as they shuffled up the streets of Saginaw to the great tent in the dark of morning."

The bitter family story was that their father had been made to promise at his father's death bed to give up his medical practice to run the brewery. Even more bitter to Grandmother's sons when they were older was the disclosure that their father's two sisters disposed of their brother's will at his death; they thought his young widow would marry again and take the brewery out of the Schemm family. Due to the law at that time, Grandmother's sons were made wards of the state of Michigan, and money was doled out to her to care for them. "Therefore," my uncle said indignantly, "she had to account for the purchase of every button!"

Grandmother's grown sons spoke with awe of her heroic decision to sell the grand house in Saginaw to support their education at the University of Michigan. She went to live as a house mother in a sorority in Ann Arbor. After she left that position some years later, she would live for several months at a time with each of her married sons. My brother Christopher was just a few years old when she died, but for my brother George and me, she was an island of affection when she lived with us. When we were small, she read stories to us on our big, blue-black horsehair couch, which had been hers, hugging each of us tightly to her, but still managing to hold the book so we could both see the illustrations. A photograph of the three of us like this on the couch shows clearly beneath her blouse the large round hearing aid she always wore. She taught us outrageous songs and even more outrageous faces we could make at inopportune moments. From all my mother has told me over the years, she and Grandma became close friends while Grandmother lived with us. "She told me the most about her family in answer to my questions," Mother said once, "when I was brushing her long hair for her." Much later, when I learned that Grandma had read *The Brewers' Big Horses,* published in 1940, I asked Mother how Grandma had responded to the novel. "She said she had not realized how much she had told me," Mother said.

Grandmother Schemm was one of four daughters and two brothers. It was a family of mischievous gaiety as well as genteel behavior. Grandmother would address her siblings and later her sons and grandchildren by outrageous nonsense names. She wrote to her brother Henry, a career army officer, as "Norty Niddle Nad." When Great-uncle Henry was stationed at Fort Missoula in Montana, he wrote to her that he had to give up dancing "because the ladies mistook his asthma for passion."

When Mother spoke to us about Grandmother, it was usually with affection but also awe that such a ladylike woman could infect the household with sailors' songs and enthrall her grandchildren. Mother also indicated that having Grandmother with us as she aged became a burden. But in those earlier years in Montana when Grandmother lived with us, Mother was vigilant in introducing her to people who were her age and maintained the customs of her generation. Mother must have taken her every week to make afternoon calls on some of these acquaintances. I can still remember the small white oblong cards, engraved, that were carried to leave on brass trays in a front hall if the woman of the house was not at home. I remember especially because Mother had such a tray in our front hall and intimated that this was part of the necessity of being seen as a "well-brought-up" woman. A bit of Saginaw came to Montana with Grandmother Schemm.

I am convinced, too, that when she first married, Mother took care to adapt the social rules of Saginaw to the lumber community along Lake Superior. As a young wife, then mother, she observed the other residents of Big Bay with humor, curiosity, and a sense of being quite apart from them; theirs were not the lives she wanted or intended to live. Once she told me: "We just had the kitchen table next to the window to eat at, but carefully set with candles. I served our coffee in demitasse and asked Ferd to leave the curtains open so people walking by on Main Street could see we were different."

Another story she told was of an evening when Dad asked her to sit with the wife of an injured lumberjack who needed emergency surgery. "Of course, I sat her down by the warm fire, served her tea, and tried to make conversation," Mother said. But the two women sat silently until Mother said that it must have been hard to see her husband so badly injured. The woman burst out, "Oh, blood don't bother me none! But snakes? Golly!" I remember Mother telling this story at dinner parties out in Great Falls when I was a youngster. Her listeners always laughed at the incongruity of the woman's horror and seemed to take it as a characterization of the Upper Peninsula's people.

The community was mostly of Finns, and my father became fond of them. Nine years after he left Big Bay, he would name our log cabin in Montana the "Tupa," a Finnish word for a one-room cabin. The title of one of our storybooks was *Tales from a Finnish Tupa*. Dad must have spoken often with Mother by their wood stove about his Finnish patients. Mother told me of his coming home deeply saddened one night. He had attended a young wife whose first baby was stillborn. Father had enjoyed knowing the young man and wife for a year or more and had admired the beautifully carved cradle the young man was building. As my father walked away from tending the young woman, he heard the silent young husband chopping the cradle to pieces.

In the winters, Dad often had to snowshoe to the lumber camp to care for injured loggers, sometimes crossing over the tops of fences in the snowdrifts. The loggers and their wives thought well of Dad, especially because the doctor before him had often neglected them, often been off on a "bender." When I was born in 1929, the loggers came in from the camp to congratulate him. He liked telling us about one tall Finn who tossed me in the air and pronounced, "Damn fine baby, Doc!" When Dad took all of us back to Big Bay twenty years later, we were introduced to two men my age who had been given the name Ferdinand.

We have a photograph of Mother wearing a bulky raccoon coat, holding me as a baby on the ledge of my parents' open front porch. Her hair is drawn back smoothly from her face as she smiles into the sun and what must have been a chill breeze from Lake Superior. That raccoon coat was a legend in our family. When Mother and Dad were stuck on the road in a blizzard, coming home from Marquette, they wrapped up in it together to last the night in the car and survived. From her telling of these stories, I think that Mother enjoyed the excitement of those moments, what she thought of as frontier life.

Mother often spoke of the hilarity and unexpected moments that Dad made part of their lives. Once he assured her that spirits in moderation were the best of tonics, that one was a warmer person for it. Another time, as they were driving from Big Bay, Mother saw a deer leap across the road in front of them, and she commented that it must be difficult for the deer to give birth to those hooves. Dad agreed, adding, "Their antlers make giving birth even more difficult." Mother confessed that she believed Dad for a few more miles, and told the story on herself.

My parents' stay in Big Bay might have gone on longer than my mother wanted it to, except for a dismaying result of Dad's work. Although X-ray machines had been proven in Europe as early as 1904 to affect their operators with radium poisoning, purveyors in the United States in the 1920s sold the machines to construction and logging companies for use by their contract doctors. After three years of working with one of these, holding the injured limb of a man steady with his left hand under the rays, Dad's fingers developed blood poisoning with the danger of gangrene setting in. Mother never mentioned to me her horror or Dad's at what had happened. They must have decided to leave as quickly as they could because Dad could no longer do the delicate work of surgery.

That took them "across the Straits," a term Mother uses in her first published novel, *Fireweed,* set in the Upper Peninsula. After Dad was treated and informed that he would always be subject to recurring infection, he returned to the University of Michigan to study internal medicine. But first he wanted to observe at St. Bartholomew Hospital in London, known for its diagnostic advances. He and Mother took their savings, left me with my maternal grandparents in Germantown, Pennsylvania, and went to live in a boarding house in London for four months.

Mother wrote in the boarding house while Dad was at the hospital. She learned to join the other women, also boarders, by the fire when the winter days were too cold to work in her room. Mother told me that the women "looked askance" at her for leaving her nine-month-old daughter behind. When she showed them a photo at their request, that didn't seem to satisfy them, she said. She omitted telling them that she was carrying her second child, my brother George, who would be born six months later back in Ann Arbor. In the boarding house Mother finished her first novel, "God's Elect," the bound manuscript that was turned down. But it was returned from Harcourt, Brace with the request that she submit her next novel to them. Now, having found it in her saved papers, we know that it was an autobiographical novel of a minister's daughter.

Mother and Dad had one excursion during their stay in London in a small plane that took them across the English Channel. In a sudden storm, the plane stuttered and seemed to them to be going down, so they returned by a boat train. It was Mother's first trip to Europe, but my father had been stationed in France with the Expeditionary Forces in 1917–18 as an ambulance driver. He told us that Paris was a different world in 1930. He never told us about his experiences in the front lines, only about the last months spent near Dijon, enjoying the French people who befriended the young soldiers and taught them the virtues of good wine. I have a small watercolor of a thatched-roof farmhouse, in golds and soft browns, that he purchased on a later trip with my mother.

My father believed until the late 1930s that he had fought in "the war to end all wars." He let us dress up in the jackets of his old uniforms and wear two helmets he had brought back. At the cabin in a large bin stowed under a bunk, he had kept his army issue backpack, and my brothers used it for their early backpacking trips into the Wilderness. None of us was ever told any of my father's war experiences; he made that experience seem a private matter that he didn't want any of us to understand. But when we were all driving together, he taught us some roisterous songs with memorable lines like "Oh, the Infantry with dirt behind its ears / never could beat the artillery in a hundred-thousand years!"

As soon as they had returned from England and settled in Ann Arbor in the summer of 1930, my father enrolled Mother at the university where she studied for a master's degree in literature with an emphasis in creative writing. Her professor, Roy Cowden, became her mentor and a lifelong friend. Letters from Cowden to Mother, preserved in the archives, show that from the beginning of her writing in Montana, she sent Cowden her manuscripts to read and comment on. He and my father were her only readers before the novels were submitted to her editor at Harcourt in the years following.

From 1930 to 1933 my parents were devoted to their work and to lively social events with their university friends. It must have been a contrast to their first three years together in the Upper Peninsula. "We all had very little money because of the Depression," she remembered, "so we entertained by serving waffles for dinner." My father's studying and teaching in the medical school, and the stories told by their medical friends, were of great interest to Mother and would become the subject of her third novel, *Dr. Norton's Wife,* published five years later.

Mother juggled classes and studies with caring for two children. She hired students during the day, she told me; after a year, at my father's insistence, she hired full-time help. By the time my brother and I were one-and-a-half and three years old, Mother devised a method of putting us behind her in the large seat of a wing chair, so she could go on typing in front of us. She was writing the novel *Fireweed* at the time.

Mother's determination kept her going. At one point she became ill with fever for some time and had to recuperate. When she started going to classes again, she said, she was furious to find that all the books she needed to finish her master's work were checked out of the library. She berated the librarians, then felt guilty when she found all these books were already in her home. From the stamped-in dates, she saw that she herself had checked out the books when she was in a delirious state. The books had to be returned surreptitiously, one by one, and then checked out again as the librarians let her know the books were available.

In the spring of 1933, my father was deciding where to begin his new practice. He considered openings at Duluth, Minnesota, Portland, Oregon, and Great Falls, Montana. My parents made a trip to look at each location, and at the time, Mother said, she thought Great Falls the least desirable. But my father preferred a place that seemed more open to new ideas. And a Michigan colleague of his who was already practicing at the Great Falls Clinic urged him to come because they needed a cardiologist.

In the same spring, Mother received her master's degree in literature, completed her novel *Fireweed,* and received the Avery Hopwood Award of $1,100 at Michigan. She submitted the novel to Harcourt. Harcourt took the novel and, in the contract, opted for the next two novels they were sure she would write. Harcourt would publish all twelve of her adult novels, from 1934 to 1970. The sale of *Fireweed,* Mother told us, paid the expenses of moving to Montana in the fall of 1933. She was twenty-eight years old when we set out for Montana.

4
The Midwest Novels

While participating in a panel discussion at a Missoula, Montana, writers' conference in 1950, Mother was asked a question by another panelist, Joseph Kinsey Howard: "How did you know to have Sue [the sufferer of multiple sclerosis in *Dr. Norton's Wife,* published in 1938] long to be able to walk downstairs by herself and cut a cold sliver from the evening's roast?" Mother gave a ready answer that she repeated with a sly smile: "Why, I just thought if I were a cow, where would a cow go?" She said her answer was received as if it were frivolous by both Howard and another panelist, A. B. Guthrie Jr., the author of *The Big Sky.*

A large part of Mother's writing depended on both her strong sense of empathy and her keen self-observations. These two strengths seemed to give her a sense of sureness as she wrote. Each of her first four novels, set in the Midwest, would have women as protagonists. None of these protagonists would live lives like hers, but she knew where each would go.

In those first six years of marriage in Michigan, Mother found the lives and incidents she chose for each of her first four novels. *Fireweed,* from her three-year experience in the Upper Peninsula, explores the life of a young woman contemporary to Mother and living in a village like Big Bay. The next three novels take the stories of older women whom she admired: *Light from Arcturus* from long talks with the wife of a Marquette doctor; *Dr. Norton's Wife* from observations of my father and his medical friends in Ann Arbor about the invalid wife of a much-revered retired doctor; and *The Brewers' Big Horses* from my paternal grandmother's reminiscences about her life. These older women's stories must have been firmly in her mind when she left for Montana.

Fireweed and *Light from Arcturus* have protagonists who yearn for certain kinds of lives. In each novel these young women, both seventeen years old, are beginning their marriages with decided ambitions about where their lives will take them. Each woman loves her husband but expects him to raise his status in life. How these ambitions are realized is a source of suspense in each novel.

Celie Henderson of *Fireweed* is introduced by the narrator as confidently at work in the lumber mill's company store, aware that she is going to make something of herself: "Someday they might need an extra girl in the office next door, who knew? Pretty Celie Henderson was there to watch her chances" (10). And Julia Hauser of *Light from Arcturus* at seventeen is already on her wedding trip, married to a dependable older man of thirty-five from Nebraska: "Julia Hauser reached out to all that lay ahead. She wanted things to happen; that was the expectancy in her dark eyes. She had no fear that perhaps she would not be equal to them. . . . That confidence was the secret of her poise" (3). The differences between the two novels are in social status and time: The reader sees Celie for about four years of her life (1929 to 1933) as a lumber mill worker's wife in a contemporary setting and Julia for sixty-seven years beginning in 1873 as a wholesale producer's wife. After the first four years of Celie Linsen's married life, she realizes she may never get "across the Straits," away from the Upper Peninsula to Detroit, but Julia Hauser leaves Chicago for Nebraska, and returns, several times.

Because of events that are significant to the plots of these novels, each ends in 1933. In *Fireweed,* the Depression and lack of trees have caused the lumber mill in Celie Linsen's Flat Point to close and a newspaper nearby to print an obituary to the town. In *Light from Arcturus,* Julia Hauser, whose life has revolved around the occurrences of the world's fairs—the first in 1873, the second in 1893—has just attended her third in 1933 and thinks as the novel ends, "It was something to have seen three Fairs."

About *Fireweed* and its setting in a logging community, Annick Smith says in her introduction to the 1994 University of Nebraska Press reprint, "Working people who harvest natural resources have always balanced their attachment to place against the certainty that the logs will run out, or the iron, the oil, the gold." Smith pursues the author's use of the wildflower fireweed as the metaphor for the young wife and husband who, vulnerable to the company's supply of timber, stay with the country as the milltown begins a decline. Of the author, Smith writes: "Imagination, observation, and empathy are a writer's renewable resources. Mildred Walker was well endowed with all three."

There is a constant and rapid motion in *Fireweed* between what Celie aspires to and what she has. In the third person Celie thinks steadily about a house she prefers to the one she lives in. In the next moment, Celie takes pleasure in having their own house (though she will replace that bedspread soon) and in greeting Joe with a fine noonday dinner when he comes home from work (though she wishes he could become a bigger man at the mill). Her children make her feel discouraged about ever getting away from Flat Point, but she turns to them more and more for comfort toward the end of the novel.

The way life is in Flat Point is told consistently through Celie's thoughts in the third person except when the thoughts of other characters are described or when the narrator interprets Celie's state of mind or the village's appearance. The narrator is intent on including characters Celie might turn to or from. But some seem included, in this novel, out of the narrator's fascination with "those sorts of people," a phrase Mother used in explaining her social distance from them. The narrator's representation of the villagers' speech is intended to depict the uneducated experience and foreign backgrounds in the village. There are lives in the village that the narrator renders as a counterpart to Celie's thoughts— sometimes bluntly, sometimes harshly. The reader is directed to the very minor character of Anna Andres, "a big woman with classic, regular features, a look of complete peace lay on them although it had nothing to do with the few thoughts and petulant animal nature behind it." She is watchful as her husband, home from work, puts "his [pay] envelope . . . on the shelf over the sink as usual."

Her husband, hearing that she is going to the company foreman's house to help put on a dinner, says he has heard a rumor from the company timekeeper about less work for the men:

> *"You keep your ears open an' hear if they do any talking about a cut."*

"Did he say how a person could live?" asked Anna grimly.

"Naw, they don't think of that, them city guys." (200)

The scene changes then to the dinner party at the foreman's house where Celie is seated as a guest, hoping to further her husband's promotion at the mill with the owners. One man points out about the work schedule, "We'll either give a cut or run four days a week." After more conversation that underlines in Celie's mind the crassness of the mill officers, the point of view shifts again: "Anna Andres, putting away silver in the dining room, listened to the talk. That littlest brat of hers needed cod liver oil like the doctor said; what did that man from Detroit mean about four days' work a week?" (206–07)

The depiction of minor characters in *Fireweed* includes every possible kind of person who might make up such a village. Each woman's view of her domestic situation there, each man's sense of the work he is doing—even those who do not touch Celie's life. This is an effective device to underline Celie's feelings about Flat Point. She is a sympathetic character, a youngster really, who delights in taking the boat out on Lake Superior with Joe, driving to town with him, watching their babies grow, and loving Joe for himself at saving moments. Just as often, the lake seems an unrelenting gray and its wind bitter, their drives back from town spoiled by Joe's silence in answer to her dream of moving out of Flat Point, the babies crimping her social moments with other young wives, Joe seeming thoughtless or taking a drink. The effect is to emphasize how small the scope of her life is in Flat Point. It is also a reminder of Mother's early essays in "Time in Vermont," depicting the villagers of Grafton. Even more so, the device is reminiscent of her college essay, "Gargoyles." In one swift instant, she characterizes a person and takes on the attitudes or feelings that would be hers if she were that person.

This unerringly effective device for the novelist, Mildred Walker, is not the approach I saw my mother, Mrs. Schemm, practice in ordinary moments of a day on the streets of Great Falls, Montana. Instead, there were "those sorts of people." Too often, to my resentful self, it had to do with clothes: A man in a three-piece suit striding along the sidewalk earned a cordial nod; a man sloppily dressed, slumped on a bench, was "a ne'er-do-well." Once, perhaps in my first year of high school, when these comments were applied to my school friends, I cried out in frustration, "How can you know that?" Unperturbed by my desperation, she smiled, saying, "It's so obvious, dear. You'll see it yourself someday." I remember vowing silently that I never would see it someday.

But under the spell of the narrator of *Fireweed,* I do see it as it affects Celie Linsen, whose cheap rayon dresses and high spiked heels ordered from the catalog are mentioned often by the narrator. As the lumber mill shuts down, the jobs end, and the houses on each side of them stand empty, Celie comes to admire Joe's ingenuity in providing for the family, and she finds ways to work with him. In the last chapter, Joe and Celie lie in the warm grass while the children sleep, and soon Joe sleeps with his head on Celie's lap. She looks down at him affectionately, thinking: "He wouldn't go very far, maybe, but he was hers, anyway. . . . She had known they were not going to get away from the Point." In her mind, she goes over their lives to come:

> She and Joe would always live there. She would grow old
> the way Christina had, but they would be independent
> like Christina and Ole; Joe would always make a living.
> She would always have to work hard; there would be more
> babies and she would look tired like Christina did, but it
> wouldn't matter, so much. (313)

Her children would go away, make a success, come back, "and wonder how she ever stood it up here. It was all right; plenty of things were left to her, after all." In and out of these thoughts, Celie watches the tall blooms of fireweed, thinking how sturdy they were to grow "in that burned out ground."

Early in Part I, when Celie's mother, Christina, tries yet again to prevent her husband, Ole, from continuing the dangerous work he does for the mill, the narrator comments: "Christina Henderson would go back to her work grimly. Whatever fears she had she shut her lips tightly upon, in the habit of a lifetime. What else to do?" (18). This is a mannerism of her mother's that the narrator has Celie notice earlier, but now, on the last page of the novel, it becomes Celie's: "Whatever fears Celie had for the future, she shut her lips tightly upon, like Christina. They would manage all right, she and Joe" (314). I have come to realize that as a novelist, Mildred Walker not only became her characters but also felt a warm kinship with them however unlike her experience theirs might be. Halfway through the novel, Celie has found Joe sleeping, his boots knotted in the bedspread and alcohol on his breath. A moment before she had hated him, but now seeing him so vulnerable, she kisses him: "A strange new feeling for him rose in her. Celie Linsen had left her adolescence behind. A girl grows into a woman early in the country of the sticks" (145). It was only as a woman bent on achieving an important social status that my mother insisted on a right and a wrong "sort."

In the Upper Peninsula, my father had as a colleague the head doctor of a tuberculosis sanatorium in Marquette. Dad consulted with Dr. Lojacano about a number of his tuberculosis patients from Big Bay, and my parents became friends of the doctor and his wife, visiting them whenever they were in Marquette. Marie Lojacano became a compelling influence in Mother's life. The Lojacanos' style of living captivated Mother. Through the years, Mother instructed me in "the little touches" that Marie insisted upon for a dinner party or a living room arrangement: small bowls of matches placed on a coffee table; the wicks of new candles always burned, then snuffed out a few moments before guests arrived. "True elegance has a look of casualness about it," Mother explained to me.

Before her marriage to the Italian doctor, Salvatore Lojacano, Marie had been a settlement worker in Chicago. Her stories about her mother's life that took the mother from Chicago to Nebraska and back again to Chicago were Mother's inspiration for her second novel, *Light from Arcturus*. I know of Marie from black-and-white photographs: a large, dark-haired woman, usually seated in a wooden armchair on the lawn, and smiling widely with her head thrown back. Her husband usually stood beside her, his bearing erect and his dress impeccable. In several snapshots my brother George and I are small children in the foreground. While Mother and Dad lived in Ann Arbor, they visited the Lojacanos regularly. Later, growing up out in Montana, I knew of them as my godparents.

Marie Lojacano's telling of her family story must have suggested to Mother a much wider scene than she had been working with in *Fireweed*. As the novel *Light from Arcturus* opens, Julia Hauser, newly married to Max Hauser, is on her wedding trip from Chicago to Philadelphia to visit the 1873 world's fair. Its splendor will always be a touchstone for Julia. Philadelphia is imagined from a horse-drawn cab, forty years earlier than Mother's own childhood. The Hausers' route takes them to the elegant, glamorous places—down Chestnut Street, across the new Girard Avenue Bridge, to stop at the lighted doorway of Lafayette House. Julia approves the luxury of their rooms, and in her mind is already planning a drawing room for the new house Max has promised to have built in far-off Halstead, Nebraska. Max's mild protest that people in Nebraska don't have drawing rooms doesn't deter Julia. The first twenty-some pages of the novel establish Julia's priorities.

After the wedding trip, the Hausers are settled temporarily in a rooming house in Halstead. As a surprise, Julia visits her husband's flourishing wholesale general store—"MAX HAUSER—PRODUCE." When they leave the store together, Julia sums up the situation to herself:

> *Julia felt a sense of security and ownership as Max locked the door behind him then, quickly, a little feeling of superiority to the small store. Max must become something more than a wholesale produce man in a prairie town. The granddaughter of an official at the court at Prague slipped her hand into her muff. Max took her arm and together they went along the frozen ridge of the road that served for sidewalk. (33)*

The reader discovers through the narrator that Julia is intent on "something more" in every aspect of her life.

Mother's character, Julia Hauser, reacts fiercely to the rawness of the midwestern town. Published just two years after Mother was settled in Great Falls, *Light from Arcturus* reflects Mother's early impressions of living out west. She minded the lack of culture as Julia had. Mother had in mind Portland, Oregon, or even Duluth, Minnesota—places where she and my father might have settled. Earlier, she had envisioned her husband establishing his medical practice on Chestnut Street in Philadelphia as her father had proposed. Much later, she told me these thoughts, but admitted, as if to herself, that Montana had been good for her writing.

Mother kept a low profile as a writer in Great Falls. Instead, she maintained vigilantly what she thought of as her social role—that of a doctor's wife. Her character, Julia Hauser, also has a social role to live up to in Halstead—that of the wife of a successful merchant who is well thought of, eager for progress in the raw new town, and who encourages confidence in his fellow townspeople. Julia is able to respond to that role with a lively, observant watchfulness. She makes friends with her husband's friends, enchants others, and entertains their concerns. But she has an inner world of thought and ambition that absorbs her, that she works on each day.

Julia Hauser's inner resource is not the work of writing but of comparing the lacks of Halstead with the advantages of a city like Chicago. Through the narrator's eyes, Julia is aware not only of her new home's lack of culture but also of the discouragement of those who have lived in Halstead longer than she has: the wife who no longer paints; the well-educated doctor from Edinburgh who is impatient with the lack of a concert hall and a good restaurant that might serve lobster; the husband who eases his boredom by being unfaithful and is shot to death. There are personal excitements in Julia's life: Once, she defies her social set by taking into her home a visiting actress who has become ill and who stays on after her convalescence. But her driving ambition after twenty years in Halstead is to get her children back to the opportunities of Chicago and to persuade her husband to move there permanently.

I venture the comparison between Mildred Walker in her new setting and her character Julia Hauser in her new setting because each has a sense of managing in the midst of what seems to them the pettiness of small town lives. Mother's development of characters was thoroughly based on empathy. She had the story in mind when she arrived in Montana in 1933. She told me once that shortly after their arrival in Great Falls, she felt lonely because my father was gone all day, seeing patients and driving long distances to the ranches of those critically ill. "So I wrote," she said. Mother could easily have empathized with the feelings of Julia Hauser in her raw midwestern town, a town without culture.

At the first, in 1876, Julia tries to imagine Halstead becoming a city. But in 1933, in her seventies, with a moment to reflect as she is borne through the sky on her first airplane, Julia remembers, "Halstead was worse than she had feared, not even dangerous nor rough, just cramped, already set in its narrow rut. She had tried to live there" (343). A year later, as their home is being built for them, Julia insists on certain amenities, including a drawing room. She overrides her husband's objection this time; she wants their house to "make a statement" to their friends in Halstead. This kind of statement will influence Julia's choices throughout the novel.

My family lived for the first year in Great Falls in a rented house not far from the hospital where my father treated his patients. I remember the house as tall, two stories, with a tree surrounded by cement so that my brother George and I could ride our tricycles around and around the tree. I especially remember an upstairs room where Mother wrote. There was a Valentine's Day when Mother gave us red paper and white doilies, paste and scissors, and sat us in a three-sided window seat. Mother sat typing at the table behind us. The sun shone in, tall elm trees swayed in the February wind, and I felt secure—because we were there with Mother. I was going on five by then, and my brother was just three and a half, so the year must have been 1934.

Usually, we were taken care of by the young woman named Dorothy who had come with us from Michigan on the long hot drive. Mother later told me that Dorothy had pleaded to come with our family to start a new life. My parents agreed because Mother needed her to keep house and to have uninterrupted time to write. And, Mother told me, the fact that my parents brought "Help" with them impressed other doctors' wives. As I grew up, I was always aware of Mother's ways of impressing others, and that is why I compare her situation to that of her character, Julia Hauser. In the twenty years of living in Halstead, of raising four children and later of making new lives for her children in Chicago, Julia kept her mind on impressing others.

Again, as for Celie Henderson of *Fireweed,* there are members of Halstead's community whom Julia never meets, never needs to impress, but who comment on Julia's life. As Marthe Polkas and her husband, Stanislas, in their wagon full of produce, drive by the Hausers' big green house and see it in the upheaval of packing for Chicago, Stanislas tells his wife that Max Hauser is going away:

> *Then Marthe Polkas's brown weathered face expressed an emotion; dismay, suspicion as to the future showed in her slackly opened mouth, in her eyes. Marthe Polkas had no trust in people or fate. Only eight years of taking farm-stuff in to Max Hauser's store, getting solid silver dollars for it, made the universe secure. Now he was going away. That was where he lived. She stared from under her black wool shawl. . . . What did people move for when they had a house like that and a store? It was a queer country. The green wagon jogged around the corner of Omaha Street, Stanislas Polkas and his wife on the front seat, two peasant figures against the wide blue sky and the flat land.*
> *(205)*

This device, a kind of chorus on the lives of the protagonists in a novel, Mother will use in most of her early novels. Most often, the chorus is made up of briefly introduced characters who don't begin to understand the intricacies of social pressure that propel groups of people who are not like themselves.

Of her first two novels, *Light from Arcturus* would probably be of more interest than *Fireweed* to present-day feminist readers. Celie Linsen begins by being conscious of her social status, of wanting to "be different" than her mill town counterparts. But in the end she recognizes that she has changed; she accepts staying in her husband's world. Julia Hauser leaves Nebraska to gain what she feels is a superior social status for herself and her children, but at the expense of her husband's world.

Mary Swander, who wrote the introduction to the 1995 Nebraska edition of *Light from Arcturus,* finds the concerns of a current feminist viewpoint at work in Julia's situation. She asks, "For a contemporary reader, why does this story still have such a hold?" and goes on to propose an answer:

> Light from Arcturus *not only gives us a historical perspective on "trailing spouses" but on women's self hood. . . . But don't many still feel they must justify their own steps by seeing them as ultimately for the good of others? Aren't women still socialized to give up the self in the service of family or the larger community? (x)*

Swander's reading of this novel considers Julia's closing thoughts on what she has done with her life "an enigma." Of her decision to uproot her family from Nebraska for the culture they would gain back east, in Chicago, Julia muses: "Everything she had done had been for the children. . . . Or was it for herself, after all?" (343). Julia's only regret is that persuading her husband away from his successful business and wholehearted support in his community had left him without purpose in his life. Swander suggests, "Some will say Julia muddled her way through to selfhood in a milieu of feminist unconsciousness" (xii).

But when Mother, at age ninety, read the introduction by Swander, that suggestion did not interest her. Instead, she burst out to me, "I thought it was a tragedy! That women would drag their husbands back east for the sake of culture, force them to give up the lives they had made out west!" Did Marie Lojacano, Mother's older friend back in Michigan, tell her family's story as tragic? Or did Mother conceive of it through the nature of her character, Julia Hauser? I think the answer lies in one of these two questions because we children never heard her discuss feminism in the 1960s and 1970s and never in terms of her own novels. Julia Hauser had an agenda, and a reader has followed Julia's narcissistic certainty that her own life will be much more interesting in Chicago than in

Halstead. Mother seemed to conclude, in her last chapter of *Light from Arcturus,* that it was done at the expense of Julia's husband's self-respect, thereby being "tragedy." Perhaps she would say that the tragedy was caused by feminine selfhood.

Harcourt's writer for the dust jacket of *Light from Arcturus* used a term similar to selfhood: "This story of a woman's self-realization . . . recalls the early novels of Willa Cather in background and characterization." But I think the term was probably of less interest to Mother than the comparison to Willa Cather. I remember finding Willa Cather's novels and short stories in Mother's bookshelves.

In August 1934, Mother published a short story, "Comfort Me with Apples," in the *American Magazine.* The magazine gave the story a billing: "The author of *Fireweed,* the Hopwood Award Prize Novel of 1933, presents here her first short story" (49). The story is written in the persona of a young Philadelphia woman who describes herself as living in a small apartment in the city, teaching "English language and literature to the youth of the nation in one of the larger high schools of the city" (48). The young woman's tone is urbane, often self-mocking, and yet she admits to being vulnerable to a college friend's lovelorn tale.

The Philadelphia setting in the beginning plays off the situation of Mother's older sister, Margaret (whom we knew as Aunt Peg), who was teaching in Philadelphia in similar circumstances after a disastrous early marriage. On her wedding night, Margaret's new husband, a minister, exhibited such psychopathic tendencies that she escaped to the family home a few blocks away. After her father arranged for an annulment, Margaret taught in one of the "Fresh Air Schools" in vogue at the time, which she described to me as so bitterly cold that she provided all her students with mittens. After she survived a bout of pneumonia, Margaret was encouraged by her father to take a Ph.D. in history at the University of Pennsylvania. She was one of the first women in Philadelphia to accomplish that degree in the late 1920s, and she went on to teach history at "one of the larger high schools of the city." I have copies of some of the professional papers she published following her move into counseling inner-city students. Mother told me how she admired her sister, but was always sorrowful about what had precipitated her sister's career in teaching.

Katherine, the speaker in "Comfort Me with Apples," listens to her friend's bitter story of her fiancé's breaking off a long engagement and thinks her own thoughts: "I looked at Marge's face and then back at the fire. It seemed to me that women are pitiful, they're so easily hurt and there's so little they can do about it. There almost ought to be a new kind of insurance established. Of course, teaching makes you feel a little that way" (50). Then Katherine brings herself back to her friend Marge's statement. Marge says she had asked her fiancé if he no longer cared for her: "And he acted as if I'd committed a breach of etiquette. He said, 'Oh, Marge, don't be like all women'" (50).

The speaker in this short story has a silent dialogue with herself while she listens sympathetically to her friend. She thinks about the man she loves and how they will soon marry. In the central drama of this story, Katherine takes Marge for a weekend to her family's Vermont farmhouse. Katherine is happy because the man she loves, and intends to marry, will also visit. But she becomes afraid that he is falling for Marge. The story ends with her bitterness as they eat apples by the fire. She remarks, "Know that verse from the *Song of King Solomon,* 'Comfort me with apples, for I am sick of love?' . . . I picked up another Spy, raised it to my nose in mock salute, and sauntered up to bed" (129).

This story is about two smart career girls. Does it suggest a feminist outlook on the writer's part? Other than Katherine's thought about "insurance," each woman seems to be looking at the possibility of not marrying the man she loves. Why do I pose this question about feminism? The time is the early 1930s when, according to Betty Friedan in *The Feminine Mystique,* large numbers of women had begun to have a sense of themselves as having the right to be equal to men. If, as Katherine thinks, "women are pitiful," is Mother making a statement, or is she toying with the idea of a career as "insurance"?

In Mother's acute sense of whom she wanted to be, she had exacted my father's promise that she would be unimpeded in her writing by domestic duties. She was a feminist in a personal sense. As for her characters, in her first novel, the woman feels trapped, at moments, by raising children. Her later heroines, I think without exception, find ways not to be trapped by domesticity because of their natures or because of their financial circumstances. Yes, Mother believed in her right to pursue her writing career, but as my friend Claire Davis, author of the novel *Winter Range,* said, "Well, it was your father who was the feminist."

In *Dr. Norton's Wife,* Mother's third novel, a woman's personal right to selfhood is not the issue. Her oppressor is an incurable illness. This novel departs from the ambitions of young wives intent on living their lives as they had dreamed of doing. It departs, too, from the social drama of maintaining a household in a certain way. Instead, it studies the effect on a household of living with the sorrow of an incurable disease. Each of the three parts of the novel begins with a quotation from Sir Thomas Browne's *Religio Medici.* Browne, an English physician in the mid-seventeenth century, wrote that contrary to contemporary thought doctors were not godless; rather, they hoped for a miracle but were forced to contend with much that was hopeless. The epigraphs to Part I read:

> *I am not only ashamed, but heartily sorry, that, besides death, there are diseases incurable.*

> *Men that look no farther than their outsides, think health an appurtenance unto life, . . . but I that have examined the parts of man know upon what tender filaments that Fabrick hangs.*

Sue Norton, a woman struggling with the indignities of multiple sclerosis, is the protagonist of *Dr. Norton's Wife.* The novel opens as she awakens at dawn and notes how slowly time passes and how uncomfortable she is. But at this moment she feels rested, strong enough to attempt walking down the short hallway to the room where her husband now sleeps. She longs to overcome the separation from him that her illness has brought about, to "break the cage that this sickness has thrown up around her." She thinks, "It was unbelievable that Dan Norton's wife should be an invalid, practically bed-ridden. That happened to other faculty wives" (5).

Sue makes progress, supporting her unwilling legs by leaning against the wall as she moves. Almost to Dan's bedroom, she leans on a small table so hard that it crashes to the floor with her awkward weight. The noise brings the rest of the household—her husband, her sister, Jean, and the housekeeper, Agnes—to rescue her. She is unable to get to her feet without help, and she sobs with disappointment as Dan carries her back to her bed.

As the novel continues, Sue's helplessness increases until her speech becomes slurred—a characteristic of the disease—and, at inappropriate moments, she erupts into embarrassing, involuntary fits of laughter. As an admired member of the medical faculty, Dan inspires the student doctors. They have become accustomed to dropping by the Nortons' house. But as Sue's disease progresses, Dan discourages those gatherings because it bothers her so much to be seen changed. Much worse for Sue is her awareness that Jean has come to love Dan and her certainty that Dan has turned to Jean. Sue begins to hate them, helplessly but bitterly. The depiction of what multiple sclerosis does to its victim in *Dr. Norton's Wife* was so accurate that, soon after its publication in 1938, the novel became required reading for student nurses across the country.

The novel was chosen by the Literary Guild of America as its January selection in 1939. The Guild's publication, *Wings,* announced:

> *Mildred Walker is a writer who has been known to only a few devoted readers. We feel safe in predicting that with the publication of* Dr. Norton's Wife *she will become one of the American writers of front rank importance. . . . We believe that Guild Members will find this book so much above the ordinary level of fiction writing that they will share our enthusiasm. Besides the thrill of discovering unusual talent, they will enjoy the simple and direct writing, the distinguished and restrained treatment of the plot and they will respond to the intellectual and emotional appeal that makes the book so outstanding and interesting. (1)*

The same pamphlet for promotional purposes includes a brief introduction to the novel by John Beecroft, who writes: "She will not only win praise for its sensitive, balanced and honest writing, but will be established as an author of unusual ability and a master of the novel form" (2). He notes the quotation of Shakespeare's sonnet at the end of the novel—"Let me not to the marriage of true minds / Admit impediments. Love is not love / Which alters when it alteration finds"—and terms it "her inspiration for this novel."

Two more selections follow in the pamphlet, both written by Mother, the first with the title, "I Have Written What I Saw," and the second, "All about Myself." In each brief selection she describes her familiarity with the medical world. In the first, she gives a summary of her life with my father, saying that the novel came from

> *the medical environment in which I have lived for the last eleven years. In a sense, I have been the wife of three different doctors: for three years the wife of a country doctor, for three years the wife of a doctor teaching and learning in a large medical school, and for five years the wife of a doctor practicing a specialty with a group of associates in a city. (4)*

She goes on to say that she had read many novels of "medical background in which the doctor moves from one dramatic success to another; novels in which the patient always seems to recover." But she had observed, sadly, that this was not always what happened; instead, the doctor "has often, after he has used all of his skill and knowledge and wisdom, to turn away in defeat." In the rhetorical question that follows, she states the impetus for this novel:

> *What effect does that have upon him? Here, it seemed to me, was another story worth telling . . . what has concerned me in this book is the problem that arises from the doctor's struggles against the still numerous diseases for which he has, as yet, no cure; what happens, moreover, when the disease strikes in his own family. (4)*

She ends this selection with the disclosure that "I started out with a problem or situation but I had come to see it in terms of Dan and Sue Norton" (5).

Mother's second selection in *Wings* is, in contrast to the first, autobiographically arch and jaunty about the details of her life. By way of introduction to her life, she characterizes herself as beginning to write "at the tender age of seven, . . . and now, twenty-seven years later, I have not left off writing." She concludes by referring to the subject of *Dr. Norton's Wife:* "It was probably inevitable that it would have a medical setting with my eleven years of exposure to doctors and their jargon." The novel is dedicated to my father.

Almost sixty years later, in 1997, David Budbill, the poet, has written an introduction to the Nebraska reprint, commenting, "Simply put, Mildred Walker culls beauty from sadness." In writing of the irony of this tragedy in the midst of a thriving medical research community, Budbill points to the title of the novel: "There is more than a little here about the doctor's wife as an accouterment to the doctor's career. Even the title of this book can be seen as a statement regarding Sue Norton's place in the scheme of things in this medical-academic world" (ix–x).

Of course, I imagine that is how Mother first heard the story and gossip of the doctor's wife who suffered that illness. Mother would say to me, much later in the 1980s, that no friends from Ann Arbor's medical community wrote to her after the publication, that perhaps they felt she shouldn't have written the novel. She also said that even my father, after having provided her with the accurate details of how the disease progressed, and after suggesting those quotes of Sir Thomas Browne, didn't talk much about it with her. "I wrote too much about medical matters," she said glumly.

When she said that, she was including a later novel, *Medical Meeting*, this one also set in the Midwest and published in 1949— ten years after *Dr. Norton's Wife*. What binds these two novels together is a rendering of a medical community. In each novel the wife has fully supported the husband in his medical research during their first twenty years of marriage. Dan Norton presents his findings before the medical school faculty of a university resembling the University of Michigan; Henry Baker in *Medical Meeting* presents his findings before a medical convention in Chicago.

Perhaps the similarity would not be worth noting if it were not for the occurrence of a phenomenon in research that happens to each of the doctor husbands. Having given his important lecture, with Sue present in a wheelchair, Dan Norton acknowledges to his audience that a doctor in Norway has reached the same finding: "'I take the keenest scientific pleasure in this added proof of my hypothesis, but, naturally, I cannot in honesty claim the priority for which you have honored me tonight.'" In spite of his disclosure, Dan is awarded the medal to the cheers of the audience, but Sue Norton thinks, "Their medal was too like giving a reward to a good boy for effort rather than accomplishment. Dan must feel let down. They didn't understand. She understood."

In *Medical Meeting* Henry Baker listens to the papers given in the morning before his own presentation. A distinguished head of a team of university specialists presents another form of early antibiotic that is more far-reaching than the form that Henry has developed. Henry has worked in rural isolation in upstate New York, with his wife, Liz, as his lab assistant, hoping his work will become a significant contribution to the treatment of infection. Disheartened, he goes ahead with his afternoon presentation but knows it is anticlimactic.

At the last moment, Liz comes to hear his presentation and is stunned by the description of one of the cases in which deafness occurred. It is their own daughter's case—and her admiration of her husband turns to bitterness. Not until the Bakers have returned to their rural home does Liz understand how Henry used the new antibiotic to save their daughter's life, not knowing that it would cause her to be deaf.

This second "medical novel" written in the late 1940s drew upon how my mother saw my father's experience with the research he carried out. As a cardiologist, he treated many patients for edema, an incapacitating retention of fluids in the body's cavities or tissues, often due to an injured heart or kidneys. This condition could become life-threatening if excess fluid accumulated in the space surrounding the lungs. Relief required passing a needle through the chest wall into the space around the lungs and drawing off the fluid. This was standard treatment, painful, and frequently necessary to do repetitively. The cause of the edema was retention of salty fluid. The main problem was salt retention, not water. But until the 1940s, the main treatment for preventing edema was to withhold drinking water from the patient, even though the patient might complain of great thirst.

The condition of edema, termed "dropsy" in earlier times, had been described by physicians since the days of Hippocrates. My father had always been interested in medical histories, and he read of early treatments for edema which prescribed large amounts of water to rid the body of harmful brine or salt accumulations. Too much salt prevented fluids in the body from passing through membranes to be excreted as urine. My father's treatment relied on these early observations, increasing ingested fluids as a means of relieving edema in his many seriously ill patients in Montana. In his relatively obscure practice in Montana, he amassed enough cases to convince a significant part of the national medical community by the early 1940s. He began reporting his findings in 1942.

By 1950 *Time* printed an article by Joseph Kinsey Howard on Dad's work in which it quoted him as saying, "Restriction of water is useless, harmful, and a cause of suffering." In that same year he was invited to present his treatment at the International Congress of Cardiology—the first congress to be held after the Second World War—in Paris and at the Hague. He was thrilled with the opportunity and chastened by the controversy that his findings prompted. But it was a thrill for my father that his talks brought him widespread correspondence.

In the mid-1940s, a doctor doing research at a university in upper New York state had been working along the same lines at the same time, and after learning this, my father had corresponded with him. The doctor's research corroborated my father's work, but my mother thought of it as a scoop of my father's work. She was maddened by it. My father treated it as the nature of research—a need or possibility that occurs to more than one researcher simultaneously. But the doctor, Mother told us, was credited in the academic community with his findings in a way that my father was not.

Although Mother never mentioned a connection between the subject matter of *Medical Meeting* and the outcome of Dad's work,

I cannot help seeing the impulse on her part to take it on. It was a violation that she deeply resented. She had had a part in his work, urging him to prepare his papers for publication. She was also haunted after my father's death by the thought that her urging him to write the papers that would ensure his importance in his field had put too much pressure on an already hardworking man. "I wonder if I pushed him too hard," she would ask herself aloud.

But among Mother's notes is a calendar page with the printed date "Monday, April 6, 1942." First in pencil and then in ink in her smallest handwriting she made this entry:

> *This has been a good day, close to Ferd. We had dinner together in the hotel & tonight while he has been working on his introduction I have walked softly or sat close by him mending so he could feel me with him. By 1 o'clock he had really finished his introduction and was elated and a different person. We were both hilarious & felt like the Curies. Moments like these I would rather be I than anyone else in the world.*

I know that Mother had her typewriter along on these trips and typed up new pages and changes at the last hour for my father to read at meetings. This passage reveals how much she enjoyed having a part in my father's work and how proud she was of his success.

And I think this closeness to the medical community in her own life gave her a particular certainty with which to characterize the two doctors' wives in *Dr. Norton's Wife* and in *Medical Meeting.* Each wife is aware of the lives of other doctors and their wives, and each novel goes into those lives thoroughly, vividly. And minor characters, given their own points of view by Mother, react to the disappointment and imagine the discomfort of each wife.

But in the later novel, *Medical Meeting,* Liz Baker has a deep bitterness about her husband's research because it has been the cause of their daughter's deafness and because she has so totally devoted her days to assisting her husband in the research. When the Bakers return home, a small house on the tuberculosis sanatorium where Henry sees his patients, Liz purposefully goes into their laboratory rooms, when Henry is not there, and pours out all the jars of molds. On the blackboard, where they had left working notes, she writes "finis." All that work for nothing, she thinks. Henry hadn't "made his mark," after all. Their reconciliation will come about by the end of the novel because Henry will make her see that his work will assist in the final effective form of the antibiotic, and he will make her remember that their daughter would have died if she had not been given his form of antibiotic. What I remember is that my four-year-old cousin died of pneumonia—"before there was penicillin," my father said later.

I recently found a lecture Mother delivered on May 1, 1969, about how she pursued her writing career. She called it "Speaking of Writing." Her comments are typewritten on five-by-seven-inch ruled notecards with additional remarks added in ink in the margins. She saved it all these years as if to remind herself of what she had thought at the time. Many of the cards are written over or added to as if she used them several times for different talks.

Among these cards is her description of deciding on a revision of the first manuscript of *Dr. Norton's Wife*:

> *So I wrote a third [novel]. My publishers sent it back with a letter so kind the kindness burned. There were good things in it, but the subject matter (hopeless illness) was dubious. That was in the '30s. Nothing is now. A slow beginning; a slight confusion. But I was more my own woman by now. That novel said something I wanted to say; I believed in one character especially. Finally, I could bear to lay out the manuscript on the living room floor, in chapters.*

> *(I hasten to say that the children and my husband were all away.) Suddenly, I began to see. What if (a great phrase for the novelist), what if I began with chap. 3? I put the first three chapters on the piano. And I began to find out that as Shorer says: "Writing is discovery of your meaning." You see, as you write, things you didn't know were in the material. Oh, you find yourself saying, that's*

what it's about. In this case, instead of being about the
young people around a medical center, it was about the
older doctor and his wife. I went through it again, with
my new perspective, sold it and had my first real break be-
cause the Literary Guild took it and quite aside from the
useful money it brought, I was assured a modest public.

She must have felt justified in those changes she made when she received a letter from her former teacher, Roy Cowden, soon after sending him a copy of the revised manuscript. It read:

Dear Mildred,
There have been times in the reading of this story
when I have thrown my hat to the ceiling for the way
you have done things, and never more often than in the
last hundred pages. Dear Lady, you are on the way to be-
ing a great novelist. This book is so far above the others
there is no comparison. . . . Don't mind the fact that
your days of easy writing are over when the other kind
takes you in as deeply as you are here. Your last chapter
brought hot tears to my eyes, partly for the story and
partly in elation over your success.

He goes on to answer questions she must have sent with the manuscript:

All the major operations are successful. There are adhe-
sions here and there to be attended to, and now and
then a plastic that may make the patient look better.
Let's answer your questions first.
Chapter 10 is satisfactory. It does enough.
Chapter 16 would be better, I think, with the interns'
quarters out. It emphasizes the play side of the life and
there is enough of that in the games at Dan's.
Chapter 18 is all right.

The second page of this letter is missing from Mother's papers, but a second letter written after the publication of the novel is equally jubilant. First, Cowden notes all the favorable reviews that appeared in the *New York Times Review of Books*, the *Herald Tribune Book Review*, and the *Saturday Review of Literature*. And he adds to the last, "Had my own delight in seeing your picture on the front cover. It doesn't do you justice by a long shot, but there it is anyway." His final comment about the novel must have done much for Mother's self-confidence: "You have written a story about complex people that goes down to the very depths of their nature and that is enough for any writer of fiction."

Mother's "modest public" for *Dr. Norton's Wife* was considerable. The reviews praised the steady delicacy with which she presented the Nortons' irreversible sorrow—how it changed the man and wife but not their love for each other. One observation that occurred in a number of the reviews must have pleased her: "For those who are interested in unuttered thoughts, *Dr. Norton's Wife* will prove an absorbing study" (*New York Times*).

A friend who came originally from Denmark, Ranveig Schmidt, sent Mother a translation of a review from "Denmark's oldest and most important newspaper." (However, the two pages of translation Mother has kept with her papers do not note the newspaper's title or date.) The friend's translation of the review reads in part:

> *Even a critic tired of books reads her novel with relaxation and pleasure as it is a marvel of psychological art and wisdom which does not demand any plot or thrill but the talent. She describes beautifully and delicately the psychological catastrophe which is the fate of the three persons and the value of the novel brightens still more by the swift but marvelous portraits that Mildred Walker draws of the extra persons, the young M.D.'s and their medical friends.*

The records at the archives show that a translation of *Dr. Norton's Wife* was printed as early as 1939 in Sweden and Norway and perhaps near that date in Denmark. A paperback of *Dr. Norton's Wife* appeared in Portuguese in 1941.

The Brewers' Big Horses was Mother's fourth novel, published two years after *Dr. Norton's Wife*. Again set in the Midwest, this was her second historical novel. This was the novel based on my paternal grandmother's reminiscences of her life and her family in Saginaw, Michigan. The dedication of the novel is to "M.R.S. [Maude Ripley Schemm] who is intolerant only of knaves and intolerance." In Mother's imagination the adventurousness of Grandma Schemm's own story became the absorbing plot of Sara Bolster's life. As Sara's surname suggests, her family comes from New England. She marries a young German doctor, Wilhelm Henkel, from the other side of town, who is heir to the Henkel Brewery. My grandmother's family came from New England, and she married a young German doctor, George Christopher Schemm, from the other side of Saginaw, who was the heir to the Schemm Brewery. The novel opens in the Bolster household when Sara is eight with the same sad family loss that occurred in Grandma's girlhood. Events of Grandma's own life are pivotal events in Sara's life: her job with the newspaper, the two families' objections to the marriage, the young doctor's need to promise his dying father that he would take over the brewery to the exclusion of his medical profession, and the doctor's death when he is a young father.

Grandma's young husband became ill with pernicious anemia, then untreatable, and died when the oldest of his three sons was only five—before he was to take over the Schemm Brewery. In the novel, Sara Bolster's husband has suspended his medical practice and taken over the running of the brewery. He is killed saving his small son from the stampeding brewery horses. His second son is born a month early, two days after his father's funeral.

In the novel Sara Henkel does run the brewery, to her own family's dismay. She impresses the loyal men who work the brewery; she relies on their experience, and together they accomplish daring successes with the business. At first, she has to struggle with the Henkel sisters, who sit on the board of directors and want to sell the brewery. But the strength that Sara's ventures bring about for the business finally win over the sisters. It is her own family who feels publicly shamed. The parents can't bear to speak of it, and her sisters are outspokenly opposed. Ironically, Sara's brewery comes to be the support of the women in both families.

I have mentioned earlier that my grandfather's will could not be found at the time of his death. Since he had inherited the Schemm

Brewery, his will specified that the ownership would go to his wife with the understanding that she would distribute the income to provide for his mother and sisters. Grandma had seen the will because he had explained it to her. Grandma concluded that his sisters had destroyed it, and her three sons grew up with that suspicion. After the publication of *The Brewers' Big Horses,* the sisters were in their eighties and living in California. Henrietta, an artist, wrote to my father, apologizing for the disappearance of the will and explaining that she and her sister had feared that their brother's widow would marry again and take the brewery with her. Both my father and mother were astonished that the novel had prompted this disclosure.

In the novel, Sara Henkel's sisters-in-law vote to sell the brewery, but Sara's vote and those of the men representing the workers prevail. For a long time, Sara is aware of the two sisters' suspicions of her competency, but in the end they concede that she makes good decisions for the business. Sara comes to defend the work of her husband's sister, Ottilie, whose commissioned sculpture has been turned down by the Women's Century Club of Armitage City because, as the sister Marie explains bitterly, "'My dear Sara, the name is too German. The committee seem to feel it would be unwise to have it made by 'a Hun.' Marie's voice was like a sharp draft cutting into the warm October afternoon." The year is 1915.

Sara's sister Belle becomes an avid supporter of the Women's Christian Temperance Union (WCTU). They are such an angry opposition that during a Fourth of July parade, they form a shouting crowd to block the brewery wagon and the big Clydesdales. As a woman who runs a brewery and a beer garden, Sara is the target of bitter animosity. The move to prohibition causes the abrupt shutdown of the Henkel Brewery and brings the novel to a close.

There is an earlier scene in which Sara watches the fervent WCTU advocates glowing in the presence of Billy Sunday, who speaks in support of their cause. Watching them, Sara thinks: "That man, Billy Sunday, had no right to talk that way. The brewing business was an honest business. . . . It was more honest than his revival meeting. What did he make but a heady drink of emotionalism that people drank down like whiskey until it made them drunk?" (368). Then the crowd in the tabernacle, "fifteen thousand voices," bursts into a rallying song with the refrain "But the Brewers' Big Horses can't run over me!" As she drives away angrily, still hearing the singing, she becomes sure that prohibition really will come now: "She would lose everything. *The Brewers' Big Horses* were going to run over her in the end, crushing her down into worry and want, just as they had crushed William. There was nothing she could do about it. The horses were symbols of some terrible fate; they were fate" (369). But as she drives away, she determines that she won't be "run over." She will learn how to do something else; she will start a restaurant. She takes the refrain of the raucous song for her own.

The introduction to this new University of Nebraska Press reprint, again by the poet David Budbill, describes Sara Henkel as "an epical, feminist heroine for our time" (xiv). Budbill ascribes "the same boldness and daring" to the creator of Sara Henkel in taking up the social themes covered in the novel:

> *In* The Brewers' Big Horses *Mildred Walker—like her protagonist Sara, between whom one suspects there is a deep autobiographical connection—challenges established and establishment views on everything from the rights of laborers, to the arrogance of the upper classes, to the misuses of art, literature, music, clothing, and food—to create an elite, to bigoted attitudes toward "the foreign element," to the narrow-minded attitudes of prohibitionists, jingoistic warmongers, the* WCTU, *and turn-of-the-century evangelist and charlatan Billy Sunday. (xii)*

Mother, who at age seven had once sat on the knee of Billy Sunday, at age thirty-four sees him through my grandmother's eyes.

Many of the early reviews described Sara Henkel as a strong, purposeful protagonist to be admired. The *Dallas Times Herald* announced, "Sara is Miss Walker's masterpiece" (September 15, 1940). The novel was favorably reviewed in the *New York Times Book Review* (August 11, 1940), and enthusiastically boosted in the *Brewers Journal* for its treatment of the brewery business. The front cover of the *Brewers Journal* declared:

Not only should it be read by every brewery executive, every master brewer, and member of the allied trades, but we all should boost the novel at every opportunity. . . . Nothing that has ever been written can produce the favorable attitude toward brewers and the industry better than this book can. (August 15, 1940)

This enthusiasm would have amused Mother, but that would be all. She registered on every reservation expressed by a reviewer, even if the review was generally favorable. One review in the *Michigan Daily* (September 11, 1940) would have annoyed her deeply: "Mildred Walker needs only to lose the slight twinge of effeminate timidity with which she looks at the world, and she will quickly leave the 'goods' and take her place among the 'greats.'" But a review that looked unfavorably on her technique always stung her the most. An undated review held in the archives written by a W. K. Kelsey announces: "Mildred Walker still has to learn the art of omission. She likes to let herself go; she prattles. She should study Edith Wharton, who cared nothing for dialog unless it was significant." Mother did study Edith Wharton. A boxed four-volume set, handsomely "decorated" as the publisher, D. Appleton, states, of Wharton's *Old New York* novels sat on our bookshelf when I was a child.

What I wonder about now is Mother's reaction to a September 12, 1939, letter from her mentor, Professor Cowden, preserved in the archives. It gives her his view of *The Brewers' Big Horses* while it is still in manuscript:

Now about your story. . . . I don't think this is a greater story than Dr. Norton's Wife. *It is a different story and many readers may like it better but it is not as great, not yet. Greatness here means greater treatment and I didn't feel that you have gone as deeply into the character of this woman as you did into the character of Sue Norton. I do think this woman has the potentialities of character to be plumbed, but you haven't gone down where her nature is put on track. . . . One needs to come to grips and be moved by the forces that compromise this woman's integrity, her own sense of integrity. The greatness of this story rests upon the greatness of this woman's character. Great character proves its greatness by being hardly tried. This woman needs to be hardly tried. . . .*

. . . I have no objection to the materials of your story and I think there would be a distinct loss of interest if you took out the beer and the prohibition problem, but the moving story involves the character of the woman. . . . I had a feeling that you could get more deeply into her than you have. . . . We need to see very clearly the effect upon her sense of her own clear conscience, of drifting into a situation in which a part of the world thinks she has compromised herself.

Three months after Cowden's letter, she heard from Chester B. Kerr at Harcourt, Brace. He writes: "Let me tell you straight off what a grand book I think *The Brewers' Big Horses* is. Several of us have been reading it with considerable pleasure and excitement and, even in so short a time, the group enthusiasm begins to grow." After explaining his plans for publication, Kerr concludes, "Let me emphasize again what a superb book we think you have turned out—a grand character, a fascinating atmosphere, and a heart-warming story."

There's no way of knowing how Mother may have deepened her protagonist's character in response to Professor Cowden's remarks before she sent the manuscript to Harcourt. But, given Harcourt's enthusiasm, she must have decided to go ahead with the publication. Harcourt published *The Brewers' Big Horses* in August 1940.

In Great Falls, Montana, my brothers and I would come to know the importance of Mother walking up the wide cement steps to the post office as she mailed off a thick manila envelope while we waited for her in the car. My brother George and I were reminding each other of moments like that the other day when he remembered going to the local brewery with Mother. He must have been about nine years old. He said she wrote in a notebook while she asked questions of the brew master. George remembers a copper cauldron "as big as a room" where the brew was mixed. And with a smile, he repeats Mother's story about the brew master in the Schemm Brewery in Michigan who used to hold up a sample glass to the light and murmur, "Ah, the color of angel piss."

The brewery's sign, "Great Falls Select," is still on the old brick building standing on the west shore of the Missouri River. Years later on a visit to Great Falls, I met an old friend of the family who wanted to recite his poem about the long-closed brewery. The poem was about the ducks who drank at the outflow of the brewery and swam up and down in a drunken state.

5
Great Falls, Montana,
1933–1944

Great Falls, Montana, was Mother's first western town. It was laid out in what she saw as an uninteresting grid, patterned after St. Paul, Minnesota. Most of the residential streets had one-story bungalows, set squarely to the street on narrow lots. Tall elm trees paced each boulevard, a narrow strip of grass between sidewalk and street curb. Mother must have seen that as an amenity. But my brother George and I were more interested in riding our tricycles over the cracks made by the tree roots at intervals along the boulevard.

A busy street ran at the east end of our block straight to the Missouri River, but a large milling company and train tracks divided the town from the river. Across the bridge was the towering smelter stack of the Anaconda Copper Mining Company and next to it an oil refinery. On the right wind we could smell their fumes at our house. Further upstream was the Great Falls Select brewery. The graceful curve that the Missouri made around the town must have seemed to Mother abandoned to commercial uses.

My father, who loved rivers from his canoeing days in Michigan, took us all for picnics downriver from the town to the Giant Springs. The clear water, coming from an aquifer, burst up out of the earth just before the river's edge. It was surrounded by a small green park—the right size for children chasing balls and cooling off in the shade of willow trees. Farther downstream Dad showed us the swallows building their nests in the cliffs high above us and the series of falls for which the town had been named. Even though dams had been built at each falls, the river's water boiled over in a great drop at each.

I don't remember Mother ever commenting to us children about her disappointments in living in this new country. She did say much later how raw the town had seemed to her, the plains too wide and windy, and the people "lacking." Perhaps her early impressions had a part in her turning to midwestern settings for her first three novels written in Montana.

On every summer vacation to Montana, Mother's sister, Peg, brought her movie camera along to record the great sweep of country and her sister's family in it. The first film is as early as 1938, recording the train trip out west and panning the very long train ticket necessary for the trip. It is a record of small rail side towns, immense piles of tumbleweed, more vistas, then suddenly all our grinning faces. And in the later films, when Grandfather and Grandmother Walker and Aunt Peg begin to come by car, there are numbers of shots taken out the car's windows and more scenes of our family's antics.

As the family shots begin, they are full of clowning, and my parents look very young. In 1938 Christopher is one year old. He is adorable. My brother George and I are old enough to be awkward and leggy, but we are all grinning obediently. A later film shows only Grandfather and Aunt Peg because Grandmother Walker has died. Grandfather died a year later. After a few years' lapse, the films begin again, this time with Aunt Peg and her new husband, Homer. The films cover western trips made by the eastern family into the early 1950s.

I don't think these silent films were intended to be the record they became, except that Aunt Peg painstakingly spliced them all together and included hand-drawn maps, dates, and rustic illustrations. Recently, Christopher had the spliced films made into a video for each of us. And now when we watch it, we have the chance to point out to our children all these people who were important to us in Mother's family.

The video interested Deirdre McNamer, the novelist who wrote the introduction to the University of Nebraska Press reprint of *Unless the Wind Turns*. McNamer's description shows Mother as I remember her:

> *In those films, we see a handsome, steady-eyed woman with a distinctive, sensual mouth. She walks with a limber, athletic stride. Something, a kind of lanky exuber-*

ance, evokes film images of Amelia Earhart. She shep-
herds her children around her. She triumphantly hoists a
dead fish. She waves to the world from atop her cantering
horse. Then she disappears—and we get a slow pan of
stern gray mountain tops, an endless sweep of grass, no
humans, a sunset like streaked blood. (xiii)

At an early age I was aware of my mother being as McNamer describes her in the film. And responses to her by family friends, and
by parents of my school friends, underlined her exuberance. She
felt that exuberance was natural to her personality. She was just
turning thirty-three that year, but she looks even younger in the
film.

Mostly, we children were aware of her being in what she called
"high spirits" at the family cabin, especially when my father could
be there with us. Soon after my parents were settled in Great Falls,
they began looking for ways to be in the mountains. They were invited by new acquaintances on weekends to canyons on the Rocky
Mountain Front, west of Great Falls, where they stayed in cabins
and rode horseback. Soon my father found a family cabin to lease
where we children could join my parents. I remember going to the
South Fork of the Teton River as early as when I was six, only two
years after our Great Falls arrival. It was eighty-six miles from town,
the last twenty-seven miles rocky and slow. By 1937, we had the
one-roomed log cabin that is so prominent in this film sequence.

We had important adventures with my father along the small
Teton River that runs by the cabin: how to cover our tracks so
he wouldn't find our hiding place along the "crick," as the river
is called locally; how to start swimming upstream of where we
wanted to land on the other side; and how to huddle under a great
pine during a rainstorm and shave its bark for a small warming fire.

On winter weekends, the road deep in snow, we sometimes
snowshoed or skied into the cabin, leaving our car outside the canyon. I remember the New Year's celebration when Dad and Mother
carried frozen cracked crab and champagne in their backpacks.
Dad often showed us feats of what he called "derring-do" at the
cabin. One cold bright afternoon when the river was frozen almost

across, Dad hauled George and me along the ice on a sled in exciting circles until one spinning arc launched us into an open stretch of water in the middle. Horrified, Dad pulled us out and ran for the cabin with one of us under each arm. We were soon wrapped up in warm blankets and holding our feet to the airtight wood stove. Best of all, my father solemnly introduced us to the medicinal benefits of having a "Grizzly Bear" after enduring a cold plunge. The drink was really a hot toddy with a pat of butter floating in it. We glowed with the initiation. I was aware of Mother shaking her head at Dad, but smiling.

I remember how wonderfully uncomplicated the hours seemed at the cabin. After our evening chores and a bedtime story, George and I were sent to our upper bunks where we could look down on Mother and Dad reading and talking at the oilcloth-covered table. The log walls and red Hudson's Bay blankets were warmly lighted by the hissing kerosene lamp on the table. Christopher slept in a crib in the corner, and my parents slept in the lower bunks. Later, when Chris was moved to a lower bunk, they slept in a Morris bed that stood flat against the log wall during the day but folded out to a double bed at night. I remember being intrigued to watch Mother pull a large flannel nightgown over her head and undress beneath it. In the morning she reversed the amazing process.

My parents were always gleeful at getting away to the cabin, Dad away from the constant needs of his patients, and Mother away from her self-imposed social obligations, perhaps. They always seemed glad to be off by themselves, and whenever Mother spoke aloud her sorrow that my father had been gone for almost forty years, she usually remembered moments with him at the cabin.

I am sure it was easier for my parents to be tolerant of us children at the cabin than in Great Falls. Dad used to put out a large jar of Horlick's Malted Milk Tablets at night so that when we climbed down from our bunks at first daylight, we would grab a handful each and slip out the door without waking them. As we grew older, my parents became very inventive about guiding us to civilized behavior. We bickered and punched, as I remember. My father hung a mountain goat head inside the cabin over the front door, telling us that the goat watched over the cabin to keep it a peaceful place.

He named the goat Æquanimitas after a book of essays by Sir William Osler, the famous physician who strongly counseled an evenness of mind and spirit in the medical profession. The tradition remains, and it works most of the time; not only my brothers and I but all our children remember Dad's admonition and salute Æquanimitas each time we arrive. (The trophy had been presented to my father in 1933 by a much older doctor as a welcome to the West.)

My mother's solution to our quarreling, on the other hand, was to order George and me to memorize passages from Shakespeare and the Bible, to go off by ourselves of an afternoon and to sit bent and resentful over a large open book for what seemed hours. We have told her since that she was lucky we grew up to enjoy reading Shakespeare.

Only years later would I come to understand what I hadn't about my mother in my childhood. I remember that she exclaimed at events or sights with wonder or hilarity, but uncertain as I was of pleasing her during those years, I rarely trusted her responses as a moment for me to join in. I would only be freed from that uncertainty, some thirty years later, by seeing my nineteen-year-old son's delight in her outburst one morning at the cabin.

Matthew was carrying buckets of water up from the creek just as Mother stepped out on the porch with her cup of coffee. The early morning was chill but brilliant with sun striking the front porch where she stood. She lifted her head to cry out in a jubilant voice: "This is the day that the Lord hath made. Let us rejoice and be glad!" I saw my son's broad smile of approval even though he hadn't been raised on biblical cadences as Mother had. I would find later that he recorded that moment in his journal. Mother was seventy-five that summer morning, visiting the cabin from Vermont, and I realized that she must be responding to the beauty of the morning there just as she had in her thirties.

I have a small black-and-white snapshot, still in its original silvery gray frame, taken in 1938. It shows my father with his three children, kneeling on the walk in front of our house in town on a summer afternoon. George stands behind Dad with his hands resting on his shoulders; Dad, wearing a suit and kneeling, is holding

Christopher, about one year old, upright; and I am kneeling in front and to the side in one of the smocked, gingham dresses that Mother had me wear for "best." Mother may have been taking the picture to send back east. My being in a dress means it was a special occasion because otherwise I was always in pants and shorts like my brother. (I once heard Mother explain to her friends that it was easier that way—even if I were in danger of becoming a tomboy.)

The white house behind us in the picture was called a "sturdy bungalow," a common house design brought from the Midwest: a single story with a full attic and a dirt basement. It was our home from 1935 to 1944, a place where we children were growing up and going to school when we couldn't get away to the cabin. But for my mother and father, it was a place from which they did absorbing work. My father had patients in the town's two hospitals and an office in the Great Falls Clinic downtown. By the mid-1940s he had a research unit in the nearest hospital where he treated his patients who suffered from edema. Mother wrote and published five more novels from the little house on Fifth Avenue North. She also conducted their social life and their three children's proper growing up. I use the word *conducted* because that is how I felt she went about things.

The shape of our house was transformed because, as Mother explained, it "wasn't just what one wanted." The wonderful roofed porch, which ran the full front of the house and was wide enough to pedal tricycles in sweeping turns, was the first to go. We children watched with dismay as the porch came down and a tidy little box of a foyer replaced it. As I grew older, I could see how Mother felt more gracious bringing visitors into the foyer for a moment before erupting into the living room with them. Years later, she would murmur with regret at having to burst into my living room right from the front door. But my clever sister-in-law used a corner of their long house porch for a foyer, designing it so that the rest of the porch could stay. It was very much approved of by Mother.

Later on Dad had the attic remodeled, a bedroom at each end with wonderful sloping ceilings and a small room in between that was Mother's study. I don't remember her working there much, but it seemed perfect. My brother George had the best room, I thought, because Dad and the contractor, who was a family friend, built in a secret cupboard for him; he needed it to protect his treasures from his little brother. Still, my room had a dormer with a window seat, so I felt myself very lucky. George and I had to give up our prized rooms to house guests. My worst moment of outrage was finding that Mother's visiting college friend had left her high heels on my bookshelf. The nylon stockings drooped down in front of my favorite books! I would remember this surrender of my room whenever I had to ask my son or daughter to do the same.

Mother usually wrote at the desk in her bedroom at the back of the house. She wrote at a desk with secretive pigeon holes. (She was sitting at that desk when I leapt in through her unscreened window and scattered the piles of newly typed manuscript.) In the year when my Grandmother Schemm was dying, she was given the back bedroom and my parents moved into the smaller bedroom opposite the dining room. I remember Mother writing there during the day.

Sometimes we heard my parents talking in that bedroom, sometimes arguing, their voices raised. We so seldom heard their voices raised to each other that we were awed when we did. Several times I remember hearing Mother object to a suggestion that Dad made about a character or a scene and Dad defending his idea. Once I heard Mother plead angrily with Dad and then slam down a book, saying, "If you don't get started on it, you'll never do it. You'll never make a name for yourself!" I was about ten at that time, and I remember wondering what "make a name" meant.

Dad began then to write up his research on edema, and Mother typed steadily for him. That is what she had spoken so adamantly about. And by 1942 he published his first findings. At the same time, they were living through the Second World War. Many of the doctors in Great Falls entered the military service. Dad was one of the few left to take care of a large population in the area. Although he had served in the First World War and wanted very much to be part of the Second, he was turned down, partly for medical reasons but also because it was determined that his particular abilities were necessary to the Great Falls area. We children became used to my father being called out at all hours of the night—to birth babies, to tend accident victims, to comfort bereaved families, as well as to care for all his cardiac patients. It must have been hard for him to have enough stamina to do all that, but Mother supported and encouraged him steadily.

George and I remember the war years from that house. We had blackout curtains, sugar coupons, gasoline coupons. We were trained as bicycle couriers; our fleet was stationed at the nearby hospital to carry messages in case phone connections should be severed. We were also taught to recognize the smells of poisonous gases. When we went to movies, we learned the propaganda of the war effort. I was so impressed by the menace that when the visiting art teacher to our seventh-grade classroom asked for a large drawing of three sunflowers from each of us, I included the cartoon faces of Hitler, Hirohito, and Mussolini in the centers. I remember that she was not pleased.

In those days Great Falls lived in the shadow of the newly built East Air Force Base. The base was the last stop for "lend-lease" planes being flown to Russia when that country became one of the Allies. There were Russian pilots in the town and, often, Russian interpreters. We children used to know them by their distinctive walk and dress. Mother enjoyed her role as a civic-minded woman in Great Falls and, at some point around 1943, was asked to give an afternoon tea for Anna Louisa Strong, a well-known lecturer who had fled Russia after the Russian Revolution. She was an imposing woman with a very erect bearing and white hair, I remember, rather disdainful of an awkward child passing cookies. But Mother told me later that the lecturer was offended by the presence of another Russian woman whom Mother had invited. Mother had thought the two women would enjoy meeting each other. But neither enjoyed it because the lecturer was "White Russian"—of the exiled aristocracy—and the second woman was a "Red Russian," connected to the Russian Air Force. I remember the second woman, small and tense, dressed in uniform. The two women glared at each other across our small living room, causing uncomfortable silences among the five or six other women present. When Mother told about it as an amusing story at evening parties, I would remember the discomfort I had felt—rather like Alice distressed by the Red Queen and the White Queen quarreling.

Mother often told me when I was grown that I was "a very grave child." I suppose that could have been so because I was preoccupied by what everything she was telling me meant. My sense is that my two brothers and I rarely seemed to Mother to have the impulse to hilarity and exuberance that she and my father had. Years later, she would speak of this as a disappointment to her. I know that we were watchful; she would bring us up short when we said or did something heedlessly. "You should know better" or "How could you!" always seemed to me unfathomable, unfair, and grounds for silent rebellion. By contrast, Dad's way was to explain why we wouldn't want to do "that" again, and we clung to that kind of reasonableness.

But Mother liked to have things go according to a plan at home, regardless of surrounding events. At our family suppers, she carried on sprightly conversations, all the while aware of conducting the meal. By that I mean, upon seeing that each of us had finished our plates, or been chided to finish, she inched forward on her chair, reaching her foot to press a bell concealed under the rug and gave me a significant look. That was my signal. (In those older houses, the sound of the bell was to summon the "Help" from the kitchen.) Mother watched carefully to be sure that I did not stack the dinner plates. Instead, I was to hold one dinner plate in my right hand, the silverware firmly under my thumb. One butter plate and butter knife were to be held in the left hand in the same way. First, I should remove my father's plate setting, then my mother's, then my brothers' plates, and last, my own. I was to bring in the dessert and serve it in the same order. If I did it correctly, I was rewarded with my mother's approving smile as I sat down. The only other compensation was that no one could begin dessert until I was seated. We children understood that Mother considered it a privilege for us to eat with our parents. We were "excused" after dessert, when I removed the plates and brought my parents their coffee. Then we could hear them from the living room as they settled down to their talk, to their shared concerns.

I know that I watched and learned Mother's wishes with an intensity of wanting her to be pleased with me. When I didn't perform these tasks correctly, she reproved me with a pained silence or eyes widened with disbelief. In my rebellious teens, I came to believe that these household insistences were matters of faith for her. If these tenets were followed, then life would be good (and of the "right sort") in our family. Now, so many years later, I realize that I did understand what she wanted; I just couldn't understand why it was so important to her. And I admit that I have been newly outraged in these later years when she attempted to impose on her children's daughters what she had thought appropriate for me.

During these years of living in Great Falls, Mother seemed always in the midst of social activities. There were afternoon teas at which I, in my painfully awkward childhood, had to pass cookies—with mishaps. She also made afternoon calls on older women whom she admired or whom my father asked her to befriend, usually because the women's husbands were his patients and they were from out of town. At some point I realized that these were not the doctors' wives who came to our house for teas. Each of these other women had interests that intrigued Mother. We had glimpses of these interests because we were sometimes taken along to sit quietly and eat cookies.

Ranveig Schmidt, who was raised in Reykjavik, Iceland, was one of these older friends. She and her husband had fled Europe, perhaps Denmark, in Hitler's early years. I don't know what brought them to Montana, but he was selling hearing aids in Great Falls when he became ill. Ranveig was the friend who translated the Danish review of *Dr. Norton's Wife* for Mother. She must have been a rare friend to whom Mother spoke easily about her writing. I say this because one of the short stories Mother had printed in *Woman's Home Companion* in November 1941 was based on conversations with Ranveig.

The story, "Vienna Child," is a tragedy of a young German soldier stationed in Copenhagen during the Nazi occupation. As the story begins, young Lieutenant Kurt von Jagen anticipates being welcomed by the Danish family who had fostered him during the First World War when he was sent over from Germany:

> *He loved this city, this street, this door as he loved Berlin.*
> *He had come here to the house when he was eight, a thin*
> *hungry lad, afraid and lonely at leaving home. . . . His fa-*

ther had sent him away as the government ordered, be-
cause people in Norway and Denmark were willing to take
in children who were starving in Vienna and Germany.
Vienna children, they were called. (31)

During the Second World War, the Nazi government has stationed many of the grown Vienna children in Denmark because they speak the Danish language fluently and know the customs. But the young lieutenant is turned away by his foster family, who now consider him an enemy of their country, and he is not allowed to see the family's daughter Inge, with whom he is in love.

The lieutenant sees from the first that "on every side he and his troops met with cold unseeing hatred. People on the street looked through them as though they were not there." And he rehearses in his mind the premise on which they were sent: "to protect Denmark from British aggression. It was English propaganda that made Germany appear an aggressor and, in reality, the Fuehrer was only protecting them from the British" (31). When he has doubts, he reminds himself, as he sits at a table outside a cafe, of the Fuehrer's accomplishments: "Had he not knit [Germany] into a great world power! The occupation of Denmark—suppose it were not just for her protection; if it were part of a plan for a greater and a united Europe it was a noble plan" (111). After a few months the hatred of the Danes for the occupying Germans boils over on the celebration of the Danish king's birthday. Kurt von Jagen is killed by a German bullet meant for his foster brother.

The painful discovery by the lieutenant that he no longer belonged in Copenhagen is the main focus of this story, even more than the strongly imagined characterizations Mother has drawn. Ranveig must have related the misery of the Nazi occupation in Denmark but also have spoken of the beauty of the Copenhagen she missed. Long before she visited Denmark, Mother told us it was a beautiful city.

I remember Ranveig as a smiling, warm woman with a hearty laugh. My brother George remembers seeing in the Schmidts' apartment a case of six or seven Scandinavian knives, one with "a wavy blade about two feet long." He says that Mr. Schmidt told him the knife with the wavy blade was to be plunged in just behind the collar bone.

A letter from Ranveig to Mother, written from the Mayo Clinic, where my father had encouraged the Schmidts to go when Mr. Schmidt's illness worsened, gives me some idea of the strong friendships with women that Mother formed while we lived in Great Falls. Ranveig says only that her husband is dying as she sits by his bed. Her tone is of raw, unflinching pain. It is written in pencil on a small scrap of paper that Mother had kept all these years.

I have found a response to "Vienna Child" in a letter sent to Mother in December 1941 by Roy Cowden, her University of Michigan professor of creative writing. The response comes at the end of a letter about the strengths and weaknesses he finds in her latest novels:

> *Yes, I read your "Vienna Child," and think it the best short story of yours I have read. But I'm beginning to wonder about the effect upon a novelist of trying to write short stories. The two ways are so different. Short stories seem to me only rarely to touch the emotional depths easy to attain in the novel. And a novelist must retain the capacity to reach the depths of emotion and to convey experience to others out of that depth. I think the idea in "Vienna Child" would move me more if it were done right in a novel.*

Mother discontinued writing short stories after the war. In answer to my question just a few years ago as to why she had stopped, she said the stories weren't being accepted by magazines as well as they had been at first. I wonder, now, how much these questions that Cowden raised about her stories had influenced her decision to stop.

Another interesting friend of Mother's lived in an apartment just around the corner from our house. She was the artist Fra (pronounced fray) Dana, whose paintings are now a collection at the University of Montana's Museum of the Fine Arts in Missoula. I remember Fra Dana much better than Ranveig Schmidt because we went to see her in the early 1940s. Christopher was her favorite because he was much the quietest—and cherubic looking. Otherwise, Fra Dana did not care for children, Mother told us later. I remember her as distant, elegantly frail, and often turned to the window with a look of melancholy.

Mother's relationship with Fra Dana was of a different intensity than with her other women friends. Fra Dana must have read Mother's early novels, and she spoke to Mother as one artist to another. Apparently, she exhorted Mother not to become too enmeshed in domesticity to write. Mother told me years later that Fra Dana once said vehemently, "You must be ruthless, ruthless!" She was passing on the advice given her by the painter Mary Cassatt, with whom she had studied in Paris.

In 1986, when Mother was eighty-one, she came to live near me in Missoula. Later in that same year, museum curator Dennis Kern was preparing an exhibition of Fra Dana's paintings. Suffering from ill health in 1948, Dana had given her collection to the university museum. To Kern's dismay, the collection had been stored away, unnoticed for nearly forty years. He let it be known that he was preparing the paintings for the exhibition and that the collection contained paintings by other very well known artists whom Fra Dana had studied under—J. H. Sharp, Alfred Maurer, William Merrit Chase, and Mary Cassatt. Kern invited people to add their privately owned paintings to the exhibit.

At the time when Fra Dana's husband died, she had given a landscape by J. H. Sharp to my father to thank him for caring for her husband. I grew up knowing this painting, and when I married and left home, my father gave it to me to remind me of home. In response to Kern's invitation, I told Mother that I was going to lend the painting. Then Mother remembered that she had a notebook of entries she had written down when Fra Dana had insisted that Mother read her journals.

When we told Kern about Mother's notebook, he was overwhelmed because he had not been able to trace the original Dana journals. Mother typed four single-spaced pages of excerpts from Dana's entries, covering from 1907 to 1913. These entries are invaluable for understanding how Fra Dana managed to assist her cattle rancher husband in southeastern Montana with his seasonal work and at the same time see clearly with the eyes of an artist, longing for time to paint. One entry reads:

> *Today is Velasquez' birthday. I always keep it in my heart. But I speak no more of my vanished dreams. We spayed 68 heifers this morning. It took from six o'clock until eleven of hard work. I tallied & got hungry & sleepy—so sleepy that I fell over against the gate post of the corral. It was while tallying that I remembered it was Velasquez' birthday & a strange place it was to remember. I was cold, wet, tired & dirty. All was rush and hard work.*

When Mother was later interviewed about Fra Dana on video camera by two members of the Art Department, I think she was amazed by the sudden closeness of those days in Great Falls to her new life in Missoula. In the interview she said suddenly that Fra Dana didn't think much of her novels because there were no "wrenching scenes" in them. Mother was clearly disappointed, remembering that remark, but then said, with a wry smile, "I thought that might not be the case," referring to the wrenching scenes.

In the Great Falls days, when Mother filled small notebooks with material for her novels, novels that were published almost instantly, and when Dad was working very hard, Mother continued to conduct herself as an interested socially correct doctor's wife. Her membership in the Junior League mystified me in my teenage years, but now I realize that it was part of the role she wanted for herself. A good number of doctors' wives in Great Falls belonged to the League. It meant to us that each summer she and another doctor's wife sold tickets to the state fair. Smartly dressed, they sat at a card table on a sidewalk of Central Avenue, the main street. Mother usually wore a red bandana tied around her neck. In a quick study of her in my aunt's movie, Mother is handing over tickets, taking payment, and smiling broadly. She's wearing well-cut gabardine riding pants and cowboy boots as part of the fair's theme. I remember thinking, when we stopped by her table, that she was in costume, pleasant and direct with everyone who stopped to purchase a ticket.

Mother really did everything with a flair. Her hats, for instance—she had one for every occasion. Photographs show her in an elfin felt hat embellished with a curled feather, or a broad-brimmed dark hat with the turned down brim elegantly shadowing the upper part of her face. The most interesting was a soft leather skull cap, a warm brown, with a pheasant feather rising from it. I could see that she was pleased with "the effect." I think that this was a side of her own mother that she admired. Mother always adapted her hats to "say something" about herself.

When she was readying herself to go out for an evening with my father, she sometimes called me into her bedroom. Along with telling me that I must do this and that in the way of behavior, she would invite me to see how she dabbed perfume behind her ears and at her wrists. I was overcome with happiness when she placed a moist dab behind my ears. And I saw how she expertly applied red lipstick. She didn't wear any other makeup that I knew of, but these were the arts she consciously imparted to me. I was entranced, feeling myself poised on the threshold of womanhood. It would be from my high school friends that I learned about curling eyelashes or wearing blush. But Mother was adamant, when I was older, that "a lady" should never have a shiny nose but should always powder it vigorously. I was to wonder about that proscription, even into my forties, and decide against it.

Mother gave dinner parties in response to invitations she and my father had received, and I was very aware of these parties because, as I became less of a domestic hazard, I was required to be present. Not seated at the dinner table but waiting in the kitchen for the ping of the bell. When conversation was vigorous, the bell was heard only in the kitchen. I entered to clear the dishes, to bring the next course, to refill water glasses, all according to the practice Mother had given me during our family meals. Alice Miller, who lived with us at that time and who prepared dinner according to Mother's directions, would have everything ready. It was my job to do the rest.

Afterward, perhaps at supper the next evening, Mother would discuss with Dad the details of the party—especially how scintillating or how dull the conversation had been. What I remember is Dad making funny remarks in response to Mother's more serious comments. But I remember both Mother and Dad having delight in some of those parties. One night they were returning a dinner invitation to the man and wife who lived across the street—two lawyers who worked for the powerful Anaconda Copper Company. (The Glovers were what my father had taught us were HDWBs —"Highly Dignified Waddle Bugs." In other words, people so concerned with matters of decorum that they suffered from self-importance, a condition that his mother had taught him merited that description.) At the end of a dinner, the Glovers had served to their guests what looked like an iced dolphin in the middle of the table. Their ten guests went on talking, not knowing what to do about the presentation. After quite a few minutes, Mrs. Glover graciously spread her fingers, one hand at a time, over the dolphin's back, then wiped her fingers on her napkin. The guests followed her example with relief. I remember my parents being convulsed about this incident and plotting at our supper table what they might do to "one-up" the Glovers. They decided that a finger bowl with a goldfish should be set at each guest's place. And I had the honor of bringing in the bowls! I remember being filled with the importance of my task. As I passed each glass bowl at the end of the meal, I was concentrating so hard on not spilling one that I don't remember noticing the guests' consternation. But out in the kitchen, Alice and I had giggled while we listened to the exclamations going on in the dining room. Mother told us the next day that the surprise of the goldfish was a huge success.

The journalist Joseph Kinsey Howard, who had become a strong family friend of Mother and Dad's, did not fit into the social framework of those who were invited for goldfish in the finger bowls. We children knew him at that time as the rigorous newspaperman who wrote for the *Great Falls Leader*. His sense of world history was so acute that he was required to remain in Great Falls during the Second World War so that he could give daily statewide radio broadcasts.

We knew Joe first as our parents' friend. He used to come by the house in the afternoons to talk with Mother about books and reviews, sometimes about publishers. Mother told me with amusement years later that Grandmother Schemm didn't think that "looked well" when my father wasn't at home. When Joe came in the evening, he talked eagerly about history, knowing Dad's interest. Joe was working on his book *Montana: High, Wide, and Handsome,* his journalist's interpretation of Montana's history, published in 1941 by Yale University Press and still in print in the 1990s. Joe had been the first national journalist (his article was printed in the *Atlantic Magazine*) to expose the oppressive corporate power brokers in Montana—the Anaconda Copper Mining Company and the Montana Power Company.

George and I listened at the edge of some of these conversations—especially to stories Joe told about the local newspaper where he had worked since he was just out of high school. As we grew older, Joe took time to talk with George and me about what we were doing. George sold copies of the *Great Falls Leader* on a downtown corner and told Joe of his trouble from time to time with bullies or told him of a book he was reading; I told of winning in a school footrace or showed him my first poems. When I graduated from high school to go off to college, Joe gave me deerskin gloves to remember the good smell of home; when George was away in college, he received cryptic postcards, usually quotations from W. H. Auden that Joe thought apt. And George remembers Joe telling him once, "Music is the only unpunished rapture." I think now that Joe was the first adult outside our family to whom we could tell our serious thoughts or of whom we could ask our serious questions. Mother used to look on with amused tolerance, but George and I felt we grew up by knowing him. I was six years old when I was first aware of Joe and twenty-two when he died of a heart attack in 1951. He was only forty-five years old.

Mother thought of Joe as a literary friend who brought interesting friends from back east to Montana, who arranged literary conferences (scarce events in the Montana of the mid-1940s), and who listened sympathetically to her complaints about her unfavorable reviews and, often, her publishers. He interested her in going to the Bread Loaf Writers' Conference in Vermont the summer of 1949. In Montana he brought writers together to give workshops attended by regional participants interested in writing.

Some of Joe's correspondence with his mother, Josephine Kinsey Howard, is collected in the Montana Historical Society in Helena and describes moments in our family that amused him. These are excerpts from a letter written in 1937:

> I went up there yesterday to return some photos and found the two, Mrs. Schemm and the doctor, peeking warily from their lattice; it seems doctors who wanted to go to the fair could get off and of course he promptly went home and hid in the piazza [Mother's name for the small brick patio at the side of the house].
>
> They have decided it's high time Christopher was weaned though it's only five months, and the doctor also decided bottles were a lot of foolishness so yesterday Christopher, in one stride, went from mother's breast to milk in a cup. This he grasped firmly with both hands and drank nobly. They're so proud of him they're fit to burst, the doctor remarking frequently about the "two-handed drinker" they have produced in the best Schemm tradition, and Mrs. Schemm again wearing that somewhat strained look she gets when she wonders how she could bear such extremely odd children. . . . Now the Schemms are considering a vacation in the Sierras with friends, leaving all three kids at home (which is why the weaning) with Elsie.

Joe comments that he "dozed in one of their chairs while the doctor earnestly studied 'The Care and Feeding of Infants,' working out Christopher's formula."

Mother's parents and sister had been visiting for two weeks in the little house at this time, and Joe has a good time describing the scene:

> Walkers are leaving Tuesday and that night Schemms are to celebrate by coming up here [Joe's apartment] and lis-

*tening to music. Mrs. Schemm says she'll even take Gil-
bert and Sullivan. Her father annoys them both to distrac-
tion by his insistence upon fixing things up: he has
painted both porches twice, renovated all the flower-beds
and now has taken all the weeds out of the lawn. Minus
weeds, the lawn looks pretty much like a field in summer
fallow. Mrs. Schemm came home the other day from
someplace with a bunch of women and found all the
porch furniture on the front lawn and no way whatever to
get into the house—because of paint—except through the
basement door and the laundry. Dr. Schemm has played
bridge until he's blue in the face, and his hospital visits
are taking up more and more of his evenings.*

Joe had no family of his own, and he supported his mother, sharing a small apartment with her not far from our house. That may be
why they both seem to have taken a great interest in the domestic
hilarities of their friends with growing children.

Ten years later, Joe is still describing our household, this time to
his friend Jean McReynolds, the artist. She had known us all these
years and apparently shared the Howards' interest, but she had just
recently moved to California. Joe records that I have just been accepted to college, that Mother, Christopher (now called Kit), and I
have driven to Minnesota to bring George home from school, but
that Kit will want to stop at every possible scenic attraction along
the way (he is now ten years old):

> *There's cause for alarm, as he is the most thorough inves-
> tigator I ever saw. The other day he lost a book which had
> been given him at school to bring home for Mildred's
> auto-graph, so she took him in the car to retrace his path
> after school. He had made seven stops—at plumbing
> shops, garages, the city library (to go to the toilet), loading
> racks in groceries, the ten-cent store, and others. They did
> not find the book and Mildred had to buy one—The
> Quarry—to replace it, which did not please her.*

The next year (1948), Joe wrote Jean what he had heard about Dad's work from friends they shared in Chicago:

> Did I tell you that the Rogers' doctor friend Wolf in Chicago, when Ginny mentioned Ferd, said: "You mean Ferdinand Schemm? Why he's internationally known!" I told Mildred; she like to bust with pride. Apparently Ferd's regime has caught on splendidly and has been listed by some world authority as among two or three of the greatest revolutions in medicine in many years. I don't know anyone for whom such recognition could make me happier unless it were you [for her painting], and I imagine you feel about the same way. He has earned it not only by the real nobility of his character but by his remarkable courage.

Joe's affection for my parents is evident in these lines. And it's fun to think of Mother being "fit to bust." Dad had endured a lot of ridicule from members of the medical profession in the United States for his clinical observations that the current treatment for edema was unfounded. In particular, his evidence was not assembled in a university hospital setting; and practicing medicine in a remote area, according to his detractors, could not place him at the forefront of investigation.

As a "stringer" (a reporter who wrote stories of interest to news magazines back east), Joe wrote an article for the *New York Times Magazine* about Dad's work. It was 1950 and Dad had been invited to the International Cardiological Conference, the first one held since the war, to deliver a paper in Paris and in Amsterdam. The article's accompanying photograph showed Dad sitting at his desk in his small hospital office.

In January 1940 Mother was revising her fourth novel, *The Brewers' Big Horses,* to be published that summer. I have found among her papers eighteen small pages torn from "The Standard Diary" for 1939. But she has crossed out "1939" on each page and written in "1940"; she begins on January 1. I had never known that she kept a diary before I found these pages, only that she kept small notebooks for her novels. And from these diary pages I have learned that she could have moments of deep dissatisfaction with her life. I had never imagined her with self-doubts.

> *(January 1) A plain day not glorified by sun nor transformed by snow. All that is ugly is ugly—fences and alleys and garbage cans. What has attraction of its own stands out. A good day to begin the New Year. I haven't made resolutions—and yet I do instinctively because I am that sort of person; mostly that I shall have more equanimity, more leisure of spirit out of which comes graciousness with Mother, more honesty in writing. Perhaps it is good that I have a job already to my hand in finishing the revision of the book. Then will come the heart for the new book—of Montana—I can put off a little longer the pain lest I have no more to write.*

On the next day she records my father's sadness at the death of a patient and friend and their drive down along the Missouri "to shake our depressed mood." She writes, "Sometimes I hate him being a doctor." The entry continues: "Got contract back from H.B. & Co. 15% after $5,000. Scares me to ask for things—always the fear that the spring might dry up, yet why should it?" On January 3 she mentions going to the vacated apartment of an elderly friend to make "a stab at writing." For January 4 there are only two sentences: "I worked in the morning in an uninspired way. The afternoon & evening were full of domesticities." On January 5, after a brief entry describing their friend's funeral, she adds, "Ferd made a call at 12:30—I dressed and went with him."

On January 6, Mother's observations become almost wholly a self-analysis:

> *Outside the window the snow was deep and clean as it used to be in the Upper Peninsula. It made me homesick for those years, that way of living. Some joy that was part of that is hard to hold on to now. I mustn't let my discontent with myself, my lot, my work grow into a habit of mind. People are divided into two great classes—those*

who find life good and those who scowl at the bitter taste. My tradition is of the former; I mustn't lose it. Loon Feather *(Iola Fuller) came and gave me a jealous pang for its beauty & skill & inevitable success. Ferd knew it. I am ashamed & have now fought it down—how vile I am. I must have beauty in my next book—beauty of the world—that is the most satisfying part of life. I must finish getting the opus ready to send off—today.*

The entries for January 7 and 8 are brief descriptions of the scenes that delight her outside her window. She writes: "Joy is in the sky—the snow—the morning. I mustn't lose it today." And for January 7: "The day ended with bridge at Lymans'—'young married people at play.'" She is quoting the narrator's observation in *Dr. Norton's Wife.* In describing her feelings in these early days of 1940, when she herself is just reaching thirty-five, she touches on the diverse activities of her day. They surround her discontent at not being absorbed in writing; they would have mattered less, perhaps, if she were "at work."

A week lapses before she writes again on January 13: "The north light is dismal this morning and my mood is gray. Elsie in one of her deep Slavic grumps—Ferd & I weary & dispirited—the opus about ready but full of weakness & I wonder about the whole thesis—ish! I must keep quietly to myself until the mood is past." Elsie was the woman keeping house for us at that time, a woman who was very possessive of my brother Christopher, just three years old that year. I remember Elsie as constantly peeved by the way I did the tasks she directed me to do in the kitchen. Even at eleven, I was mortified when she criticized the way I broke eggs into a bowl. I may never forget that.

But what is important is that after five more days, on January 18, Mother records another dimension of her life:

> *Yesterday we drove to Helena (one hundred miles from Great Falls) to see Eva Le Gallienne in* Hedda Gabler. *On the printed page it was hideous, a play of weakness & selfishness and boredom fanned to desperation. On the*

stage it became a play of three men and a woman; a
woman driven by uncontrollable forces in herself. The
scene of her burning the manuscript was unforgettable. It
seemed, as it was meant to, like murder of something
living. We drove home through a world that was cold &
moonlit and frosty.

Mother could not have imagined then that fifteen years later Le
Gallienne would star in the stage version by John Cecil Holm of
Mother's novel *The Southwest Corner*. A letter Le Gallienne wrote
expressing her fondness for playing the character of Marcia Elder is
stored with Mother's papers in the Wyoming archives: an excerpt
is quoted in her introduction to the University of Nebraska Press
reprint of *The Southwest Corner*.

The next entry is two weeks later, but her mood has not light-
ened. The diary pages have become a record of her dissatisfactions
with herself and include, again, comparisons to other writers
whose books she is reviewing:

I'm no good at diary writing, never have been. The days
escape into nothingness. I got the manuscript off. On re-
reading it seemed dull and pointless. I was and have been
low as the dust, since. I read Loon Feather *(Iola Fuller) &*
wrote the warm praise I felt for it, but a sneaking envy
gnawed in my soul. Then, Darkling Plain *(Wallace Steg-*
ner), as different as it could be—and it too disturbed me.
Its setting was Montana and Canada—and he wrote
wonderfully of the dry, hot wind and sun—of ditches and
coulees and prairie and isolation; the sort of thing I want
to get into my next book—but I haven't found the story
yet. I have been resting too long since, losing ground,
maybe. I must write. I want my sentences to be less
clumsy, my words more unusual. I want to learn to man-
age the "She got up"—"He rang the doorbell"—more un-
obtrusively. When I am reading I forget to notice.

Two paragraphs follow. One is about an account of her father's
boyhood in Illinois that she plans to type and work over; she writes

halfheartedly that it will be "good stuff to fill in with." The second is about a chinook (a warm wind off the mountains) that has arrived and will leave soon, "like an unreasonable hope." But then she returns to problems of living in the house: "I tell myself the clutter of too small rooms—makes my mind cluttered; that it would be better for the children if they had more room; but would it? after all? It is my equanimity & spirit that makes their lives. I know all this and do nothing about it! Indecision grows on me." By March 1, she is so dispirited that her self-analysis has become self-laceration:

> My spirit is choked with frustration, irritation and discouragement. I am a complete failure at human relationships. Looking back it seems to me I have always been. It grows out of selfishness, ambition, insincerity and an inability to stay even. Perhaps I should keep Elsie for the discipline on myself; force myself to get along pleasantly—ignore sullenness and rudeness. Mother rubs me the wrong way till I could scream! And then I wallow in the mud of my own shame until I have no self-respect left. And yet I have great affection for her and tenderness—it makes me crawl to say love as though love should be free from such anger. The quiet steady full feeling of work progressing is gone. I can't remember how it felt. Now I am going out to lunch. I shall try to keep still & look into other women's lives. I'm going to see lots & I shall try to look at the sky and feel the sun—ish!

The diary's final entry is April 16, a kind of assessment of what she has written, and perhaps an explanation of why, over fifty years ago, she tore these pages from the standard diary and stuffed them in with other pages she kept:

> As I read over the last few entries I find all of that still true. And it is spring. The crocuses are past, the grass is greening. Still I am not quietly at work. Unless I can put in honest effort this afternoon—be in Mother's words,

*"worth my salt," I shall have to go away to the Tupa until
I am really organized. I shall write again today—not just
the start of a mood.*

I don't know whether Mother actually went to the cabin, or
Tupa (the Finnish word my parents used), for the serenity to write
that spring of 1940. Dad and Mother often went together for a few
days at a time when either one had a deadline to meet. They also
spent weekends in town in a hotel room when Dad couldn't leave
town. It amused them when Dad was told by a colleague that he
had been seen entering the rather shabby hotel with a strange
woman. Mother told us this story years later, saying that Dad was
flattered at being thought to have a double life and never explained
who the strange woman was.

When I was about eight years old, Mother and Dad were away all
of two weeks in the Sierras, but in that time I came to a serious understanding and remember being very wistful about it: Mother and
Dad had their own life apart from us. They could have exciting adventures without us, come and go whenever they wished to without us, and most dismaying of all, they had fun without us. Remembering back to this realization, it seems to me I whimpered a
little inwardly. I understood it to be the way things were—inevitable. What I didn't realize then was that Mother had a private inner
world, too, teeming with her characters that never included us.

Always, I have known that Mother seized upon enlivening a
moment in the midst of others with an electrifying observation or
lively interjection of an anecdote. As an older woman, she had a
flair for sardonic rejoinders and, now that I think of it, a sense of
the drama that was required for the moment. She needed to make
a vivid impression on others, I felt, not only on social occasions but
in our family moments, too. When we were youngsters, she made
wonderful use of her girlhood memorizations prepared for recita-
tions. Rising suddenly to her feet, she would throw back her head
and begin:

*I want free life, and I want fresh air,
and I sigh for the canter after the cattle,*

The crack of the whip like shots in battle,
The medley of horns, and hoofs, and heads,
That wars, and wrangles, and scatters and spreads;
The green beneath and the blue above,
And dash, and danger, and life and love,
And Lasca!

Mother had become the rough-riding Texan with all the descriptive expressions of galloping over the plains, his beautiful Lasca "on a mouse-grey mustang close to my side / In Texas, down by the Rio Grande." We would be startled out of our doldrums, thrilled at the spectacle of our mother declaiming one verse after another until the fearful end when, shuddering, her arm flung across her face, she would hurl herself back into her chair, crying out, "Lasca was dead!" Our father would begin clapping, freeing us from the tragedy. Then Mother would change to merry laughter.

When I was grown, I used to wonder how the Philadelphia school system had come to reach as far as the Rio Grande for this selection, but recently I read a brief account of the history of "Lasca." The writer of the song was a Frank Desprez, an Englishman who had spent three years, in the 1870s, herding cattle in Texas. Returning to England, he worked in the Savoy Theater and Hotel for D'Oyly Carte, writing "curtain-raisers" to fill the time before the main theatrical event. One of his compositions "opened the first Gilbert and Sullivan opera produced at the Savoy," according to Michael Korn, a former folklorist for the Montana Arts Council. (Korn's article "Lasca" was printed in *Rural Montana,* November 1987.) Korn writes that the song was first published in November 1882 in *London Society: A Monthly Magazine of Light and Amusing Literature.* "Lasca" was first printed in the United States in the *Montana Live-Stock Journal,* June 1888, and could have been submitted, Korn suggests, by one of the many Englishmen arriving in Montana in the 1880s. However, "Lasca" reached Philadelphia in time for Mother's high school elocutions; she was to perform it more than once back in Montana in her own living room for the entertainment of her children.

In the late 1930s and 1940s, she and my father staged their own dramas in a Great Falls event called the "Fortnightly," a costume ball of sorts. There is a photograph of Mother dressed in a deerskin shirt and tan tights. She wears a snugly fitted hood securing a pair of antlers on top of her head. She is "the deer who got away," accompanying the notorious Irish remittance man, Sir George Gore. (He was said to have hired a train for himself and his friends from which to shoot into buffalo herds grazing along the train tracks on the plains.) A friend who attended the affair, Pat Brennan Taylor, described the scene for me recently: "Mildred minced behind His Royal Self in the Grand March, eyes downcast." His Royal Self was my father, dressed in hunting breeches and a tweed hunter's cap, carrying a rifle. There is no photo of him, but I can remember him twirling a false mustache. They won a prize for that one and for another one that required their three children. Dad went dressed as the artist Gaugin, and Mother as his native wife wearing a sarong. She carried my baby brother in her arms; George and I followed behind wearing loincloths. Mother was stained a dark brown, and so were her three children. But after the parade, and winning the prize, we were delivered home to be scrubbed raw in the bathtub by Elsie. Throughout our misery we knew that Mother and Dad had gone back to dance.

There were other times when our parents conspired against us. I remember a night at dinner when George and I must have been about nine and ten. Mother and Dad announced that they were taking our places. We were startled but played along. Then they began their imitations of us: slouching, reaching across the table for serving bowls, talking with their mouths full of food, bickering: "Did!" "Did not!" They appealed to George at the head of the table. At first we giggled with recognition, but then became embarrassed for them. Still, we got the point. Mother was obviously the instigator of this demonstration. Once, driving home with Mother, I listened to her telling about something amusing she had seen. I don't remember the story; what I remember was her insistence that I not repeat it because she wanted to tell it at the supper table that evening. I was old enough to realize that she liked to enliven an occasion, even supper, when she had an audience.

At the same time, I was learning about my mother in a different way. In each kitchen I have known in my mother's houses, she hung three small framed pictures. They seemed to have come from paintings that had been reproduced in a newspaper. One was a hearty looking woman holding a large loaf of bread against her stomach as she cut into the loaf. She was dressed, as I thought later, in a Flemish costume: a long black dress, a wide white apron, and on her head a peaked white fabric cap that curved outward at her cheeks. Her expression was pleasant and concentrated. The second shows a similarly dressed woman turned toward a window full of light. She stands next to a table with one hand resting on a handsome large pitcher; her other hand is deep in a pocket under her apron. These pictures comforted me, as if solid good women were contentedly in the midst of their households. I used to look up and find them with my eyes when I was most nettled by whatever I was being told to "get on with" by whomever was in charge in the kitchen.

But the third picture was my delight and, somehow, a secret revealed about my mother. The same kind of tinted reprinted painting, it was of a young woman seated in the long grasses of a hillside, facing forward. Her long skirt is gathered around her knees and a light wind curves tendrils of hair around her face. She is blowing soap bubbles into the sky for a group of four or five children looking up at her, spread in a semicircle on the grassy slope just in front of her. The focus of the painting is on her pleased face, slightly tilted upward.

Why did these pictures tell me something that I almost, and quite shyly, understood as some aspect of my mother's feelings that I never otherwise saw? Homely moments of a woman cutting bread for her family, or pausing by a window as she readied a table, or entrancing a group of children? They reassured me, I know. And finding them also hung in the Vermont kitchen when Mother was retired, I was convinced that they were moments she wanted to return to at times.

Now I see those pictures as being like the postcards I have kept taped inside the kitchen cupboard doors in my own homes: the interior of the Trinity College reading room in Dublin; the view of the sea from Nathaniel Hawthorne's desk in the Salem, Massachusetts, counting house; and the vivid colors of small Parisian chil-

dren tumbling from the dark schoolhouse door out into the sun—
a print of Honoré Daumier's painting *Coming Out of School*. My pictures are intended to present me with spaces outside the domestic
world, spaces that I could rediscover as I worked in the kitchen. I
wonder if Mother and I were alike in this, each of us indulging in a
private drama.

I have handwritten notes between Mother and Dad dated only
"Dec 18." This is George's birthday, still when we live in town and
when Dad was in the hospital as a patient for treatment of his
hand, so this was probably written in 1943. A day earlier, Dad and
George had been wrestling around on the living room floor when
Dad stopped suddenly and Mother drove him to the hospital. Dad
didn't want George to know about the injury during their play, so
we were only told that his hand was acting up again.

Over the years the fingers on Dad's left hand had to be amputated one by one down to the lowest knuckles whenever gangrene
set in from his prolonged X-ray use in the Upper Peninsula. At
this date his little finger remained, but because it had become very
brittle, it was broken in the wrestling. After all four fingers had
been amputated and healed, Mother had Dad's left-hand gloves
cut down for him.

This exchange of notes that Mother kept for more than fifty
years must have brought Dad closer to her each time she read
them.

> *Dear Doc,*
> *A highly satisfactory day so far. George just glowing.*
> *Wasn't he cute to rush over to see you before breakfast?*
> *I hope he didn't get in the way. He was the first one*
> *dressed and came in my room while it was still dark and*
> *said, "I'm going over to see Dad." He reports that you*
> *are doing all right. Are you truly? Did you have a good*
> *night?*

Mother goes on to say how much George enjoyed opening his
birthday gifts, that she'll "get the papers typed," and that Kit was
coming over to the hospital, five blocks from home, with this note.

She ends: "Could give him a note to bring me [on the other side]? All our love, dearest, if you have ANY time when you're let alone get the implications done—let's get it off before Xmas. Your silly, Rib." The implications Mother refers to must have been necessary for the papers she was typing, papers on his edema treatment that he was submitting for a medical meeting. Dad's reply on the other side of the notepaper reads:

> Dear Madame:
> (1) Very good night
> (2) Painless dressing—looks fine
> (3) Enjoyed George's visit
> (4) Kit is having his [?] repaired by the supervisor
> (5) Have papers out—but usual interruptions
> (6) Prob. home tonight or in A.M. early
> (7) The implications, hidden, but already verified, are that I love you.
> Your sincere admirer,
> FRS

Dad's rejoinder to her remarks about finishing the implications reminds me of his teasing replies to her to give him some breathing space. And reminds me of her insistence that he get on with that part of his work that would help him "make a name" for himself.

During a later summer, Dad was in the hospital in Chicago for skin grafts for the same injury, and George, nine, and I, eleven, were placed in the Wisconsin camps for boys and girls called Bryn Afon, where Dad and Mother first met. Kit, three, was at home with Elsie. Mother wrote this note:

> Dear Doc—
> If I could sketch I would draw your head right now, beard and all, your aquiline nose, the shine of the gray hairs at the sides of your hair—your ears that are perfectly formed (even though they do need barbering), your hair that always breaks into separate strands like strong vital strokes of a pencil—I would get in the height of your brow with the noble places running far inward—

your sweet mouth that is so sensitive and kind and stub-
born—your eyes are on the page so I can only see the
eyelashes (not so long as Kit's) but I like the way they lie
gabled in close to your nose. Funny to be so in love with
you in jamas in a hospital room—I mean with your
Looks, not just you. I think there is not a flabby or cheap
or coarse or mean line in your face, nor Ordinary. That
was the first thing I noticed on the porch of Bryn Afon.
Goodnite—a spendthrift kiss—Mildred Walker—

I think Mother's pride in Dad was almost as deep as her love for
him. Did she sign the note so formally because she wanted to insist
on her commitment to him? If Dad saved the note, did Mother find
it after his death fifteen years later and keep it where she could find
it to read over again? Their life together had a steady strength, and
I think we children learned that as we were growing up.

6

The First Two Montana Novels

In late April 1999, I received a letter from Patricia Taylor, a native Montanan and a professional photographer in Great Falls in the 1940s. Pat had been a friend of my parents and of Joe Howard. She wrote in answer to my question about her impressions of Mother:

> One thing I think you should always keep in mind is that she was living a many-layered life: loving wife and mother; wife of a prominent doctor in a small western town; probably still reeling somewhat from the culture change—and challenge. I think she sailed through it although I was certainly not one of her confidantes. Meanwhile, those stories were rolling around in her fertile brain!

Mother may have stopped writing in the brief diary of 1940 because she found a story for her next novel. What she described as "the quiet steady full feeling of work progressing" may have returned, because her fifth novel, *Unless the Wind Turns,* was published just eighteen months later—in October 1941. Perhaps the painful months that she had recorded in her diary, waiting for "the Montana story," accounted for the swiftness with which she wrote *Unless the Wind Turns.* Forty years later, when Mother had retired to live in Vermont, I asked, very tentatively, about the subject she had chosen for her first Montana novel. She told me, instead, in a conspiratorial voice that she had written *Unless the Wind Turns* in two and a half months. The memory seemed to awe her; she added that sometimes she thought she had written her early novels too fast, but that she thought her "forest fire novel" was better than reviewers had given her credit for.

In the February 1939 issue of the *Junior League Magazine,* Mother published a short story entitled "The Knife." Its main characters were easterners on a week's vacation out west, climbing in the Sierra Mountains of California. Now that I've recently found her copy of this short story, I see that it could have had a part in her decision to choose the perspective of vacationing easterners for *Unless the Wind Turns.*

"The Knife" had its source in that brief vacation that Mother and Dad were persuaded to take in the Sierras by old friends from back east. In the spring of 1937, when George and I were six and eight, they went off in a state of gaiety that didn't include us! I think our wistfulness was increased by our realization that we were left to the mercy of grumpy Elsie, who was in charge of the house. We were probably a little pleased when they returned home gratefully; the trip had been strenuous for them, leading burros up into the high altitude. Dad had had to lead Mother out on a burro because she had become too ill from sunburn to walk. A photograph of Dad from that trip shows him sunburned, too, and very thin. The fish in the mountain lakes, he told us, were so thin you could see through them. And they both complained about the sparseness of their hiking rations.

The five-page story that I found among Mother's papers had been torn out of the glossy magazine. The columns of the story are bordered by advertisements for cruises, skiing vacations in Sun Valley, and illustrations of elegant young men and women at play. But "The Knife" is quite other than a splendid event among the leisure class. The characters are seen through the thoughts of the newly married wife of the guide. Seth Reed had urged his wife, Miriam, to come for the wonderful mountain experience. "He had no idea what a mistake it had been to bring her along," Miriam thinks. Her discomfort is acute in these opening paragraphs because she feels she doesn't fit in with the other wives:

> *Walking toward the kitchen fire she was conscious that her red slacks and rayon shirt and red sweater were all wrong. The slacks were too skimpy, and jeans were the thing, anyway. Her sport shoes were all wrong, too. Seth should have told her. But Seth thought everything about*

her was perfect. The girls had heavy bass moccasins and
wool socks and men's flannel shirts. Their heads were tied
up in cotton bandanas. They had little belongings, too,
that made a difference. Betty had a Mexican gourd that
she fastened to her belt for a drinking cup and Sally had a
snake skin belt that even the boys envied. These were the
things you couldn't fake. You had to have gone places, the
right places, to pick them up. (10)

Miriam knows the others are startled by her nail polish and her
perfume, "Flower of Love," because "these girls smell only of soap
and cigarette smoke." As each member of the party leads a trio of
mules up the increasingly steeper trails, Miriam has time to think
of how her only background has been business school and now
secretarial work, not an experience to make smooth conversation
with. Again she feels she doesn't fit in.

Trudging at the end of the line, Miriam finds a small, beautifully
carved knife that has fallen by the trail. She slips it into her pocket:
"She decided to bring it out casually some time the way the others
brought out their trophies." When she does bring the knife out to
peel an orange as she sits in camp with the others, one of the
women admires it. That pleases Miriam, and she tells them she has
had it for years. She is sure then that the knife is one of those "little
belongings that made a difference." Now she is confident enough
to join in the conversation, to feel "one of them." Now she can
even enjoy being in the high, rugged country with the rest.

But Miriam loses all her confidence when their camp is approached the next morning by a lone hiker coming up the part of
the trail they had climbed earlier. He explains that he is looking for
a knife he lost on the trail. When she is asked to show the stranger,
Mr. Green, her knife, he turns it over slowly in his hand. "Miriam
was braced, waiting for him to say it was his. She would face it out
then. . . . 'Mine wasn't so fine a one as this,' the stranger said
slowly, 'but it was on this order. I hope you have the good luck not
to lose it.' He handed it back to her and his eyes looked straight into
hers" (62).

At first Miriam's emotions are of fear, then defiance. She is desperate to get the camp packed up so they can move on. As penance,

but also to keep away from Mr. Green, she cleans up the camp kitchen: "the worst job of all; every pot and kettle had its cover, with Abercrombie and Fitch on it like a label in a high-priced dress. It was better equipment than most apartment kitchens had." When the group starts off, Miriam admits to herself that she is "a liar and a thief." Down below them, she can see Mr. Green still resting at their campsite. Finally, she decides "she was a little idiot, but was no thief." Tying the lead burro to a rock, she runs back down the trail to give up the knife. But Mr. Green won't take the knife because, he says, he knows how much it means to her. " 'I'm giving it to you; you're not stealing it.' He smiled."

The strongest focus in "The Knife" is not Miriam's shame at taking the knife for her own but her need to be accepted by the others. Soon after she had shown off the knife, the three women had taken a swim in a glacier lake. At night, stretched out in her sleeping bag, she remembers their conversation: " 'Mim, do you have any extra cold cream?' Sally asked. And when they were dressing, Betty said abruptly in that blunt way she had, 'You've got the neatest flanks on you, d'you know it?' But it wasn't what they said, it was their tone of voice, as though she were one of them" (62).

The heart of the story is Miriam's concentration on being accepted; it is stressed so constantly that the incident with the knife seems a plot device. She is much harder on herself about not dressing as well (expensively) as the other two women, not possessing "some gadget to show off with" as they do, and not having had the right experiences to make conversation that will interest them. She needs to be "the right sort" for her own self-esteem. Miriam's reiterated thoughts about not being equal to the others are almost claustrophobic when I reread the story.

I remember now that Mother came back from the Sierra trip with a Mexican gourd which she always tied to her belt when we went hiking. Had she held the gourd in her hand and seen a possible place for it in the story? Or had its reception by the other wives on the Sierra trip suggested the story to her? Could she have seen herself as a Miriam—at a disadvantage when she compared her background with that of the others? I ask these questions because, as her child and even as her grown daughter, I resented her disapproval when I didn't wear something "appropriate." As a young person just deciding what my style might be, I used to react with shame, then defiance, and finally with indifference—or take that stance, anyway. I would never have worn a red rayon shirt on a camping trip, but for years I felt hopeless about having a sense of "taste" that could please Mother.

I see now, however, coming across this short story, that these things had more significance for Mother than simply taste. And it reminds me of a moment when I was visiting Mother and her sister during a summer in Vermont. My mother and Aunt Peg, both in their sixties, argued vehemently over the curtains I was hemming for my new apartment. Mother's distaste for hems that were too "skimpy" was scathing; Aunt Peg didn't think that was important. Mother stalked off, saying, "You may not care to have things right, but I do!"

I stammered an apology for my mother's outburst that had mainly been directed at my aunt, and asked with some anguish, "Why is she like that?" My aunt replied calmly, "You know, I've always felt that your mother had an inferiority complex." It was a thunderous notion to me. I was awed by my aunt's perceptiveness, by her acceptance of what she saw as a lifelong struggle in Mother.

I have indulged in this digression because it helped me to understand my mother, the social being. And only at that late date in my own development, in my early thirties, was I beginning to allow my mother to be the kind of person she was. I have come to see about my mother, the writer, that she put this trait to good use in her characterizations—especially of her women. A woman who is her main character is especially alert to what is being said about her by other woman characters. It is that same claustrophobic emphasis which, in her novels, can have a powerful effect.

But now to the novel, *Unless the Wind Turns*. On five-by-seven-inch cards for a speech given sometime in the 1960s, she wrote about the subject of her fifth novel: "Montana was so vast and strange to me that I didn't dare to write about it for almost ten years, though I wrote about eastern dudes there in a novel called *Unless the Wind Turns*."

The title phrase was heard often in Montana: A forest fire in the mountains had a chance of being stopped unless the wind changed and took it in another direction where there was still timber to fuel it. What I remember as a girl of nine years in 1938 is the forest fire on the North Fork of the Teton River, just over the ridge from the South Fork where we had our cabin. I was waiting table in the South Fork ranch lodge where the firefighters were fed and rested, before they were sent back to the fire again. We would watch from the safety of the South Fork. We could see deer, and once a bear, racing along the ridge to escape the fire—silhouetted against towering smoke and flaring roaring skies.

But as in each of Mother's earlier works, the relationship between a husband and wife is at the center of the novel, not the occurrence of a devastating event like the forest fire. The novel opens with a quotation from *Julius Caesar*, act 2, scene 1. The quotation is a foreshadowing of the wife's discontent with her husband because he has become reluctant to confide in her and the husband's unspoken question of whether his wife has married the wrong man:

> PORTIA:
> *Within the bond of marriage, tell me, Brutus,*
> *Is it excepted I should know no secrets*
> *That appertain to you? Am I yourself*
> *But, as it were, in sort or limitation,*
> *To keep with you at meals, comfort your bed,*
> *And talk to you sometimes? Dwell I*
> *but in the suburbs*
> *Of your good pleasure? If it be no more,*
> *Portia is Brutus' harlot, not his wife.*
>
> BRUTUS:
> *. . . Portia, go in a while;*
> *And by and by thy bosom shall partake*
> *The secrets of my heart.*

In *Unless the Wind Turns,* Serena is an easterner who has agreed to take a pack trip with her husband, John. His roots are western —in the Rocky Mountains of Montana. Serena is removed from John, idly disappointed in the kind of man he seems to be. To her husband's dismay, she has invited three of her eastern friends to come along. The novel opens with the train trip that brings them west:

> *"You can positively feel the barrenness, can't you, Walt?"*
> *Lizzie Phillips turned away from the window of the club car with distaste.*
> *"It was just as bare yesterday in North Dakota," her husband objected.*
> *"Yes, but it was new then. It's only the second day that it really sinks in."*
>
> *"John doesn't think it's bare," Serena said, looking across at her husband. "I thought he was going to get out and kiss the dirt when we crossed the Dakota-Montana line."*
> *John gave no sign that he had heard. (3)*

The novel is divided into three days: "Monday" (three chapters), "Tuesday" (six chapters), and "Wednesday" (seven chapters). In the first three chapters, we are given John's point of view as well as Serena's. The intensity of John's thoughts, his hope to have the trip bring him closer to Serena, is a contrast to the carelessness of Serena's feelings for her husband. By the end of the first day of the trip, she has placed him verbally and physically at a distance.

In his disappointment, John thinks of Serena's wealth and self-assurance and feels hopelessly that she doesn't want or need his love. Instead, she seems to thrive on the small things he does that annoy her. John decides to enjoy the mountains and his old friend, Burns, whom he has known since he was a boy. Burns is the outfitter who is taking them on the trip.

One of the things John does that annoys Serena is to invite the young wife of a woodcutter to come along the second day of their trip. Rose has been cooking at the cabin for Burns and wants to be with her husband, who is cutting logs farther up in the mountains where the pack trip is headed. In the novel, it is as if Miriam of "The Knife" is cast as Rose. And Rose is treated by Serena and her friend Lizzie as "not one of them." They think less of Rose for wearing her shirt hanging outside her jeans, and she seems comfortable in the mountain world that they are leery of. What happens to Rose in the novel, however, changes Serena. It changes even Serena's thoughts about her husband. Miriam's character, so exhaustively explored in the short story, clearly seems to have given Mother a plan for her first Montana character. But we see Rose through the eyes of Mother's eastern protagonist, Serena.

"Tuesday" becomes tense and terrifying in its rapidity of events: They catch up the horses, start up the trail, taking pleasure in the mountain air, and John stops to show Serena the cabin that Burns had allowed him to have for his own as a young man. John thinks how he loved Serena so much in their early years together, but now, he bursts out, "What do we really mean to each other?" Her reply makes him wince: "Of course, there are always adjustments to be made between two personalities." And she adds, "That's true of any marriage, but ours is certainly as successful a relationship as . . ." He thinks sadly to himself that being "successful" is all that matters to Serena. "She didn't even feel any lack in their lives together. . . . Sometimes, lately, he had wondered if he loved Serena, and it was like looking down the sheer side of old Baldy. If you got down there you couldn't get back up easily" (66).

On the trail again, with John and Burns leading the pack horses, the conversation is between the easterners about their reading preferences, interspersed with comments about the bareness of the mountain slopes they're passing. As they ride up to a rocky ridge, Burns and John catch sight of smoke rising over the next reef. Waiting in camp for the men to come back from a closer look at the source of smoke, Serena spends her time going over in her mind what she doesn't like about this trip: "The whole thing seemed stupidly aimless. They were going up to the Chinese Wall. And what was that but another granite reef, standing on end like a wall? John talked about it as though it were something tremendous . . . and then they would ride back down again!" Her impatience with John has encouraged her fascination with the refugee doctor from Germany, Victor; he is one of the three whom she had invited to come along on the pack trip. But that fascination is muted when Victor comes back to tell them that there is a big fire just over the reef from them.

1. Margaret and Mildred Walker,
ages eight and one,
in Philadelphia. 1906.

2. Mildred, nine years old. 1916.

3. Mildred, known as "Pep Walker" by her classmates,
at her magna cum laude graduation from Wells College. 1926.
(Courtesy of the Louis Jefferson Long Library
of Wells College, Aurora NY)

4. Ferdinand Schemm at his laboratory desk
at the University of Michigan. 1927.

5. Mildred with her parents, Harriet and Walter Walker, at the Montana cabin on the Teton River. She is clowning for the camera. 1938.
(Courtesy of Margaret Walker)

6. Ferd Schemm with his three children—Ripley, baby Christopher, and George—at their Great Falls home. 1937.
(Courtesy of Margaret Walker)

7. Mildred in front of the Great Falls home,
holding a newly published copy of
The Brewers' Big Horses. 1940.

8. Mildred in costume as "the deer who
got away," at the Fortnightly event
in Great Falls. 1942.

9. Schemm family home on the Missouri River in Montana.
The islands called the Niña, the Pinta, and the Santa Maria
are just offshore. 1950. (Courtesy of Konrad Deligdisch)

10. Lottie Barton, former roundup
cook and prototype for Ruby
in *The Curlew's Cry*. 1950s.

11. Mildred and Ferd Schemm on a family vacation by Lake Huron in Michigan. 1950s. (Courtesy of Christopher Schemm)

12. Joseph Kinsey Howard, author of *Montana: High, Wide, and Handsome*
and Schemm family friend, speaking at the
Bread Loaf Writers' Conference in Vermont. 1947.
(Jarvis Woolverton Mason, reprinted with the
permission of the Middlebury College Archives)

13. Page of Mildred's writing notebook for *Winter Wheat* showing
descriptions of the hazards of dryland farming. Early 1940s.
(Photo courtesy of Kristi Hager; loan of notebook courtesy of
American Heritage Center, Laramie WY)

...ginss ya are.

Orks bus to cash note to Ft. Reserve m—
Orks charge 10%. — this pay only 4½%—
to to make the road

(1918 crop — nothing)
Reasonably farmer needs this 2000, if surely
mony is not that he is poss. He needs it because
he is getting such as poss. He has trouble more than a
... ... is poss it once near his land.

hire labor because he has note land than he can
farm himself for that sum a pay roll.
The more land he can swing, the more credit he
can borrow to increase scale of his operations.
the more mony he will make if nothing
happens.

But if the crop fails he will be unable to
pay his note; he will be obliged to borrow more on
a secd note to tiry off the next year's crop.
And the bote being started with him is obliged to
go on.

⑶ Kremlin — 6-8 houses, in elevator, a large
garage & two bats. hive of cars is 5 M. 25 automobiles.

"" This bad years you know, we're about to get
another crop when the grasshoppers came. The sky was
filled with them gleaming in the sunlight.
They eat everything down to misture. The land
they'd been over to as if it were summer fallow.
Well, there was a woman in there whose
husband worked on the railroad. She did the farming
She fought the grasshoppers with her boots & rags
there, surrounded by people who got so when at
all, she brought there a crop of 40 bu. to the acre
& paid off a mortgage.

End of basis Hall — The delusion that credit is
substance

14. Mildred in Vermont; the photograph was taken for publication of
If a Lion Could Talk when she was sixty-four. 1969.
(Clara S. Sipprell)

Rose, though she is five months pregnant, rides back down the trail to warn the fire guard. Victor has assured them, "There's no great danger," but Rose is worried for her husband's safety. The next chapters alternate between the men fighting their way through the fire to find the young woodcutter and the women waiting back in the camp. The details of the men struggling through the fire, nearly perishing, needing water, needing cover from the burning trees and branches falling all around them, are terrifying.

Mother learned those details without recording them in the small notebook I found with her papers. I imagine that she heard them from the outfitters she and Dad knew, that their fearfulness stayed in her imagination so sharply that she didn't have to write them down. Instead, her notes were directed almost entirely toward the character of Serena. Toward the end of the notes she observes: "Much of the strength of the story depends on how well drawn Serena is—no emergency or crisis of life ever really sufficiently challenging for her." That is true of Serena in the novel, and John knows it to his dismay, but the fire and all its distress finally is "sufficiently challenging for her." Looking back as a reader, I see how the plot of the party being trapped by the forest fire is used to intensify the characters' personalities. As Deirdre McNamer points out in her introduction to the University of Nebraska Press reprint, "the wind begins to turn for Serena" when she disdains "Victor's tendency to deal with trouble by getting out of its path" (xi). Victor has left the other men in their hunt for the young woodcutter in order to return to the safety of camp, just as he had left Europe at the spread of Nazism, McNamer points out.

When Wednesday comes, Rose experiences premature labor, to Serena's dismay. When Serena tries to comfort Rose, she realizes that she "had never in her life tried to comfort anyone." Victor seems not so interested in how, as a doctor, he can assist Rose but talks humorously about sterilizing peasant women in Europe. Serena begins to lose her admiration for Victor. She thinks, "Back home Victor's leisurely way of talking, of growing interested in his subject and running on about it, excited her. At this moment, it seemed shallow and heartless" (166).

The eleventh chapter brings Serena closer to understanding how John feels about his life. She and Victor take shelter in John's boyhood cabin because Rose is about to give birth and can't continue down the mountain in the truck as planned. Serena finds John's books and then a composition book he had used for a diary, first as a boy, then later as a young man. The last entry tells how important the cabin is to him:

> *A place that you keep going back to in your life is always more than a place. It's a kind of measuring ground and a philosophy and a hide-out. . . . This cabin's mine. When you get back to it, it makes you sort out things and leave some behind that you won't be needing. Then you take away with you what you really care about. (182)*

Serena wishes he had told her why he cared so much about his cabin, about getting back to Montana, "instead of just acting stubborn about it." Then she realizes that she hadn't been much interested at the time.

Rose's baby is stillborn. The men find Rose's husband and his horse burned to death in the forest, but they can't find John. A further chapter follows John struggling to get to safety and finally getting himself to water. Many of his thoughts are about Serena and how it must be all over between them. Serena, finally safe in a hotel down in town, learns that John is still lost in the fire, and fears what she had feared for Rose. She lets herself think how everything might have been different if she hadn't ridden right over John's hopes by inviting her friends along.

In the last chapter, when Burns has found John and brought him back alive but badly burned, Serena is newly aware of what matters to John. But the chapter shifts to John's point of view as he hears her say that he and she should stay longer and she'll urge the others to start their return journey. When his fever has gone down, she says, they'll have a few days to enjoy his cabin. The novel ends: "An uncertain smile hurt his stiff face. She hadn't even waited for him to agree, he thought. That was Serena for you!" (235).

Unless the Wind Turns was announced in Harcourt, Brace's 1941 fall list along with Virginia Woolf's *Between the Acts*. Good reviews for the novel followed upon publication. *Publisher's Weekly* (October 18, 1941) wrote of this fifth novel:

> *For character, story, and rapid-paced action, for background—the Montana Rockies with the vivid appeal of the American West—this is Mildred Walker's best novel. It is a story of modern marriage, of a couple whose personal problem is suddenly dwarfed by the impact of physical danger. Without forcing any parable or moral, this brilliant novel superbly illustrates the dilemma of an entire world today.*

The *Wichita Eagle* (December 12, 1941) wrote in praise of the author's writing style: "Mildred Walker shows a grasp of human emotions under stress and, better than most writers, can strip the urban veneer from a character, leaving the real vices and virtues exposed." But all her life, despite good reviews, Mother would remember bitterly other reviews she characterized as "damning with faint praise." Sometimes she spoke of a review as "vaporous." One like this, perhaps, by an Oliver Crawley writing in the *Winston-Salem Review* (n.d.): "Light reading and good for three hours of entertaining book-fare. . . . The book isn't pushing parables or morals. It's an intimate story of two people and their strange situation delightfully but realistically told." Or from the *Book Review Service* (November 11, 1941) in Boston: "Staccato, dramatic modern writing, solving no problems but airing them, at least."

These reviews, we children came to know, caused Mother great distress. We would hear her railing to our father against some reviewer's comment and other times see her sitting dejectedly, staring out the window or rereading an offending comment to herself. We would rarely hear her express delight about a review. We were also aware of our father's attempts to defuse her disappointment. It was our cue to disappear quietly.

When Mother was in her eighties, I asked her one day if she had read the novel of another writer also publishing in the late 1930s and 1940s. She smiled and said, "No, dear, I was too busy writing to read other people's work." But the entries in her working notebooks show that she was reading other writers on their views of writing. In an explanatory description of her three-by-five-inch notebook for *Unless the Wind Turns,* when she sent it to the archives in 1971, she writes: "This end of notebook contains notes in preparation for *Unless the Wind Turns.* The other end is filled with quotations about writing." In one of her entries she paraphrases Bernard De Voto from his *American Novels* (1939): "A novel must have drama or else is something less—no matter the symbolism, no matter the writer's conviction." She must have been applying De Voto's admonition in her fifth novel.

Mother's sixth novel, *Winter Wheat,* published in 1944, would be wholly concerned with Montana characters surviving and triumphing in that country. And it has the "drama" that De Voto insists must be present. Natural events surrounding her characters are also essential to *Winter Wheat.* Recently, I found it helpful to read Mother's short story "Rancher's Wife," published in 1940 in the *Junior League Magazine,* because it reads like a rehearsal for this sixth novel. It takes up those Montanans who live in what Mother first saw as barrenness. The short story is a kind of query into who a woman living in the West might be, and it is told entirely from the point of view of Bella Meyers, the wife of Will Meyers, who grows wheat on land sixty-seven miles out of town. As the story opens, Bella, waiting in the front porch swing for Will to come in from the ranch, notices that "he looked more tired tonight, more stooped, it seemed to her." Before his arrival, she has been thinking back to her luncheon at the country club and an afternoon of playing bridge. Now, as he approaches, she thinks: "He never looked real slick like the men who had positions in town. Most of the time, she forgot he was a rancher, the ranch was so far in the background, providing the comfortable income back of the pleasant life on Elm Street." After a silent supper, Will explains the discouragement that Bella has seen in him. The drought has been so bad this summer that there is no wheat to cut, and so, he says slowly, he has had to rent the house in town: "I rented it from the first of next month. I thought you could put up with a year on the ranch, till spring anyway. . . . After all, Bella, you're a rancher's wife."

The rest of the story is of Bella's disbelief, expressed only in her thoughts, that she must give up her town activities, must endure the ugliness of the ranch house way out there with no trees, "only a gangling row of cottonwood saplings planted along the road." She panics at the thought of not being surrounded by her fine china, her kitchen conveniences, her shady porch. As they drive toward the ranch, Will's assurance that they can bring out "maybe a truck load of things" she will want to have, including the "Beauty Rest" mattresses, is not enough: "But the women who lived on these ranches weren't like her, Bella told herself; they were used to this sort of life. They liked it. She saw them in town or at the State Fair. She had never thought of herself in the same breath as a rancher's wife." Will tells her, "You can see the mountains from here, anyway," but she knows that she has "never been one for looking at mountains." Once there, she feels even more strongly her dread of the wide bare hot land surrounding her. Only when the sun has begun to go down and the dry country seems less harsh can she appreciate the sight of the mountains. The story ends with Bella's reluctant discovery that when she sees Will riding in on his horse after the long hot afternoon, the country doesn't make her so lonely.

Mother's short stories written during the Great Falls years (1933–44) seem sharp glimpses into lives that "said something" to her. Now they seem almost autobiographical descriptions of her interests. The plot of "Rancher's Wife," for instance, depends on the depiction of how a woman of what Mother called "shallow interests" (chiefly interested in her luncheon at the country club or the view from her front porch) might respond to the crisis of having to move to the ranch. I can see how this heroine might not have been a character who would be complicated enough for Mother's sense of what she would want to accomplish in a novel. But a Bella or a Miriam would continue to be present as minor characters in Mother's Montana novels.

As a writer she could imagine the feelings these women had, depict them with what seemed to me pitying accuracy. But in the world she inhabited as a nonwriter, they were of little interest to her. She took pains to dismiss them from her vibrant life with her husband and friends. And in the years that followed, she would wonder aloud at her children's association with and affection for men and women who struck her as being "of that sort," of less value in her eyes than those she felt to be vital and accomplished. Such remarks of hers would cause wild resentment in me, but also leave me defenseless. This reaction on my part was beside the point to her; she made clear all through her life that she made such a statement "for your own good." No wonder my reading of her novels, not until my thirties and forties, brought me up short: Which perception of human beings was hers? Why could she empathize with them on the page and not in her own life?

I admit that my resentments were my own problem. I still relive a rainy afternoon in the car with Mother on Great Falls's Central Avenue. I must have been about thirteen. As she stopped for a traffic light at the intersection, a tall young woman in a long bright red raincoat wearing high black heels crossed in front of us. I exclaimed at the wonderful air of the woman, the raincoat sweeping out behind her and the rain glittering off her black heels. As the light changed and Mother started up the car, she said in a dismissive tone of voice, "I don't think that. I think the red makes her look quite common." Of course, I have remembered the scene all these years, even the smell of the rain, because I was so shocked, and chagrined, at what seemed to me Mother's dismissal of this woman for the clothes she wore. It didn't occur to me that I was really resenting her disapproval of my delight. I raged silently that Mother was unfair. And yet I would realize years later, reading her novels, that she used an observation like this to evoke the personality of a minor character.

In *Winter Wheat,* the protagonist is a young woman, Ellen Webb, who looks forward to college, to a world encompassing more than the wheat ranch of her childhood. Mother surely understood this yearning from her own eagerness to be off to college, away from the Philadelphia parsonage of her own childhood. And yet Ellen would find herself sustained by the country when she returned. Mother's notes for the novel suggest she valued the drama of her heroine's life, increasingly, as she wrote of the effect of the country on Ellen.

In the Wyoming archives I found a typescript of a statement that explained how she came to write *Winter Wheat*. It had to do with the country first, then its people:

> *In an old notebook I came across a few scribbled notes I made back in 1933, the first year I lived in Montana. I realize now that they were the beginning of this novel that I didn't write until 1943.*
>
> *A ranch laid out on the flat prairie, a cluster of unpainted buildings without a tree or bush, so ugly it takes willpower to make yourself look at it. A woman and two children, clothed in drab-colored garments, are guarding a fire of tumble-weed along the edge of the road. The fire leaps out of the dull background free, vivid, beautiful. . . .*
>
> *A man rides his tractor along the edge of his field while, on this side of the fence, walks his woman, come to fetch him since it is too dark to work any longer. Both figures are bent, dumpy, wedded to the brown furrows, but escaping drabness because they are together. . . .*
>
> *These tiny wildflowers growing heedlessly out of the dry dirt of the flats are pure color: blue, such a bright yellow, red. They grow so low you might miss them easily. You feel them more than you see them. . . .*
>
> *A grain elevator standing up like an obelisk, functional but not beautiful, yet fitting, after a while, into the land; dominating the country around as cathedrals the old world towns and as white, spired churches the New England villages. . . .*
>
> *I saw a teacherage today, a one-room school house, three miles from any other dwelling. There is a second room behind the schoolroom where the teacher lives. The teacher is usually a girl fresh out of normal school, eighteen or*

twenty years of age. From the time the school closes in the middle of the afternoon until the children come the next day, she lives there alone. How does she stand the loneliness, fall and winter and spring? What does it do to her?

Each of these observations comes alive in *Winter Wheat* ten years later. Her main characters feel a closeness to the kind of country that they, by turns, rail against and cling to. When Mother received word that *Winter Wheat* was a Literary Guild selection, she supplied an author's sketch requested for publication in the Literary Guild magazine, *Wings* (February 1944, 4–9) and called it "How Winter Wheat Grew." Mother uses the above descriptions of her first reactions to the country and adds two anecdotes about its people:

> *A girl from a ranch came to see me about work one day, a healthy, hearty looking girl of twenty with a strong smell of perfume and bright lips and earrings and a green bag that matched her scarf. She looked like the sort of girl who would be crazy to live in town.*
>
> *"I could work till April. I'd want all April off," she told me.*
>
> *"Why April? What do you do in April?" I asked.*
>
> *"There'll be lambing and planting and things green up. I wouldn't want to be away from the ranch in the spring," she said firmly.*
>
> *A girl worked for me who learned so quickly and did things so effortlessly that it was a joy to have her. She told me about her family who lived in two rooms on a dryland farm up near the Canadian line. They had had such a succession of bad years she had had to stop school and go to work. But after three months she told me she was going back home. "I can't stand being cooped up in town any longer."* (Wings, 6–7)

When Mother has described a few more of her observations of how people in Montana lived on the land, she observes of herself:

"I had looked on the bare ranch dwellings we could see from the highway and thought how terrible it would be to live there. Maybe I was wrong. The people who lived there liked it. Why did they?" Her explanation is that "people were different out here, at least some of them."

The article "How Winter Wheat Grew" lets me see the use Mother made of these observations as a novelist. I had only heard her repeat these conversations to regale dinner guests when I was a girl, waiting table. Mother's spirited telling of the incidents was received with laughter; everyone seemed to appreciate the oddity of the commitment of these young women. To my hypersensitive thirteen-year-old ears, Mother's retelling seemed to belittle their lives. I remember my resentment back then, not because I lived as these young women did but because I was growing up with their same commitment to the country.

Ellen Webb is a complicated heroine, wanting to understand her parents' relationship to each other and to understand her own relationship to the country that holds for her, at different times, both despair and hope. Every opportunity in her life so far has depended on the health of her family's wheat crop from year to year. And the harder she works for its success, the more hope she feels for her dreams.

As a novelist, Mother explores this yearning: The more clearly she depicts the details of ranch work, the closer she comes to explaining why "the people who lived here liked it." Of Ellen, she writes a note to herself in the notebook: "May even need to begin with childhood to show how much country means to her." Of herself, a few pages later, she writes: "I have to say that the sky is endless out here, nothing can contain it, not even the eye or mind of man; that the sun is bright, too bright for despair, the smell of sage is clean & health giving & the lesson of the mountains is the lesson of aloneness." With this response to Montana as a place in which to live one's life, Mother seems to understand in herself a loyalty that one born to the country might have. Her statement seems, too, an acknowledgment of the beauty she finds in this kind of country. In a lecture given to an audience in Helena forty years later, Mother explains her interest in the characters in *Winter*

Wheat: "I thought I'd like to tell you about the four novels I've written that take place in Montana. Not that I set out to write about Montana, but that the characters I was moved to write about happened to live in Montana and were shaped by their environment."

Directly following her personal observation above in her notebook for *Winter Wheat,* she writes:

> *I have a story to tell of two people of vastly different natures & backgrounds thrown together by the last war [First World War] but in a union made of distrust, hate, bitterness & sickness; of the child of that union who can find no faith or trust in herself until she finds the abiding under-current of faith and love between her mother & father, neither acknowledged nor recognized by them, that has grown steadily with the years. This is the seed. In the beginning the girl has only superb strength to give, which alienates the man she loves; later she has a faith to give.*

In none of the rest of her notebooks for each novel does she set forth such a comprehensive statement of a story line. Her underlying metaphor of the seed is also in place.

The notebook has numerous entries on the makeup of Central Montana's population in the wheat country in the early 1940s—largely, groups of people who have come from Central Europe and Russia. She heads one entry "Russian Information." Two detailed handwritten pages follow about an American Expeditionary Force of men from northern states like Vermont and Montana, recruited to fight in Russia in 1918. (Forty years after Mother came by this information, my son, interviewing old-timers for an oral history of their lives as Montanans, heard the same story from several of them.) They were recruited because theirs was a homeland similar to that of Russia and because they were presumed to be hardy and to be familiar with rugged country. Mother quotes an unnamed source: "They fought for a cause never fully determined to their satisfaction. The Force was called the 'Polar Bear.'"

In *Winter Wheat* Ben Webb, Ellen's father, describes being recruited from Vermont for that force, engaged in fighting in Russia, and receiving his painful shrapnel wounds there. The nurse who cared for him in the hospital in Russia is young Anna Petrovna, whom he marries and brings to Montana after the war. At the end of this particular entry, Mother observes: "Might turn out to be the story of Anna and Ben—of a love that hardly knows itself." But ensuing entries, some that become passages in the novel, make clear that the story will become their daughter's.

The next notebook section is labeled "Home Life in Russia." One entry reads: "Somehow—Anna has memories of visit to Little Russia. Vast steppes, houses on klati: built of earth, thatched with fresh straw . . . Anna's background." In the novel, Ellen shares Russian words of endearment with Anna and always with a feeling of warmth or pleasure:

> *Mom's hair was still down her back in two thick black braids. She looked younger than she was. I could almost see how she must have been as Anna Petrovna.*
>
> *"You're pretty, Mamushka," I said lazily, calling her by the name she had taught me when I was a child.*
>
> *Mom made a little face and brushed my compliment away with her hand.*
>
> *"Don't talk such nonsense, Yolochka." I had that queer feeling I have, sometimes, with Mom that we were both talking Russian even though we had said only two Russian words.*

An entry early in the notebook, one which does not appear in the novel, imagines a night in Russia when Ben makes love to Anna:

> *He had known he would love her the night he walked across from the hospital. She had known, too, not this night, maybe, but soon. They had lain against a haycock, a miserable remnant of one, in the warm dark but he was not unique in this. She had expected it. If she had not wanted to—he excused himself. But still he was from Plainville, Vermont. A man who had intercourse with a girl out of marriage was wrong. He must marry her. Because he, Wayne Webb, had come way out here in the army he was no different.*

From day to day in the novel, Anna's stamina for doing heavy work because it must be done characterizes her as Russian for her daughter—as coming from a people thought to be good at endurance. Mother's notes also quote writers on the characteristics of the Russian people that have made them take to life in Montana.

Ben's roots are New England, a source of friction because the mother feels the father sometimes longs for that more silent and bookish life. Knowledge of a New Englander's nature needs no note taking for Mother and is used to magnify what the daughter perceives to be a source of distrust on her mother's part. When Ellen is angry with her mother, she thinks how much more like her father than her mother she is: "She was Russian; I was not." Toward the end of the novel's first part, her mother tells Ellen that the wheat crop has not brought in enough money to send Ellen back to college and that there is an opening at Prairie Butte School for the coming year. Ellen is angry: "Mom went on sitting on the top step of the porch. I was so angry for an instant I think I hated her. I thought of her scheming to make Dad marry her. Now she was scheming to have me stay here and earn my own living. What could she know about an education?" (145). Earlier, Ellen has overheard Anna angrily tell Ben that she had told him she was pregnant so that he wouldn't leave her back in Russia. Ellen thinks it so scheming of her mother that she does not hear her mother say, "Because I love you so much."

Early in the notebook the names for the mother and father are Marieto and Wayne Webb, but they change to Anna and Ben Webb. The daughter's name of Margaret changes to Ellen much later in the notebook. It may be that Margaret became Ellen when Mother decided to dedicate the novel to her sister Margaret or when Mother discovered the Russian equivalent of Yelena for Ellen.

Late in the notebook, Mother changes her protagonist's point of view from third to first person without giving a reason for the change. "Have Ellen speak in her own voice" carries a note of excitement that is followed by more entries now in the first person. Because this is the only one of her thirteen novels with a protagonist whose story is told in the first person, I imagine Mother becoming the character in a personal way. Mother's own girlhood must have provided her with a sense of how Ellen could be drawn back and forth between her mother and father, too. Her empathy for her characters in this novel is acute and perhaps sharpened all the more by her own experience. She too loved her parents but always spoke of them as very different from each other and as having a life that she grew up not wanting to be hers.

In her notebook Mother paraphrases, unattributed, a statement describing the seed as a spiritual metaphor: "Kinship between seed which is good news of kingdom of God & soil which is soul of man." This entry is followed by the reading she took notes on for the metaphor of the seed that becomes wheat. From the English translation of Antoine de Saint-Exupéry's *Flight to Arras,* she quotes numerous passages. The epigraph for the novel is Exupéry's statement, "There is but one victory that I know is sure, and that is the victory that is lodged in the energy of the seed." The epigraphs for *Winter Wheat* are also quotations from Saint-Exupéry:

> *Part 1: "I shall not fret about the loam if somewhere in it a seed lies buried." (2)*

> *Part 2: "The seed haunted by the sun never fails to find its way between the stones in the ground." (143)*

> *Part 3: "Sow the seed in the wide black earth and already the seed is victorious, though time must contribute to the triumph of the wheat." (257)*

In his introduction to the Nebraska reprint of *Winter Wheat,* James Welch cautions the reader: "Don't overlook the brilliant metaphor of winter wheat." The quotations from Saint-Exupéry prepare the reader for the depth of the metaphor in the story of the Webbs.

Ellen Webb explains the importance of the metaphor to her own life in the first chapter of the novel. A type of wheat just found successful in Montana was called winter wheat because it could be planted in fall for early germination, die back in the winter cold, but germinate again with a double yield in the spring. Reading the notices on the wall of the grain elevator while she waits for her father, she says: "There was an advertisement of Karmont wheat that Dad says was developed especially for me because it has Russian and American parents, too—from Karkov and Montana. He calls me Karmont, sometimes, to tease me" (2). But later, when she has overheard what she calls the "scheming" of her mother, Ellen thinks of herself bitterly as the seed of parents wholly unlike each other, parents filled with distrust of each other. When she has learned more about love, herself, and her parents' enduring relationship, she can accept the metaphor on a deeper level.

The novel spoke to unexpected readers, perhaps, soon after it was published. *Winter Wheat* was one of the first American novels to be printed in a paperback edition for distribution overseas to the armed forces. Mother received grateful letters from soldiers stationed in Europe and thirty years later sent the letters to the American Heritage Center at the University of Wyoming. Two of the letters express thanks because the novel brought them home to Montana. The first was sent by Sergeant Edward Urbanich on December 20, 1944, from "Somewhere in Belgium":

> *I wonder if, when you wrote* Winter Wheat, *you realized that it would be read by one of America's soldiers in far-off Belgium? I picked the book out of the [Special Services] collection mainly because of the title; I almost knew those two words meant home. They did, too, for I call Montana—Great Falls, to be exact—my home. Although I am not too familiar with wheat farming, I have associated with enough folks at home to know that you have captured all that there is in what might be termed Montana's greatest contribution to the world. I have felt the life at home even more vividly than memories can bring it, just by reading your magnificent novel. . . . I can appreciate your comparison of the wheat and life—it was very good. Somehow, I had never stopped to think about it. . . . I like the thought so much that I know I shall think of it many times in the future.*

Urbanich adds that he has already passed his copy of the book on "to another soldier reader." A second letter came from George Smuik, also stationed in Belgium, dated January 9, 1945:

I'm writing a few lines to let you know how much I en-
joyed your most recent novel, Winter Wheat. *It so well*
expresses the average life in Montana, the trials and woes
of a dryland rancher. Each page was like a day of my
youth before me. They recalled the days spent at our ranch
near Neihart. I liked best the description of the land. The
detail brought out so clear the feeling one gets when
standing on a high hill, and can feel the earth and sky. It
fills you with an awe that is rather hard to express. You
achieved that in your book. One part that amused me was
"The Farmer's Noon Hour." I can remember it so well.
The same voice, the same thing every day.

Smuik adds that he hopes to read more of Mother's novels, and he ends his letter, "Thank you for the furlough home."

In a letter from occupied Japan dated December 6, 1948, Wasuke Soramoto identifies herself as a teacher "of the normal school at Mihara near Hiroshima and my teaching subjects are principles and methods of education. We have 358 girl students who are all going to become teachers of primary schools in towns and country." She states that Japanese education is making rapid progress toward democracy under the very kind guidance of the experts from America and explains how she received a copy of the novel:

The other day an U.S. soldier came to our school to give us
some advices on our education and then he gave me the
Winter Wheat *of armed forces edition. I am very much*
interested with the story of Ellen Webb in Prairie Butte
School. It is one of the best novels which I have ever read.
I am sure it would be very interesting and suggestive to
my students and young teachers in service. So I should
like to quote some parts of the novel into my book which I
am wanting to write on new educational ideas for them
to read. Please permit me to make some quotations from
your novel. I should like to know much more about Ameri-
can democratic way of life. If you have written some other

novels of this kind, please be generous enough to send me
some copies and help me in my work for the understand-
ing and realization of true humanity in our country.

Mother must have been touched by these letters. I wish she had felt she could tell my brothers and me about them. But they belonged to her writing self, which was kept separate from the life she shared with us.

Perhaps most telling of all are the statements of two women writers who were raised in Montana and who remember reading *Winter Wheat* when they were young. They both told me separately that the novel made details and people of their own lives fictionally viable for them. When the University of Nebraska Press reprinted Mildred Walker's works, they were pleased to write introductions: Mary Clearman Blew, whose early short stories and essays are rooted in central Montana, wrote the introduction for *The Curlew's Cry*, a later Walker novel with a Montana setting; Deirdre McNamer, whose first two novels are set in north-central Montana, wrote the introduction for *Unless the Wind Turns*. Both of these writers depict in their work the contemporary life of rural and small-town Montana in dryland ranching country.

We children didn't see a copy of *Winter Wheat* when it was published. Mother never let a new novel lie on a coffee table, for instance. But we were aware that in December 1943 the *Ladies' Home Journal* featured the "Novel Condensation Complete in This Issue" of *Winter Wheat*. I recently found a copy of the magazine in Mother's papers and discovered both a photo I'd never seen of her and a brief self sketch on the Contents page. The photo shows her partly in profile against a Montana skyline, sunlit clouds behind her head. She is dressed in jeans and a light tailored shirt with the sleeves rolled up above her elbows. A red bandana is tied at her throat. This is just how I remember her dressed when she sold tickets at a card table on Central Avenue in Great Falls for the Montana state fair. Seeing this photo gives me a chance to contrast my mother the Junior Leaguer with my mother the novelist, her eyes searching the distance.

The self sketch printed beneath the photo is two paragraphs. The first describes in an amused tone her early attempts to become a writer; the second, sounding equally amused and downplaying her success, finishes by describing why she writes:

> *I grew a little more, at least in years, and a long-suffering husband, with an unfailing sense of humor, and three children assisted the process. Somehow, in between the hilarious and strenuous business of living, five novels—* Winter Wheat, *Literary Guild Selection for February, published by Harcourt, Brace & Co., is the sixth—found their stubborn ways between covers. I'd rather write them than struggle with the fall canning, and I like to think they are as important as canning, but on a cold and hungry winter's day I wouldn't want the other members of my family to vote on it. (*Ladies Home Journal, *December 1943, 3)*

Mother's depiction of herself in this way must have delighted her readers. I remember her as being fully aware of having good nourishing food on the table for her family. With each woman who worked for us she held daily morning consultations: what she would like prepared for supper and how it should be prepared. I remember hearing these stipulations delivered with what I thought of as a grand lady-of-the-manor air. But, clearly, this way of conducting her household justified her feeling that she should then be free for the rest of the day to write. And often, as I remember, she had a yearly ritual of canning not tomatoes but brandied peaches—always appreciated "on a cold and hungry winter's day" as we children grew older.

When Mother took over in the kitchen, usually on the Thursday evenings that she spoke of as "the maid's day off," she produced delectable treats. She moved about with an air of pleasure and confidence that made my father mischievous with all of us as he sat in anticipation at the kitchen table. As she told me years later about the dinner parties she put on in her retirement, she loved to make the evening "a real success."

Whenever I reread *Winter Wheat*, I enjoy the moment in the opening chapter when Ellen, in the kitchen, becomes aware of her mother outside calling in the turkeys and her father turning on the grain market news in the next room:

> *I washed some cucumbers while I was waiting. They were bright-green and shiny in the water. I used to play they were alligators when I was a child. Then I fenced them in with my hand and poured off the water into the kettle on the stove. When you have to carry every drop of water you use half a mile, you don't throw away any. (3)*

One day in Grafton in the early 1960s I was visiting Mother with my husband and two children. As I washed cucumbers for our family's salad in the long oblong soapstone sink, she told me about the alligators. "Yes," she said, looking into the distance out the small kitchen window. "I put it in my novel once—*Winter Wheat*." It marked the moment when I first wanted to read her novels. Why? Because the scene in the novel was so vivid. And why else? Because for the first time it seemed to me she spoke as a novelist, not as my mother. She admitted me to her writing world.

In all three parts of *Winter Wheat*, Ellen's voice moves the events of the novel, simultaneously describing the details of working the family dryland ranch and confiding her feelings about that from day to day. Her encounters with people and places not part of the ranching experience, new in her life, she sees in comparison. In part 2, Ellen's voice describes, again in a confiding tone, the details of her teaching in the Prairie Butte country school and her over-whelming feeling of loneliness when the children have left for the day:

> *Time filled the room and lay across the empty prairie and pushed against the window. There was so much of it that it had pressure and weight. But it was empty. Somewhere there were people who didn't have time enough, who forgot time and themselves. I wanted to get away from here, to go home and pack my clothes and go back to the city to college. . . . It seemed the thing I wanted most in the world. (158)*

She leaves her small room to walk in the night, saying to herself, and somehow to her listener, "I would stop at whatever house
I came to. I had been here five weeks and already I craved people, grown people." She comes to a ranch house where she is
invited in by the grandparents with whom one of her students
lives.

By the end of that chapter, Ellen has returned to the teacherage,
to her room. She bathes in the washtub she had brought from
home, and enjoys the moonlight shining through her window,
deciding, "I didn't mind being alone here anymore." Many readers
of this novel have asked me if it is autobiographical, and I have assured them that it isn't, that as a novelist Mother grew into the
situations of her characters intimately. While I believe this about
each of her novels, I have to say that Ellen's responses to her
aloneness at the teacherage are very like those of Mother's that she
has confided to me over the years. She hated living alone, almost
despised that state. After my father had died when she was fifty,
and she lived in situations she found comfortable and appropriate
to her style, and after she retired from teaching to live in Grafton,
Vermont, she would remark bitterly, "Before Ferd died, I had never
in my life had to live alone." And how, she would ask me, had I
been able to do that—as a student in Scotland, as a country school
teacher (ten years after the publication of *Winter Wheat*), as an itin-
erant poetry writing teacher in Montana, living for a week at a time
in a motel room. Perhaps her own dread—when she was not quite
forty and was surrounded by her family—of what it would be like
to live by herself sharpened her empathy for young Ellen Webb,
not quite twenty. And then, her main observations in her notebook for *Winter Wheat* about a teacherage are how lonely living
there must be.

Perhaps Mother's dread of loneliness belonged only to her physical world where she needed to see herself in the eyes of others bustling about her. Surely she was never alone in her writing world,
which teemed with her characters. But moments after she expressed a feeling of anguish, and while I was still anguished for her,
she was finished with that thought. I learned over the years that it
was a canon of Mother's, a matter of spiritual backbone, to over-

come the day's dejection with a healthy outlook before bedtime. Hence the alchemy of a good bath and brilliant moonlight. Ellen Webb was Mildred Walker in this sense.

As to how Mother could render all the details of teaching in a country school so vividly without ever having done so herself, I can only guess. I'm sure she must have had some discussion with people who gave her a glimpse of Ellen's days—the smell of chalk dust, the school desks still alive with the children after they've gone home, the Christmas play that thrills the children and brings the families together. And, as her daughter, I am amazed by Mother's knowing the young teacher's awareness of each child's needs.

In 1952 when my husband went to the Marine Corps and later to Korea, I decided to teach in the Spanish Coulee Rural School, twenty-five miles from my parents' home. The one-roomed school was named for the coulee that ran up behind it—a deep cut in the high bluffs that had been formed by spring rains over many years. (The word *coulee* came originally from the French *couloir,* a descriptive term for a narrow place where water runs. The French was later anglicized to *coulee.*) At the foot of the bluffs Hound Creek curved around the schoolhouse and the small two-roomed house for the teacher behind the school. Two outhouses, or privies, stood off to the side. The whole was a small fenced island of grass that I shared with eight children, ranging in age from six to eleven, and my dog and my horse. I became very fond of it.

Not having read *Winter Wheat* at that time, I had no idea of how much of that country school life Mother knew. Nor did she give me any indication that she knew. Mostly, I was aware that she didn't think much of my decision to teach there and said often that she was sure I must be lonely. "What can you gain from it, dear?" she would ask me. Well, I thought to myself, I could learn from the children how to teach; I could learn what they needed to know. Just returned from studying at the University of Edinburgh for a year after college, I thought I could teach these children about distant places and fascinating subjects. But nothing I tried to explain about my excitement got across to Mother. She said in a disappointed tone, "I hoped you'd come back married to a Scotsman."

So much for my high ideals. Marriage seemed to be her only expectation of me; I was furious and hurt.

My father seemed to have accepted my impulsive schemes early in my life. I felt him to be a conspirator even when he offered me cautionary advice. His advice about the teacherage was that I take plenty of canned macaroni in case the children should be snowed in with me some night. And a big batch of newspapers to wrap up coffee grounds. And he was right about that. It didn't cause him dismay that the school had a hand pump for water and two outhouses, one for the boys and one for the girls. He liked my solution for the skunk living under the floor of my two-room house behind the school: I stomped loudly on the floor before I went out the door so we wouldn't meet each other. My father, if not my mother, felt I was doing something of value.

Fifteen years later, when I first read *Winter Wheat,* I saw that, like Ellen Webb, I too had taught eight children from five families, that I too had formed a strong awareness of each child. Why hadn't Mother talked to me about that coincidence? And I have to admit that I was stung all over again: Why, in Mother's estimation, was it all right for Ellen Webb but not for me to take a teacherage? Why, when she had taken such pains to portray unerringly each detail of an inexperienced teacher's day, was she not interested in that experience for me? Such a complaint was probably the most foolish error in my reading history. But eventually I figured it out: Ellen Webb was a heroine of fiction and a character who portrayed strength and individuality; I was my mother's daughter and had a role to play that fit Mother's idea of what a daughter of hers should be or engage in.

The teacherage experience is over by the end of part 2. In part 3, Ellen Webb, in the world of the family's ranch, understands herself and her parents in almost the same moment—true to Mother's early assessment of the story she had to tell. James Welch's response to the novel in his introduction to the reprint offers a clear summary: "It is a story about growing up, becoming a woman, mentally, emotionally, spiritually, within the space of a year and a half. But what a year and a half it is!" (viii) He goes on to point out, unlike the national reviews full of praise at the time of *Winter*

Wheat's publication, that it is "the character of Ellen Webb that lifts this novel far above the usual narratives of coming of age in a hostile environment":

> *Mildred Walker's success is in creating a keen psychological portrait of her main character. We see through Ellen Webb's eyes. We feel the stalks of wheat through her fingers, the wind through her hair. We hear the howl of the blizzard through her ears. We smell her mother's borscht through her nose. Above all, we are in her mind as she attempts to make sense of her emotions, of her relationship with her parents, of her parents' relationship with each other, of their relationship with the land. (x)*

It was 1992, when Mother was eighty-seven, that I brought the first copy of the University of Nebraska Press reprint of *Winter Wheat* to her. Because her eyesight was failing, I read James Welch's introduction to her. She was very quiet and sat looking out the window for several seconds without speaking. Then she said almost to herself, "He may be the first writer who ever saw what I was trying to do." She dictated a note of thanks to him, phrased very formally but warm with gratitude.

7
At Beaverbank on the Missouri River, 1944–1955

S outh of the town of Great Falls the north-flowing Missouri River is wide, lined often with cottonwoods, where its islands and sloughs support deer, beaver, fox, and migrating ducks and geese. My parents took drives along the river in those early Great Falls years—often, I think, to escape the stodginess of the town. In 1944, Mother's just published *Winter Wheat* became a literary success as well as a regional favorite. On the strength of its monetary success, Mother and Dad decided to move out to the river, ten miles south of town. We children understood the move was to make possible Dad's getting out in the country and to the river without having to drive the eighty miles to the cabin in the mountains. As the war continued, he had had a harder and harder time getting a weekend off. And they had already anticipated the possibilities of living on the bank of the Missouri with great eagerness, we realized, before they broke the news to us.

By November 1944, nine months after *Winter Wheat* was published, we had moved to the river. Mother and Dad bought eleven acres in a beautiful, narrow valley bordered by the Missouri and three islands on the west side, and seventeen more acres of pasture that sloped up into rimrocks across the road on the east side. In some places the river was as wide as the pasture land. Mother and Dad named it "Beaverbank" because there were beaver houses off the bank and on the shores of the three small brush-covered islands. We could see some of the beavers' woven houses from the living room window of our remodeled roadhouse and, at dusk, watch the beavers gnawing down young willow branches to carry back to their houses.

After its first years as a farm, the property had had a very different life. The farmhouse had been bought by a shady character, the story went, who turned it into a roadhouse, furnished as a bordello. The first time we children were taken to see it, floor-length velvet looking maroon curtains hung in the doorways of the downstairs rooms. Mother and Dad walked us through, raising their eyebrows as they went. I have an awed memory of those furnishings before they were removed and the house was renovated according to my parents' plans.

A large outbuilding a short distance from the house became our barn. But it had been known as the Box Elder Park Saloon, and for the first three or four years, Dad would answer loud banging on the front door of the house in the middle of the night. The man, usually already drunk, would demand that Dad open the saloon. Dad would have to stand there in his underwear and explain—several times over. In the daylight, he found it amusing.

Mother must have found the rambling house spacious after the Great Falls bungalow. The long comfortable kitchen had room for a table looking down to the river where we often gathered for late night treats and consultations. A door at the other end of the kitchen opened out on our front field and the rimrock beyond. A small pantry with glass cupboard doors led into a pleasant dining room with French doors opening onto a small front lawn. This room was Mother's pride, done in her favorite color—a warm yellow. A doorway on the opposite side of this room opened to the long living room where two large square windows looked down the grassy slope to the river.

In the far corner of the living room stood a large fireplace, its rectangular stone blocks rising to the ceiling. The stones had been quarried from the rimrock. My father delighted in the story told by our Scots neighbor down the road about the building of it. The neighbor's father had come to Montana from Scotland as a stone mason and was engaged by the roadhouse owner to build the stone fireplace, but he wasn't paid. The fireplace smoked with its first use. When the owner complained to the mason, he was told that the problem could be fixed if pay was forthcoming. Having been paid, the mason climbed to the roof and removed the large stone with which he had blocked the chimney. In this living room Mother and Dad entertained many friends and out-of-town guests; I was old enough to realize that Mother enjoyed the graciousness with which she could entertain in this room.

At the far end of the living room, a door opened out to a long, wide screened-in porch. We could look down into the river and into the tall cottonwoods growing up from the bank at the west end of the porch and across the small pasture and up to the rim-rock from the east end. It was a get-away place for my brothers and me—as the Grafton barn loft must have been for Mother—except for the coldest days of winter. On summer evenings we could sometimes find Mother and Dad out there on the porch talking and watching the river. In my homesick spells back east in college, I would imagine myself there on the long porch.

The living room also opened to a narrow hallway leading to the front door. On one side was a tiny powder room leading into a small bathroom. The powder room was one of Mother's remodeling triumphs. We used to tease her about it. Farther down the hall was the door to my father's study, a room we children were invited into by turns for formal discussions and a room where we heard Mother and Dad talking heatedly behind the closed door. I remember being shown how to balance my checkbook in Dad's study; he had a way of cajoling us into being responsible.

On the other side of the hallway, a staircase led to the upstairs. It had a sturdy newel post and spindles. I can still remember Mother pronouncing "spindles" with that tone she used for what was appropriate. It was handsome, but we liked to grimace at each other through the spindles when one of us was beating the other up the stairs. Once, when I had swum my horse across the river and hoped to hurry up the stairs undetected, my father reached through the spindles to grab hold of my sopping wet jeans.

At the top of the stairs, a small landing led to more stairs to the left to my brothers' rooms, my room, and a bathroom, and more stairs to the right to my parents' large room. Their room was big enough to include a Franklin stove, large closets, and a corner for Mother's desk from which she could see out to the river. I was enlisted to bring them coffee in bed in the mornings and would find them vulnerable but cocky. Mother's continual complaint was that the coffee had become cold. While I felt remorseful, if unfairly accused, they would allow me to huddle in front of the small fire in the Franklin stove on winter mornings.

My parents always remembered an early autumn morning when my brother George and I came into their room and held a pair of dripping ducks over their heads, gleeful with our luck at hunting with a riverwise neighbor. Mother would use that startling sensation in her twelfth novel, *If a Lion Could Talk,* twenty-five years later.

Soon after we moved to Beaverbank, a woman named Lottie became part of our household. She lived in a comfortable apartment Dad had built above the garage as part of the remodeling. Lottie was a colorful woman probably close to sixty years old, who had been a roundup cook—following the men who were rounding up cattle on still unfenced ranges and cooking for them out of a chuckwagon—and had also cooked for outfitters on hunting trips in the mountains. Since her husband had died in an accident on one of those mountain trips, she had made her home in the small town of Cascade farther south on the Missouri River. Her gravelly voice could be helpful and ironic in the same sentence to George and me as she taunted us about how we did chores around the place. George milked and cared for the two red roan shorthorn cows that Dad was proud of having, and Lottie would pointedly inspect the level of milk in the pails when George brought them up to the house. In the same manner, she taught me how to work the garden and care for the chickens. I began to understand that, as the half-grown children of parents who hired experienced adults, we were in a tricky spot. Even young Christopher came in for tirades.

Lottie's usual exasperated address to my mother was, "Dammit, Woman, I've got to have a vegetable garden!" Or looking out the kitchen window down to the barn, she'd announce a crisis by exclaiming, "By Christ, if that cow isn't lame!" I was fascinated by her cooking and her fuming in low mutters when I helped her in the kitchen. Each morning Mother would ask Lottie to prepare a dish like chicken in a certain way. Most times Lottie erupted defensively: "Dammit, Woman, I've been cooking chicken all my life. Don't you think I know how to do it by now?" "Of course, Lottie, but I like a little variety." Standing in her cotton dress, summer and winter, with a long apron, one strap off her shoulder, a lighted cigarette dangling from the corner of her mouth, and her hands balled into fists on her hips, Lottie would reply, "Hmph!" Other times, the tone of her answer, "Yes, Ma'am!" seemed a little more menacing to me.

I have wanted to describe Lottie so thoroughly because I was shocked when I first read *The Curlew's Cry* by finding Lottie there as a minor character without any fictional transformation—complete with the dangling cigarette. *The Curlew's Cry* was published a few months before Mother moved from Montana, but Lottie obtained a copy. Years later, Mother told me that she had heard from someone that Lottie didn't like herself being depicted as a fool. Mother said only, "I didn't think I'd done that."

By our first spring on the river Dad's plans for Beaverbank were being carried out. A horse corral was built onto the back of the existing barn by an old friend of Lottie's who came down from Cascade, Emil Swedebloom. Emil, too, was colorful, even comical, with a crooked grin and Swedish accent. But he liked to tease George in a bullying way that I don't think my parents knew—about how George was a sorry kind of bookish kid. Emil and Lottie both let their friends know that we were all three "Dr. Schemm's spoiled rotten kids." Emil, too, would appear in *The Curlew's Cry*, slightly transformed.

When the fencing was finished, we were able to bring our riding horses down from the mountains. Mother and Dad delighted in riding as much as we did. Mother rode her mare, Jolly Folly, with a spirited air, her head thrown back and her hand flicking the ends of her reins. Dad rode black Danny in an erect stance with his hat tilted forward almost to his eyebrows. Their favorite ride was along the river bank below the house, beneath the towering cottonwood trees, and then across a narrow channel to the long island where they could ride through a long deer meadow to the main channel.

Dad had leased three islands that came with our place, and because they were stair stepped in size and pointed straight down river, he named them the Niña, the Pinta, and the Santa Maria. We could pasture the milk cows as well as the horses on the largest island. We discovered one late afternoon that the bigger shorthorn milker had borne twins on the island. The weather was turning cold, so Dad wrestled the flatbed, really an old army reconnaissance truck, down to the crossing to the island, while George and I forded the channel. When we had led the cow down to the water, we let her go and each of us carried a calf across, George the heavier bull calf and I the heifer. Dad was at the edge to meet us and helped us lift them onto the truck. He slowly drove back to the barn while George and I held the calves on the flatbed, the cow following and bawling all the way. Afterward, as the first snow of the year began, we celebrated with Mother and young Christopher in the warm kitchen, all of us almost speechless with the wonder of the twins. We made a unanimous decision—maybe it was Dad's suggestion—to name them Ferdinand and Isabella. Among Mother's saved letters is an affectionate one from Dad in which he refers to Mother as "Isabella" and signs himself "Ferdinand." Perhaps it was a shared story between them that prompted the use of these names, but of course he was a Ferdinand, and we had the three islands named for Columbus's ships.

But that must have been three years after our first year at Beaverbank. As the years went by, we had new baby chicks to raise each summer, a sow who birthed thirteen piglets one spring night as we watched in amazement, a foal born when the Missouri was flooding so we could see the reflection of the water in her eyes, and 4-H calves that did well at the county fair. We cut the alfalfa hay in our front pasture with our neighbor Tom Rada and stacked it by the barn. In turn for his loan of haying equipment, George and I worked with Mr. Rada in his fields and helped stack his hay. I can still remember my relief when Christopher was old enough to take my place, stomping down the loose hay in the wagon. Forking the hay up to the wagon as George did was preferable to having its chaff settle down my collar in the heat. But Christopher was reasonably cheerful about it, and afterward we three could head for the riverbank, plunge into the cold water, and watch the hay prickles float away from us.

Dad made all these things happen beginning when we were fifteen, thirteen, and seven years old. We loved the commotion and surprises of the place, as well as Dad's pleasure and connivance in it and Mother's cheering at each event. We were proud that we raised a lot of our own food, hay, and grain, sold our eggs in town, raised some good saddle horses to sell, and became conversant with the ways of the river and the wildlife we shared it with.

Early in our first year at Beaverbank, Dad's two brothers back in Michigan, who remembered Dad's love of canoeing, sent my parents an Old Town canoe, complete with a sail and sideboards. Dad taught us to use the canoe safely in spite of the warnings from his friends of the dangers of the Missouri and its undercurrents. To qualify to go out in the canoe by ourselves, we had to be able to paddle out in midchannel, overturn the canoe, and right it again, then climb back in. The adventures that followed our qualifications were numerous, sometimes incredible, like the day two young piglets got out of their pen and took to the river. George and I went after them, but it became an ordeal. When I finally grabbed one by its tail, its head went under water as George paddled furiously. Desperately, he shouted, "Let go!" So then the chase continued from one shore to the other. Finally, he set me to paddling furiously to keep up with the pigs while he managed to get them into the canoe and had to wrestle with them while I slowly made our way back against the current.

I knew with a sense of underlying happiness how Mother delighted in the living at Beaverbank. These were the early years when George and I grappled with our own crises as high school students and, though I don't remember Mother expressing much interest in those matters, I do remember her proscriptions for what I should wear and who my friends should be. She kept an almost wary eye on our schoolwork; her interest was not so much in what we were working on but what the grade results were. I knew that I disappointed her because she thought I was not ambitious enough. This made me sometimes contrite, more often rebellious. At Swarthmore College I was barely a B student. That I was enthusiastic about my studies, immersed in them, was less important to her, I think, than her feeling that I could have tried harder. But looking back I can see that how we fared was a steady concern in her life.

In these next ten years on the river, Mother wrote and published four more novels. After the two novels with Montana settings, she turned for the first time to a novel set in Vermont, *The Quarry*. Had her characterizing the New England traits of Ben Webb in *Winter Wheat* prepared her to turn to her own first landscape for the first time? The answer to this question may be yes in one respect: Ben Webb had come from a village called Plainville, Vermont; Lyman Converse of *The Quarry* would live all his life in the Vermont village of Painesville. This new novel was historical because that was the period that interested her most in her own Vermont village of Grafton. In the summer of probably 1945, she made a trip to Grafton to explore further the earlier find she had made of the late nineteenth-century letters exchanged between the two cousins connected by the local quarry. And her writing notebooks show the extensive research on the history of Vermont and the operation of the quarry that she carried out at that time.

One of Mother's small notebooks for *The Quarry* remained with her personal papers. Half of it is written in pencil, half in ink, in small cursive handwriting. It contains research notes on college life at Brown University in Providence, Rhode Island, words to some of the student songs, and a description of the general disorder of the streets. One of her notes reads, "Late student would rush to chapel in slippers and dressing gown." At the opposite end of the notebook, coming forward, are entries that describe the freight routes to Helena, Montana, historical events of the 1880s out west, and the liveliness of Keno Bill's Saloon: "Every kind of gambling in full sway. Beer, straight whiskey, cigars 25 cents each." All of these notes made their way into scenes in *The Quarry*.

But this notebook, unlike those for any other of her novels, lists the chapters for "Part IV," each with a brief sketch of the events that take place. The chapters move from 1873, 1880, 1890, 1905, and 1910, to end with 1917. The events of the last three chapters are rearranged in the finished novel, and the final chapter occurs in 1914 instead of 1917. Mother must have suddenly seen the last hundred pages of the novel clearly. I say all this here about the writing of *The Quarry* because I see how absorbed she must have been those days in spite of being surrounded by our lives in Montana. Her inner world was moving up and down the main street of a small Vermont village.

We children had no thoughts about what Mother might be working on for her next novel. As I wrote earlier, that was her private world, a world she shared only with my father. We knew that an increasing number of eastern visitors to our house had to do with both Dad's and Mother's work. And most of our visiting relatives were from back east, too. Sometimes we were enlisted to take them horseback riding or canoeing on the river; sometimes up to the cabin. But mostly George and I, at least, were enmeshed in our own pursuits. We understood, though, that Mother and Dad made visitors warmly welcome.

Increasingly, Dad went to large cities for medical meetings, and Mother's letters sent to him at these times reveal both her deep affection for him and her eagerness to have events at meetings go well for him. The opening of a letter postmarked June 1946 and addressed to the Mark Hopkins Hotel, reads:

> *My very dearest dear,*
> *I've just talked to you and feel not deflated or flat the way you usually do after a call but high, singingly high! Oh Ferd no voice in the world is like yours. I hope you really are rested and taking time to breathe in a completely different new atmosphere.*

The rest of the letter speaks of her reading up on places to see in San Francisco where she will meet him for a week: "It is so extravagant to go to see you for a week but I can't *not* do it and three weeks is too long to be away from you unnecessarily. Won't it be *fun!* I'm just plain leaving—they'll all manage somehow." Dad saved this letter in its envelope. On the back of the envelope are penciled chemical equivalents. Those I can read clearly have to do with his concentration on critical elements excreted in the urine in his treatment of edema: "36 grams Cl in urine," "Cl 36 grm=1000 ME, Na 23 grm= 1000 ME." It lets me see him at his meeting. It must have done the same for Mother when she reread in the years following his death all the letters he had saved.

This break from routine at home may have given Mother a change of pace for her writing. Her later journals, kept apart from her writing notebooks, indicate that she took her current writing with her on all her trips. When she had gathered the material she needed in her notebooks, she wrote in longhand on yellow pads until she was ready to type a manuscript. She may have been thinking through last changes to *The Quarry* on her trip to San Francisco. It was published on February 6, 1947, exactly three years after *Winter Wheat*.

In the spring of 1947, I graduated from Great Falls High School and was accepted in college. George had one more year in a private high school in Minnesota, and Christopher was ten years old, the last child at home. By summer I was eager to be going to college, partly because George had already been away from home for a year. I must have been completely self-absorbed by my preparations, certainly unaware that Mother would have been working on her eighth novel, *Medical Meeting*, by then.

This novel, as I've mentioned before, was the last to be set in the Midwest. The subject was a husband and wife whose marriage survives the discouragement of a difficult medical meeting, and the writing of it became difficult for Mother, according to her letters. The letter I quote from, addressed to the St. Francis Hotel and postmarked November 7, 1947, was written to Dad, who was again at a medical meeting in San Francisco. After expressing relief that he had arrived safely, she continues:

> *Dear, I'm sorry I was so bitchy last night. Forgive me again. It's so childish of me and I seem to know it as I do it. Hated your going, hated your feeling bum; was worried about you and that's the odd way I showed it. I even regretted on the ride back under the cold stars from the airport that we hadn't loved with all that time. And when I got to bed I didn't go to sleep the way I usually do for fretting. Oh Ferd, please know how I love you, and don't think things about me or worry about me and the little hells I make for myself over trying to write. Please don't even remember, tho I spose you might as well for that's me. To show you how I love you, I'll work hard and steadily and quietly this week, every day you're gone, beloved, putting down the little words whether they add up to any-*

thing or not, without panic or frustration, or envy or self-pity—that hateful word you hurl at me in hard moments. And then you can feel comfortable about me. You may ask me when you come back and I will tell you de trut.

She then admonishes Dad to see "if you can work out a way of living that will encompass the research and papers without killing you." She adds, "But anyway, living, no matter how it is, *with you* is the only kind of living." After a few more remarks in a kind of defensive apology, she signs the letter, "Yours, Rib," and adds, "Please don't keep this letter, it's too 'open.'"

George and I were both away from home in the fall of 1947, and Christopher remembers it as a lonely time for him. When he came home from school, he told me, he would sit at the head of the stairs by the set of encyclopedia—just outside the door to my parents' bedroom where Mother wrote at her desk. He would wait, he says, until she left her desk and came out to see him. He dreaded her questions about his schoolwork because she felt he should be better at it. It was what George and I had felt when we were that age— that we must succeed in whatever we did as a matter of moral fiber.

Still enclosed in that letter of apology from Mother is a note to Dad from Christopher, written laboriously in cursive. He hopes Dad is having fun and that everything "goes ok." He signs it with his trademark of those days, a drawing of a pistol above two crossed swords, and seals the small page with copper-colored sealing wax. I think George and I never thought about how Christopher must have felt those years when we were both away.

But he has told me recently that he used to wonder why Mother often seemed so remote, working away at her desk. He remembers that one day he ventured in the doorway to where she was writing and saw wide open doors to her closet. On the top shelf he could see a long row of books in their bright jackets, many of them with foreign titles. When he approached her, he asked what they were and she replied over her shoulder, "Those are novels I have written and, someday, you children may want to read them," and returned to her writing.

If I had read *Medical Meeting* when it was first published in October 1949, I think that I would have been startled by how closely it adhered to the way Dad's research had gone. I was aware that Mother would be deeply disappointed a few years later that Dad did not receive the major credit for his findings; in the medical world, he shared credit with a physician teaching and doing his research at the Barnes Medical School in St. Louis. There is mention of medicine's current discoveries in the 1940s in Mother's writing notebook for *Medical Meeting,* and I'm assuming that Dad steered Mother through those passages in the book describing the treatment. Following the publication of *Medical Meeting,* Dad's card sent with flowers, "Rib: Best wishes for a speedy recovery from the birth pangs of #8," suggests that the writing of the novel was an ordeal for her.

In the summer of 1949, Mother was described in the *Great Falls Tribune* as giving a lecture on writing at the Montana writers' conference held in Missoula. It was a short course in writing arranged and moderated by Joe Howard. Mother also appeared with six other regional writers on a panel. One of the writers was A. B. Guthrie Jr., who had published *The Big Sky* in 1947. During the conference his recently published *The Way West* was chosen by the Book-of-the-Month Club and, a few months later in 1950, he was awarded a Pulitzer Prize for distinguished fiction.

I don't know if Mother compared Guthrie's success after two novels to what she thought of as her own lack of recognition after the publication of her eighth novel. It wasn't a subject she would have discussed with her children. But I can imagine that she did with Dad. Years later when Mother talked with me about her novels, I found that she was sharply impatient if I said that hers was a different kind of novel than another writer's. I can guess that Dad may have tried, without effect, to make that point to Mother about Guthrie's success.

But both Mother and Dad had read *The Big Sky* and shared in Joe Howard's enthusiastic pleasure in Guthrie's good fortune. And it is clear that Guthrie acknowledged Mother as a novelist. In Guthrie's autobiography, *The Blue Hen's Chick,* published in 1965, he mentions both Mother and Dad as having been among a welcoming party in 1950 for him and Bernard De Voto, the author of *Across the*

Wide Missouri. Guthrie and De Voto had been flown by the Corps of Engineers over the route of the Oregon Trail and returned to Great Falls. Guthrie writes:

> *We had quite a welcome that night. In addition to Joe [Howard], whom we liked and respected, the party included Norman Fox, a good writer of good westerns, who was even a better man than he was a writer; Mildred Walker, the novelist, and her husband, Dr. Ferd Schemm, both of whom had wide and duly earned reputations; old friends of one or more of us all, including George Jackson, my boyhood companion, who locked up his barbershop and drove from Choteau down to Great Falls. (208)*

When we children were still at home in the summers, Guthrie would occasionally come to the house with Joe of an evening. In later years, my brothers and I and our children came to know Bud Guthrie and his wife, Carol; they built a house outside the Teton Canyon where we got together whenever we were at the cabin. I was visiting at the Guthries with my two children one afternoon in the summer of 1971 about ten months after Mother's twelfth novel, *If a Lion Could Talk,* had been published. That novel, set in Montana, concerned the relationship of a missionary and his wife in the 1850s, residing briefly at a frontier fort. Guthrie referred to a description of their lovemaking in the fort under a buffalo robe, and pronounced emphatically, "I was glad to see that Mildred finally allowed herself the obligatory scene—the first time in all of her novels." He was saying that she had never dealt with a sex scene that graphically before, I guessed. It amused me and told me something about his estimation of Mother as "the novelist."

Deirdre McNamer, in her introduction to the University of Nebraska Press reprint of *Unless the Wind Turns,* reflects, "By rights, Walker's four Montana books should have established her as a major voice of the region." McNamer's following comment concerns the lack of literary recognition of Mother's work as compared with Guthrie's in *A Literary History of the American West:*

> *How strange, then, that . . . the standard reference to the region's writers doesn't so much as mention her in its thir-*

teen hundred-plus pages. Dale Evans and Elizabeth (Mrs. George Armstrong) Custer get index listings, but not Mildred Walker. . . . Perhaps the clue lies in something that happened two years after Winter Wheat *was published. A. B. Guthrie's* The Big Sky, *published in 1947, gave American readers another, earlier version of Montana: the Montana of the 1830s. . . . The fact that he set his drama a century earlier [than Mother's first two Montana novels], and that one of its driving themes is the contamination of the wilderness by the hand of man, makes it, Ipso Facto, a romance of a sort.* The Way West, *a sequel to* The Big Sky, *won Guthrie the Pulitzer Prize in 1950. In the 1940s and far beyond—arguably to this day—the version of Montana that entranced most readers was not Mildred Walker's vision of modern Americans working out their relationships with others and with a place. It was Guthrie's vision of an Edenic Montana, always long gone. (xxi)*

The presence of my parents' writing friends in our home (Dad was always included because these were not primarily literary gatherings) seemed to be impromptu. With the exception of Joe Howard, I don't remember them gathered at the dinner table. Instead, they would arrive late in the evening and settle in the living room by the fire or out on the long porch in summer. Perhaps Guthrie would be in town (in those days he still lived in Kentucky), ring up Joe, and Joe would ring our house to see if my parents were in the mood for a visit. Usually, the conversation was made up of stories about encounters with publishers or about some writer's new book, and always about some hilarious domestic crisis. From upstairs we children could hear laughter, rising voices, and the clink of ice in glasses. As we grew older and were interested in the stories, we were often present for a while until Mother would break the spell by asking if we didn't have homework to do. Often Dad, who worked long hours and rose early, would steal up the stairs to bed while the party was still going on.

As I remember, Mother and Dad gave fewer dinner parties for doctors and their wives in these Beaverbank years. But Christmas and Thanksgiving dinners always included the McPhails, another doctor's family with children close to our ages, and a number of guests who had no families at home. We almost always had Joe and his mother, Howdy. Edith Qualls, a nurse who worked closely with Dad, especially in his treatment of patients with edema, came for dinner two or three times a year. She had grown up on a ranch near Helena, Montana, and enjoyed being out by the river. We children had grown up knowing her, especially when we were in the hospital for some childhood sickness and she would sweep in with a milkshake hidden under her nurse's cape. She was quiet and smiling much of the time, I thought, but if you asked her the right question, she could make you see a vivid moment in her childhood. Mother was fascinated that "plain Edith" was the cousin of the glamorous Myrna Loy.

I was always uneasy when I heard what seemed to me Mother speaking of Edith in a condescending tone of voice. It has taken me all my life to understand this kind of ranking of people on my mother's part. I grudgingly concede, now, that to my mother a nurse was not as elevated a person as a doctor, an elementary or secondary school teacher was not as elevated a person as a professor. And somewhere in there, elevated meant valuable, meant deserving, meant having "good breeding." Once, knowing I was impertinent, I asked her what she meant by "breeding" in regard to people we knew. She gave me what we came to call her "withering look"—a look that was supposed to say more than words.

Social standing meant a great deal to her as Dad's wife, even though it meant little to him. One night when Mother had gone upstairs to bed and Dad and my brothers and I stayed reading by the fire, I asked Dad why what other people thought about us was so important to Mother. He answered in a tired voice, not looking up from his *Saturday Evening Post,* "I do not know." And it meant much to her to have a strong literary standing. But neither of these insistences on her part interfered with the strength of her novels. When a conviction of superiority was present in one of her main characters, as it would be in *The Curlew's Cry,* her novel of early-day Great Falls, that attitude would be weakened by the author's recognition of the sudden strength of the character looked down on.

Was that because these characters and their situations did not touch Mother's own life? That seems too easy a conclusion, and yet I think it might be a partial reflection of the dichotomy she felt between the living of her life and the lives of her characters.

In another letter written to Dad when he was away at a medical meeting, Mother assures him that she is resisting returning to the "black funk" she was in when he left, and adds, "No book mail either and naught in the *New York Times*. All is quiet in that respect, but I seem to have loved the day, anyway. It was warm and still and brown, except for the deep blue sky, as blue as the Kodachrome prints." This letter is not dated, but I am guessing that it is late fall of 1949 and she is referring to the reception of her most recently published novel, *Medical Meeting*. The original dust jacket put out by Harcourt, Brace praised both her writing and her depth of subject:

> *The drama in which [the husband and wife] are involved is unusual and singularly moving. . . . To the development of this drama Mildred Walker brings understanding, a style as evocative as it is honest, and a rare sense of structure and suspense. Mildred Walker calls* Medical Meeting *the "spiritual successor" to* Dr. Norton's Wife. *Its theme, the integrity and devotion of a man and his wife, and its form, which compresses all the action into a few days, combine to make the finest novel yet to come from Mildred Walker.*

This appraisal of the novel must have pleased Mother, coming just after the success of *Winter Wheat*. But of course it was not a good review printed in a national publication. Those were the comments that she coveted.

By August 1950, exciting events took Mother and Dad away from Beaverbank, traveling together. The first International Cardiological Conference since World War II was to be held in Paris and Amsterdam, and my father was invited to give a paper in each city. Mother kept a journal of their trip from the first day in New York at the Roosevelt Hotel on August 24 through their last day of flying back across the Atlantic on the stratacruiser BOAC-Cathay almost a month later. The journal is a day-by-day record of the ocean voyage they took to France, a five-day trip through the Loire Valley, the inns and hotels where they stayed, the food, the people, the weather, and her impressions of the countryside. She describes the elegance of the conferences and the doctors and their wives who entertained them from Paris to Amsterdam to Copenhagen to Oslo and to London. The journal is also a record of the hospitality they received, the interiors of each entertaining family's home, and the use that doctors in each country were making of Dad's treatment for edema. As well, it is a record of Mother's prearranged meetings with a publisher or agent in each capital where they stopped, beginning with New York's Harcourt, Brace.

Mother told me only about fifteen years ago that she had wanted to go with Dad so much that she wrote a novella, her second use of the Vermont setting, and submitted it to Harcourt, Brace as *The Southwest Corner.* When she and Dad arrived in New York City, two days before sailing to France, she saw her agent, Henry Volkening. She describes that meeting on the first page of the journal she began for the European trip: "[We] talked about *The Southwest Corner.* Sitting there I wondered how I *could* have let time go by without writing more. Harcourt's seriously interested but want twenty pages more. I am dubious but would like to sell it" (August 24, 1950). Mother finishes this entry with her excitement about the ship's accommodations: "All so beautifully appointed— our room so pleasant and comfortable with a porthole out into the sea! Flowers and fruit and a gala air. It is all hard to believe—and WONDERFUL."

The next day's entry describes the luxury of being aboard ship, the Cunard line, and her pleasure in seeing "how many ways there are of living under the sun besides my way." Her last comment for the day is "Worked over first chapter Southwest Corner." During the next two days she read a biography of Kafka and "was glad to know a little about the man. Shall try to read his writings now in his frame of reference." On August 29, "the last day of this luxurious cruise life," she writes, "worked a bit on the S-W Corner but don't know yet whether it will pan out." On August 30, land is sighted. Mother writes, "When we went up on deck we saw Land's End where we climbed & took pictures twenty years ago. Drank to it this time and to seeing it twenty years from now!"

They arrived in Paris by boat train, having shared a compartment with other passengers whom Mother describes:

> *Dr. Aldrich from Wyoming, a Mr. Sprouse who was going to the embassy in Paris for three years, & a man from Ottawa going to Geneva. We all watched for signs of France—two wheel wagons, little gardens, barns with Norman towers, round hay stacks, and old bent men and women and little French boys in smocks and shorts. (August 31, 1950)*

By prearrangement, Mother and Dad were met by "the Cook man and his sister" who were to drive them through the Loire Valley. It was the part of France that Dad remembered from 1918 as an ambulance driver in the war. Mother's recording of the sights they saw, include the comparisons she and Dad both made to Montana—in order to get their bearings: "It was cloudy all the way, but the roads between plane trees or poplars were beautiful and so different from Montana." After a "delicious luncheon at Barbizon with 'frais du Bois' and wine and hard bread," they stopped for the night in Cosne. She notes that as they strolled through the town looking for places Dad would remember, the Loire River looked "very much like the Missouri River in a low and peaceful state." She adds, "Ferd says the hotel is like the one in Stanford, Montana, French style."

Mother records this side trip with the pleasure of being in a new setting and of seeing Dad find the sources of thirty-year-old memories. She writes that Dad found two men in the village who remembered a man who was in the army with Dad; they "brought out some wine and Ferd had a good time with them." They drive on through Pouilly, Nevers, stop in Chatillon for a lunch "in courses . . . all deliciously cooked." In Beauve they stop to see the Hotel Dieu, "a hospital that has been caring for the sick since 1443." She describes the interior in a tone of wonder, concluding: "It looks so medieval & yet is still running." She continues to describe the beauty of the valley they drive through. Then she gives a glimpse of my father as she sees him enjoying this journey: "We stayed the night at the old walled city of Lampres, where Ferd stayed about a week as a soldier boy absent without leave. I could almost catch up with him walking along those walls with the same interest he has now" (September 1, 1950).

Back in Paris, she describes the luxury of the Hotel California after the village inns in the Loire and is glad they will be staying for a week. The next day they go to La Sorbonne for the first meeting of the Cardiological Congress where "all the speeches were in French or Spanish except Dr. Parkinson's of London, but there was plenty to watch in the faces of the audience, the little goings and comings." Afterward, Mother enjoys the elegance of a reception, meeting people and drinking champagne cocktails. The next day she walked and "loitered along Boulevard St. Germain on the way back." She notes that Dad worked again on his paper in the hotel room and that she typed his changes "till late." (Part of Mother's baggage for this trip was her Smith-Corona typewriter.)

Dad gave his paper in La Sorbonne the next afternoon, but Mother did not stay to hear him:

> I left Ferd at corner & took stupid bus trip around Paris—wished I'd gone anyway. Ferd gave his paper in the Amphitheatre of Liard. He got good discussion from VIPs in Belgium (Le Quieme), Italy (Poppi), and Sweden (Asp-Upmark), and a dissenting roar from Sam Levine of Boston—Ferd was noncommittal but still vibrating in every hair end when I finally saw him at 8:30. I gather he struck a blow for freedom & felt good about it underneath. What a proud thing to give a paper at the Sorbonne! Better than a pipe dream. (September 3, 1950)

I can hear the pride in Mother's words and I also have a sense that she felt about this moment the satisfaction of being married to a man who had become successful in his field. But why did she not want to hear my father read his paper? She doesn't mention in the journal that she was too nervous for him or that she was not interested in hearing him. Perhaps her first thought as she took the bus trip was to do something for herself. I just remember Dad being pleased when all of us were there to hear him in Chicago a year later.

The next paragraphs describe my parents in a much different setting—the elegance of a fashion show at "Jean Desses—a popular Couturier—a world in itself." Here, Mother gives a glimpse of herself as the models appear, "each one with dramatic suddenness, each one a different embodiment of French pulchritude."

> *And as I am with the clowns and the trapeze artists—I had to look at the models and wonder about their own lives: the little piquant one must go out to Maxim's & the Crillon for dinners—the one with the lovely eyes & faint shadows under them—close on her 30s—must have 2 children at home etc etc. (September 5, 1950)*

Two days later Mother "calls on" the publisher who "handles the translations" for Harcourt, Brace. She is received by a secretary who was expecting her and who "reported on the *Brewers' Big Horses* & *Ble d'Hiver*. . . . She explained many things about French translations I hadn't understood before and was very helpful." As the journal continues, it is clear that a very important part of this trip for Mother is to be in touch with the publishing world in each country she and my father visit.

Detailed accounts follow of the families who are their hosts in Paris and whom Mother pronounces "delightful." An interpreter who was invited to dinner at one home interested Mother particularly:

> *At 45 her mother was widowed by the 1st World War—at 45 she lost her husband in the last war but when I exclaimed she shrugged and said, "I had a happy childhood, a happy marriage—one can't have everything." She made me feel the piggish brashness of my own attitude toward life. (September 8, 1950)*

The last day of their stay in Paris, my father met with M. LaSalle, who translated his article for publication in the *Press Medicale.* Later, Mother met them and drove with them in a taxi to Mont Martre. In the journal Mother describes M. LaSalle as having seemed "expansive and shifty": "I may use something of him in this book of the West—just a line or two—an expansiveness—a gesture of the hand that the substance belies" (September 8, 1950). She was already planning *The Curlew's Cry,* which would be her third novel set in Montana.

They traveled that evening on the overnight train to the Hague and stayed at "an old-fashioned hotel, Des Indes, where many international visitors to the Peace Palace must have stayed. Much red carpet and curving stairs and polished brass. Waiters in long tails even to bring breakfast to you in your pajamas." Their hosts the first day were a family Mother describes in this way: "The atmosphere in the Snellen's home was a very happy one and the phone rang & patients waited downstairs—a doctor's household the whole world over." The handwritten pages of the journal continue with the same attention to the physicians and hospitals Dad visited, with accounts of the memorable sites Mother and Dad were taken to see, and with Mother's observations of their hosts' families and dining customs.

In addition, Mother continues to describe meetings with publishers in each of the cities they visit. She doesn't mention an appointment in Holland, where they stayed only two days, but in Copenhagen she meets with another translator: "Mr. Busch of the Danish publishing company that has translated my books met me for lunch. Next month they are bringing out *Medical Meeting.* That will make the seventh one they have published. Very satisfactory visit with him" (September 10, 1950). This is a brief paragraph in the midst of long entries of all that Mother observed in the households where my parents were entertained—the children, the paintings, the food served. In addition, she records Dad's descriptions of all the patients and their treatments that he has been shown during their four or five days in Copenhagen.

In Oslo they are welcomed into several homes of doctors for meals and conversation. Mother's description of a luncheon party given for them by the Dr. Blegen who took Dad on hospital rounds shows her total enjoyment in her surroundings: "And after the meal we went into the other room & talked—medicine & books & education—until seven o'clock—having come at 2:30. I could see Ferd having a wonderful time talking medicine—he thought that Dr. Malm had an excellent grasp of the principles of water balance" (September 12, 1950). She describes a painting that "dominated" the living room where they sat talking: "'The Dinner Party' by one of their much honored painters. It shows a group in evening dress rising in alarm as a group of naked and starving looking people appear in the garden. I took it to suggest the need for an awareness of others' hunger and want" (September 12, 1950).

During their few days in Oslo she meets with a representative of a third publishing house in Europe. Glyndendal Norsk Forlag had published a translation of *Dr. Norton's Wife* in 1939: "Talked to the man about considering *The Quarry*. He agreed to read it & discuss." From her journal it is clear that Mother had "kept her mind on"— as she used to say often to me—the advancement of her books during this trip. It was a pursuit that must have influenced the publishing of translations of her novels, those we saw hidden away in her closet at home but never heard her mention. But of course it had nothing to do with those copies of *Winter Wheat* being published in Arabic and Hindi or her other European translations in Portuguese, German, Swedish, and Italian. Almost all of those translated copies can be seen now in the Archives of the Division of Rare Books and Special Collections at the American Heritage Center at the University of Wyoming in Laramie.

One of Mother's longer journal entries is a description of the Vigeland sculpture she was taken to see in Oslo's national park:

> *He worked all his life executing the groups—all depicting human beings at every age—men and women—old men and little boys—children at play—even a babe in utero— youths dreaming—old women with flaccid abdomens & breasts—hand at mouth in uncertainty. The central focus of interest is the tremendous monolith showing the struggle for existence—one man stepping ruthlessly on the figure below him—clinging pushing reaching. . . . There are*

too many figures to take in all at once but the impact is
tremendous—it gives a sense of the vital yet minimal
importance of an individual in the life of the race—and
the unquenchable force of the urge to live. (September 11,
1950)

Reading this passage now, I wish that at twenty-one I had known Mother well enough to ask about her impressions of things she discovered on this European trip. But my brothers and I have always felt cast back in the roles of being her children rather than her confidants in conversations. Of course, she may have felt our preoccupation with our own lives. Only in her letters to us did she dwell on how she saw things or what they meant to her. In conversations I felt, or perhaps imagined, her impatience with lingering on a subject.

After Oslo, Mother and Dad's flight to London is delayed by a storm. The airline requests that two passengers stay behind to lighten the weight in the plane. They are put up for the night in an inn in Stavanger where their room overlooks the sea. They walk about two miles along the sea watching shore birds and "ducks flying as at home." Mother likens piles of barbed wire at the water's edge, left from the war, to "masses of tumbleweed."

They spend several days in London, staying at the Mayfair Hotel. Mother describes the elegance of their room, their eagerness for English food (but the hotel restaurant is French—"French with a sad difference"). She looks into shops on her own but finds Liberty's "not quite as wonderful as I remembered when I came to it with Big Bay eyes." In a bookstore she finds "a nice old edition of Pope for George." That evening they see a play by Emlyn Williams, *Accolade*. Mother records her excitement in its plot and observes that there is "a typical James character who looks on and envies his friend because he has at least 'lived.'" She follows this with her own thoughts: "I find there's something false about that. They also live who only stand and wait if that is their nature. What is living? Is it necessarily experiencing everything? or only deeply enough to fulfill our nature? Must think about it" (September 13, 1950).

The next day Mother takes a taxi to Bedford Square to visit the publishing house of Jonathan Cape. She talks with Mr. Cape, who is "very gracious & with a quick humor." He "asked about my other books and discussed what made an American book appeal to an English reading public. They are aware, at least, of my writing & interested but I need to get some smashing critical reviews in N.Y. to interest them I think & that—will I ever do?" (September 14, 1950). The journal continues with names of all the doctors Dad met with; in each instance, Mother records what Dad thought of their use of the water balance treatment. Of a Dr. Marriott at Middlesex Hospital, she writes that he "was all Ferd had hoped—somewhat perturbed by the old problem of combining practice & study." Mother and Dad's last social visit is to Hampstead to have sherry with Sir John and Lady Parkinson and two other doctors and their wives. "All quite English and delightful" to Mother, who then describes the Parkinsons' daughter, "who was interested in writing & I had a good time talking to her—even warmed to the point of telling her 'I wrote novels.'"

At 6 P.M. next evening Mother and Dad take a flight for New York. Mother notes their seat numbers on the Stratacruiser: "47–48. So funny the way every detail assumes importance." When they are rerouted to Iceland due to strong headwinds, the trip seems very long to Mother. She wonders if George and I, who are both back east attending college, will be able to meet their plane. Her last entry in the journal is "5 hours to New York, they tell us." Someone took a photograph of Mother and Dad at the airport with George and me flanking them, perhaps just as we met them. They both look at the camera directly, perhaps a little dazed, but Mother is smiling alertly. Dad wears his hat and smokes a cigarette; Mother wears a tweed suit and stands with her purse clasped firmly in both hands.

Back home at Beaverbank, Mother expanded *The Southwest Corner* and saw its publication in April 1951. At some point in 1951 she did research at the Montana Historical Society in Helena. She may have become interested in doing a monograph for the Society while she was reading background for her historical Montana novel, *The Curlew's Cry*. The monograph, *The Major's Lady: Natawista,* is a biography of the Blood Indian wife of Major Alexander

Culbertson, who was head of the fur trading post, Fort Union, in Montana in the 1840s and 1850s. The monograph was published in January 1952 in the *Montana Magazine of History*. It would become the basis for her twelfth novel, *If a Lion Could Talk*, published eighteen years later. Although we didn't hear anything in her letters about all these interests she had, it's clear that she went to work with renewed energy following the European trip.

In June 1951, Mother and Dad drove east for my college graduation and George's last year at Yale before entering medical school at the University of Michigan. It was a memorable trip for all of us. Christopher joined us from his first year of preparatory school, and after the graduation ceremony we drove on together to Michigan's Upper Peninsula. We went to Big Bay, the small lumber town on the shore of Lake Superior where my parents had begun their life together and where I was born. We saw their small wood house and Dad's infirmary, which had once been the town's ice cream parlor, and met Dad's nurse and two men my age whose parents had named them Ferdinand after Dad. The life of this town had been the basis for Mother's first published novel, *Fireweed*, in 1934. When I finally read *Fireweed* about fifteen years later, I would remember Big Bay.

Driving back by way of Chicago, we were able to see Dad give a paper on his work at a medical meeting at Passavant Hospital. We left Dad there and drove west so eagerly, I remember, that when we found the main east-west highway, we drove one hundred miles east before we realized our mistake. I wonder what thoughts Mother had as she rode across the country with her three grown children. Christopher was fifteen, George twenty, and I twenty-two. I remember moments of hilarity, temper flare-ups, and silences. Mother always felt required to orchestrate such events. What I'm sure was her affection for us often took the form of urging one or another of us to be better than she felt we were at what we did—a source of prolonged friction. After moments like these, I used to try to remove myself. I imagine that Mother in our silences must have removed herself to think about the next novel she was working on—at this time *The Curlew's Cry*.

In August, Joe Howard died suddenly of a heart attack. In October the *Minneapolis Star* printed five articles by Jay Edgerton under the title "Everyone Mourns for Mr. Montana." Dad and A. B. Guthrie spoke of the kind of man Joe was at a memorial service in the Great Falls Public Library; Dad read lines from some of Joe's favorite poems. None of us in our family could think of our lives without Joe knowing about them, but the loss was especially intense for my mother and father. Dad was told that Joe had willed him money to help with our education. Dad made sure that the money went to Joe's widowed mother, instead. But Joe and Dad were of the same mind: When Dad died four years later, Mother told me the estate lawyer expressed surprise that Dad's largest expenditures during his life had been on educating us.

Joe's importance as a writer to Mother went back to the first few weeks of my parents settling in Great Falls. Among her papers and letters, I found sets of file cards on which she typed the talks she gave over the years. These cards are typed on both sides, sometimes numbered to as many as ten to twelve cards for a talk. She kept them carefully separated into packs held together by rubber bands. In one set I found remarks about living in Great Falls as a writer, written some years after Joe's death, I think. (None of these talks are dated.) On one card, she recalls her first encounter with Joe in Great Falls's only bookstore. The owner has told him that Mother has a newly published novel; he replies that "he didn't read many women's romances." Mother continues:

> I quickly told him this was a novel about a milltown in the depression and we argued about the difference between a novel & a romance. We talked about writing from then on as long as he lived. He was a real writer and a real friend; I learned a great deal from him. He introduced me to others in G. F. who were writing. . . . We didn't get together in any writing group but we were all starting and all working. We all knew that writing was a solitary business but the awareness of the others writing was important to us.

This is how I remember those afternoons or evenings when Mother and Joe and the others sat talking at Beaverbank. And I think Dad always felt included.

My brothers and I returned each summer from school to do work on the place, working also on projects that Mother and Dad took an interest in. Maybe it was the summer of 1951 that George remodeled a car from scratch. I remember one morning when George invited Dad to climb into the naked chassis for a ride up the gravel road. It was a gleeful sight, Dad in his pajamas, and must have been a triumphant moment for George. Christopher recorded that moment with his camera as he did so many other moments in our lives in those years.

When displaced Europeans were being resettled in Montana, Mother and Dad were interested in helping them get started. Mother brought a Ukrainian couple who spoke only German and Russian to live in the apartment and work for her. They left shortly afterward, suffering from homesickness as well as the foreign environment. One young man who came, Lazlo Tetmeijer from Hungary, preferred listening to opera or playing chess with George to doing chores. Dad and Joe Howard paid for him to complete his engineering studies at Montana State College. Three young men working at the hospital came out to be near the river at Dad's suggestion. They became family friends. One in particular, Winfried Manske from Germany, came to live at Beaverbank for several years and helped Mother and Dad with things that needed taking care of, especially during the academic year. He and his wife became part of our extended family, as did Konrad Deligdisch from Rumania, whose work was in advanced radiology and who worked with Dad and George. George remembers that Konrad took him folboating on the Missouri and backpacking in the mountains.

In 1951–52, I studied Celtic literature at Edinburgh University in Scotland. Rereading Mother and Dad's letters sent to me in Edinburgh, I realize their closeness to each other. They wrote mostly of events at Beaverbank and their concerns about what was happening in each of our lives. In my case, I wrote them often of my excitement in my studies at the university, of my adventures in the countryside, and of the people and customs that I came to know. They responded with genuine enthusiasm.

Dad was especially interested in my decision to bicycle from Edinburgh to London, going by way of hostels, in March 1952. He bought a Bartholemew atlas to follow my trip down through the lake country. I had explained that it would be a kind of literary pilgrimage. His only request was that I send him my itinerary. I found a note or letter, sometimes a telegram, from Dad mailed to almost every one of the hostels where I stopped.

Mother usually added a note in response to a letter I had written to them along the way. One letter I received at a hostel addressed me as "Dearest Traveler" and said she was trying to remember that I could manage perfectly well, but "I do wish I could be sure that the hostels are comfortable and decently chaperoned—don't laugh at me! and warm. And that you have your money in travelers or Am. Exp. checks—and that you aren't exhausted pumping up hills." But Mother wrote nothing about what was happening with her writing, of course. It would be several years before she told me that *The Southwest Corner* had received good reviews and sold well. Nor did she mention that New York playwright John Cecil Holm had asked permission to write a stage adaptation.

Back home in May 1952, I made plans to teach at a rural school about twenty-five miles from Beaverbank. In July I married David Hansen, a former classmate from college, in a ceremony above the Missouri at Beaverbank with my parents' blessings. Our decision to marry was hurried by the fact that he was due to go into training in the Marine Corps. This summer would be my last living at Beaverbank with my family.

But while my husband was in training at Quantico in Virginia, I stayed in Montana to teach. Every few weekends I had the chance to go home to see Mother and Dad. And several times they made the trip out to the school to see how I was doing. Mother spoke to me about her concerns that I was way out in the boondocks and that Dad had spells of not feeling well. He had been working harder than ever and traveling to present his work at medical conventions. The next spring, 1953, my husband had returned from Quantico and we were all gathered at home when Dad flew in on the eve of his fifty-fourth birthday from an important presentation of his work in Boston. We met his plane at the airport with a makeshift red carpet and a large banner reading "Fifty-four Ferdie or Fight!" I think Mother was startled but still delighted with the hilarity of her children's demonstration.

That summer my husband and I lived near the marine base of Camp Pendleton in California before he was shipped out to Korea. My father wrote us regularly, interested in how my husband fared in the military. I returned home to work in the Great Falls Public Library and to see the town from a new perspective. I knew too sharply that Mother had pulled strings to get me the publicity job at the library, but I knew, too, that that side of her—bringing things about—was part of how she lived her life in Great Falls. What I did not know was that she was writing *The Curlew's Cry* set in a western town like Great Falls at the turn of the century.

By January 1954 Dad had convinced me to finish my master's degree at the University of Montana, about two hundred miles west of Great Falls in Missoula. I went there as a teaching assistant in English and was halfway through the semester when Mother called to say that Dad had suffered a stroke. Dad recovered shakily but not enough to return to his work. It was especially hard for him because he had just been awarded a Public Health Grant to further his work with children afflicted with rheumatic heart disease. I drove home to Beaverbank only on weekends because Dad insisted that I keep on at the university. Mother was deeply upset by Dad's illness, uneasy until she convinced him to be treated by their friend from Ann Arbor days, now in charge of a veterans hospital in Los Angeles. Winfried Manske took care of Beaverbank until Christopher graduated from the preparatory school and came home to help. In August Christopher came to cheer me on when I received my master's degree at the university.

By the end of that summer my husband returned from Korea, and we went to see Mother and Dad in California. Dad was unhappy in California, not making any progress, and Mother was irritable at the change in their lives. Back home, I helped Christopher pack up for Amherst College, but I felt his sense of loss that our parents weren't there to encourage him. In December Dad convinced Mother that he wanted to come home. They rejoiced, they told me, when they drove across the border into Montana. The whole family was home to celebrate what would be our last Christmas at Beaverbank.

In January 1955, both my husband and I went back to the University of Montana as instructors in English, grateful that we were close to Dad and Mother. Then in March, Mother told me that she was taking Dad to St. Louis, where a Dr. Schroeder who worked in the treatment of heart disease had agreed to treat Dad. In late April I took off three days to see them. Dad was very weak. I stayed with him at night so that Miss Qualls, who came from home to assist in nursing Dad, could get some sleep. One night when I was replenishing his intravenous fluid, he looked right at me to say, "I don't want this bondage." I didn't say this to Mother then, but when we talked during the day, she made clear that this way of living was a bondage—being surrounded by illness, not being at home, not being able to write—that she hated for herself. Dad died in May 1955.

The funeral and burial took place in Dad's hometown of Saginaw, Michigan, at the insistence of his two brothers. Mother and Dad's friends and colleagues held a memorial gathering for Dad in Great Falls. By mid-August the house and fields at Beaverbank were empty. I felt we were leaving behind so much that my father had enjoyed in his years there. George was the first to leave for California to his internship at Los Angeles General Hospital. David and I were bound for Cornell University, only thirty miles from where Mother would be teaching. And Christopher drove with Mother to Grafton, to meet the moving van and to help Mother move in. After that he returned to Amherst and thought of Grafton as his family home. Mother did not return to visit Montana for several years.

I think of the letter from Mother to Dad that I read only recently; she had written to Dad from Beaverbank three or four years before his death. He was away for a medical meeting: "This morning it was snowing when I woke at 9 and has snowed all day. The river is frozen half way across. It was so beautiful I felt quite lifted in spirit though the house is very different without you, and quite pointless." I understand now that Mother and Dad had lived so closely to each other in their work and in their enjoyment of those ten years at Beaverbank that to continue there without him would have seemed "quite pointless" to her.

8
The Last Two Montana Novels

arcourt, Brace and Company took a half page in the *New York Times Book Review* on March 13, 1955, to announce the publication of *The Curlew's Cry*. The announcement included a handsome photograph of Mother, taken for the dust jacket by a Great Falls photographic studio. It is the same photograph as that chosen by the University of Nebraska Press for the reprints of her novels in the 1990s. Mother is smiling and wears a dark scarf at the throat of her tailored shirt. The announcement includes a quote from *Kirkus Review:* "A deep understanding of the special quality that characterizes our frontier regions . . . a story of mood and emotions . . . that holds reader interest. Successive novels have brought Mildred Walker to a position of real importance as a regional novelist." In larger type at the top of the ad, the *Philadelphia Inquirer* is quoted: "One of the best writers of the American scene."

But a month earlier, on February 28, the *Philadelphia Inquirer* had run a review headlined "Ranch Girl's Romance." No wonder Mother had always dreaded reviews; this one must have seared her hopes for the novel. The review by Frederic G. Hyde, while perceptive enough, does inspire the term *romance* in its emphasis. But after taking note of the curlew's cry as a significant metaphor for loneliness in the novel, Hyde turns to the skill he finds in Mother's writing: "With the tenderness, understanding and admirable sense of style which have made minor classics of such of her previous novels as *The Southwest Corner* and *The Brewers' Big Horses,* Miss Walker tells here of Pamela Lacey's girlhood." I would come to know, in later years, just how resentful Mother could feel about her novels being typed as "minor," let alone "romance." The reviewer goes on to stress the novel's study—in its thirty-year span—of the growth of the small western town of Brandon Rapids: "the great changes wrought in social outlook, economies and the nature of the town's population." But he does conclude that Pamela's discovery of her feelings about her girlhood friends Wrenn Morley and Rose Guinard are "the nub of Miss Walker's story."

Forty years later Mary Clearman Blew, who wrote the 1994 introduction to the University of Nebraska Press reprint of *The Curlew's Cry*, does not see the novel as a romance. In a 1987 essay on Mother's four Montana-based novels, Blew had stressed the theme of the dominance wielded by a western man over a western woman. Blew had found that to be true in all four novels, particularly in *The Curlew's Cry*. Mother took exception to that view, and Blew revised her assessment in the 1994 introduction:

> *Mildred Walker did not intend to stress the West, in* The Curlew's Cry, *as a man's brutal world in which women have no place, or to characterize men and women as separate human beings who are basically opposed to each other's worlds. "The concept of the Wilderness grew and grew for me as I wrote, and kept changing," she wrote to me after she read my essay. "In* Curlew's Cry *it meant loneliness, being unloved and finally loving no man." (5)*

Brandon Rapids is the name Mother gives a town like Great Falls, Montana. In her third small notebook for the novel, she observes "the things women think about in the late afternoon as they walk down the street—and no one knows." The reader learns much about Pamela Lacey's attitude toward Brandon Rapids in her walks down the streets and outside the town on the prairie —thoughts that she must struggle with, thoughts that "no one knows." I have wondered often if Mother's thoughts over the twenty-two years of noticing women on those streets in Great Falls, knowing a good number of their lives, inspired her to imagine the situation in *The Curlew's Cry*—the loneliness of a single woman. And I have wondered, too, if the novel, completed only months before Dad's death, had a part in her abrupt decision to leave Montana. I have quoted her earlier as saying that she did not want "to be known as the widow."

She must have completed that novel in late 1954, at some point when Dad was not too sick to read it, because she told me years later she was glad that Dad had read ten of her thirteen novels. I think her work on this novel must have steadied her in those months. *The Curlew's Cry* was published in February 1955, just about the time that Mother insisted Dad should be treated in the St. Louis hospital. She didn't mention the publication date to us, as was her habit, but a friend brought me a photograph of a window display of the novel in a Helena, Montana, bookstore. When I wrote enthusiastically about the display to Mother in St. Louis, she replied that that was nice but the novel wasn't being reviewed well. She added, "Besides, I'd really rather know what my own thought of it." Of course, that startled me and made me ashamed. I didn't have a copy of the novel, and I hadn't read it, but neither had she ever expressed such a wish before.

In these same months while Dad's condition worsened, she was corresponding with the playwright John Cecil Holm, who produced *The Southwest Corner.* A letter she kept from him invites her to the opening of the play in New York; it is followed by another letter in reply to her letter in which she had to decline the invitation, saying how sorry he is that her husband is ill. As I mentioned earlier in discussing *The Southwest Corner,* she also received a letter from the actress Eva Le Gallienne and newspaper clippings of the performance. She must have felt that part of her life was still continuing.

The Curlew's Cry delineates a historic period in the town of Brandon Rapids. The novel's protagonist grows up in a western town and finds herself, middle-aged at the end of the novel, running a dude ranch at the foot of the mountains at some distance from the town. She sees herself as a single woman overwhelmed at times by loneliness. Mother stressed this loneliness in a brief written description of the meaning that the curlew's cry had in her novel. In the late 1980s, she showed me her description; she said she had asked the editors at Harcourt, Brace to use it as a prologue to the novel but that they had declined. Some thirty years after the novel's publication, she was still disappointed that Harcourt, Brace hadn't used it. She felt it was at the heart of the novel:

> Women in the early west often heard the curlew's cry . . . in the lonely places where the wind blows the prairie grass and weights it with the dust. Cry of the curlew . . . or cry of the loneliness those women feared . . . sharp as the edge of a green grass blade, piercing the stillness like a woman-scream, freezing the blood with an instant of fear, and making the blood congeal. But once the towns were built out west, and tied together by twin lines of steel, women lived on streets, with neighbors, and counted themselves safe from the curlew's lonely cry. They filled their lives with love and hate and talk and busyness . . . as women always, everywhere. Yet out beyond the western towns, where the prairie grass still grows, and down by the river's edge, the curlews walk stiff-legged, long-billed and curious. And a woman still may hear that cry, that harsh curlee-li-li flung back on the wind from the bird's swift flight down the sky; sharp as the edge of a green grass blade, piercing the stillness like a woman-scream, lingering on the brain longer than the wire-thin whistle of the midnight train.

The curlew's cry becomes a metaphor for the loneliness that Pamela Lacey feels more than once in the course of the novel.

In her first notebook for *The Curlew's Cry*, Mother records the changes in ranch life in the 1880s:

> *1884—peak of prosperity for younger beef*
> *1886–87—terrible winter*
> *1887—preference for younger beef*
> *1890—cattle loan companies begin to take over*

She goes on to quote specifics from *The Range Cattle Industry* by Edward Everett Dale (Norman: University of Oklahoma Press, 1930).

In the last pages of this notebook, Mother starts writing from the back with possible details of life in the Lacey family. She notes that theirs was a lineage of aristocracy in ranching families that went back to the days of the open range. Her main character, Pamela Lacey, is juxtaposed with her school friend, Rose Guinard. Mother describes Rose as "a girl of Jugoslavian family at the [copper] smelter. Wrenn Morley, the boy whom Pamela thought would marry her, marries Rose." She terms these characters "not dramatic enough; characters not sufficiently vital," and continues: "Consider: Lacey's father dishonored in some way—something about a land deal. (So Pamela learns hate) isolation—hurt pride early. Father's interest: cattle and land; Wrenn's father a lawyer." She interjects a paraphrase of Ray West's quote on Wallace Stegner: "recognized West no longer scene for heroic action." *The Curlew's Cry* will heed that observation, even in those years of early nostalgia in the West. Pamela will not extol the virtues of pioneer days.

Following these notes, Mother returns to the characterization of her protagonist: "Let's see—Pamela has to adjust feeling about father's dishonesty; mother's insincerity—own feeling of nothing as big or as fine as it should be." These relationships and the nature of the country in which they are played out become the plot of a novel that is similar to *Winter Wheat*—a daughter taking a close look at her parents. Ellen Webb struggles to understand how the country keeps her parents together out of her need to love them; Pamela Lacey struggles to become independent of her parents' disparate attitudes toward the country. In both of these novels, living in Montana is essential to plot—in the then contemporary 1940s and in the early 1900s.

A second notebook opens with details of women's lives in the early twentieth century in a small Montana town:

> *1904—girl of 21 looked older because of flying hair—large skirt, shirtwaist.*
> *Vaudeville—not motion pictures in 1904.*
> *Arc lights—not light posts.*
> *Sen-sen on the breath.*
> *People who "did hair" went to homes.*

Following this listing of turn-of-the-century details, Mother describes an older acquaintance who once lived on a ranch but has now lived in town for some years: "loves prairies, misses most the glare of the snow on a bright still day in winter."

Further notebook entries move to Pamela's thoughts when she has returned from back east and a brief marriage. She lives at home and works in the town. In the novel Pamela becomes painfully, sometimes resentfully, aware of what other people whom she has known all her life think of her as an unmarried woman. She sees herself in this position at every turn—attending meetings of the Shakespeare Club, chatting with her mother's friends on the street, or waiting on them in the hardware store where she works for a time. And underlying these self-evaluations is the antagonism she feels for Rose, who has married the man whom Pamela had thought she wanted. She lives with and expands on these resentments over the years even as she embarks on the adventure of running a dude ranch. Steadily, she rejects being pitied for her way of living. Mother draws a portrait of a proud woman, determined to be self-sufficient and successful.

Many of Pamela's thoughts about her position in other people's eyes draw on Mother's self-observations voiced in unguarded moments. She would say of a dinner party that she had been a success or had taught someone to see her differently than before. "Last night I was brilliant," she would say merrily. Of another occasion she would insist with disgust that she "had failed all evening to be spirited." In my sense of Mother's social discomforts, I read many similarities to Pamela's, each imagining herself under constant, sometimes judgmental scrutiny. When Pamela does the totally unexpected in her circle—starts a dude ranch—she sees herself as defying all her imagined detractors; Mother, fond of pointing out that she liked to "be brisk," delighted in making statements that showed her in charge of her life. I see this reflected in many of her heroines, but especially in Pamela in *The Curlew's Cry*.

Early in the novel Pamela has been invited back east to visit the family who owns the cattle company for which Charlie Lacey runs the ranch. The invitation was to thank Pamela for her bravery in saving the Randells' son, who was bitten by a rattlesnake out on the ranch the summer before. She has always thought of the ranch, though her mother has no interest in it, as belonging to her father. But, in the Randells' home, she discovers that the ranch is spoken of as belonging to the Randells. She resents this. One afternoon she follows Mrs. Randell's suggestion to look at stereopticon scenes in Mr. Randell's den.

> Then she saw the picture over the desk; a framed photo-graph, too palely gray to be distinct, but even across the room the outlines had a sharp familiarity. It was a picture of the ranch; that was King Butte in the distance. At the bottom in white ink was printed, Rocky Mountain Cattle Company. Below the long picture was a smaller one show-ing the ranch house with Mr. Randell and Slim and Papa on the steps, and Ruby standing in the doorway. She swallowed quickly. Why should he have these pictures here? He was president of the Rocky Mountain Cattle Company only. . . . The ranch house looked dilapidated in a picture. It wasn't really like that. Papa was wearing his old hat. Ruby had her apron rolled over her arms so it must have been dirty and she didn't want it to show. The brim of Slim's hat was so wide you couldn't see anything of his face but the chin. Mr. Randell seemed out of place standing there. (80)

There are moments during Pamela's visit when she feels out of place in the Randells' elegant home. Once she has taken the train and is on her way home, she is elated by the signs that are familiar to her—the space, the brisk air, the familiarity of people's speech.

I knew that Mother and Dad, especially after they moved to Bea-verbank, looked forward to the moments when they arrived home in Montana—felt less constricted by an unnecessary propriety they very often felt back east. And certainly, my brothers and I felt that way after we started going east to college and university. So I was distracted by Pamela's thoughts when I first read The Curlew's Cry, thinking that since Mother knew that feeling, how could she have moved back east permanently after Dad's death. It took me a number of years to realize that, first of all, Mother understood Pamela but she was not Pamela. Further, Mother wanted an absorbing life, a definite position that she could fill, none of which she imagined for herself alone in Montana.

There were other things about Mother's own life that affected my first reading of the novel. Soon after Pamela returns home to Montana, the cattle company owners accuse Charlie Lacey of gambling with their investment: He had borrowed money from the bank in the company's name to acquire more land. These are Pamela's first doubts about her father's integrity. This is the event that Mother uses to fulfill her plan in her notes: "Pamela has to adjust feeling about father's dishonesty." About twenty years after this novel, Mother told me in a tone of pained confession that her father had invested his Baptist parishioners' money in a coal mine's prospects and lost all the money. When I asked how he could have done that, she replied wearily, "I've never understood."

In the novel Charlie Lacey does not represent one man's dishonesty but instead is shamed by the change in the frontier society of Brandon Rapids. " 'Good God, of course I gambled,' Charlie Lacey's voice roared through the house." Pamela listens from the stairway to her father talking with Mr. Randell and his associate in the study:

> *"Gentlemen," Papa said in a quiet voice that didn't sound quite natural, "business is done differently in the West from the way it is in the East. It isn't a cut and dried kind of a deal with every transaction written down in a ledger. It rests on a man's word. If J. B. Moore hadn't known I was honest he would never have given me the loan." (105)*

Lacey's loan—in the name of the cattle company—had bought more land to feed the cattle in the drought summer. His plan was to sell the cattle in the fall and pay back the loan. Pamela believes in her father's honesty. But she reads next day's newspaper in the office where she is working: "On page two a three-column headline announced in sickening black type 'Charlie Lacey Out as Manager Rocky Mountain Cattle Company.'" The article goes on: "Claiming irregularity in management . . . , company intends dissolution after sale of cattle this fall." Rose agrees vigorously with Pamela when they talk about the newspaper article and reassures her. But when her father comes by the office later to drive her out to the ranch and reads the article, Pamela speaks to him about it for the first time: " 'Papa, it isn't true, is it, what they say in the paper?' Her voice was almost a whisper. 'There wasn't anything irregular about it?' " (117). But he doesn't say, "Of course, it isn't true," and she refuses to go out to the ranch with him. With Wrenn it is the same: "Oh, Pam, don't get so worked up. You know how your father is. He probably took a few chances and didn't expect to have them found out before he'd . . ." Pamela won't speak with him after that.

The novel's viewpoint shifts briefly to the "many versions of the affairs of the Rocky Mountain Cattle Company" held by men drinking in the bar. Sid Newton has the final word:

> What I think is . . . those Easterners want to invest their money out here and expect to make plenty more and they don't ever want to take a chance or trust anyone. Let 'em get out of the country, I say. Charlie's got his leases and his three hundred and twenty, they took the rest, or they're going to, that's what I heard. (109-10)

It will be Pamela who has to learn to put things down in black and white, not take chances, when her life brings her back to making a living on the ranch. Mother's observation for this novel—the kind of thought that she said started her thinking about a novel—was certainly of a single woman going about living in this time in a small town. But it is just as firmly about the changes taking place in a small western town in the early twentieth century that affected that woman.

Mother's papers include many notecards for talks and later for lectures, held together by rubber bands and often added to or revised for some later delivery of the same talk. Among these I found an emphatic statement about the relationship that she felt existed between character and place:

> I have never set out to write a Montana novel or a Michigan novel. My main interest is always in a character or a

*relationship; one relationship will be with place where the
character lives. You are aware of what living in Detroit
did to Joyce Carol Oates's characters. How suburban Con-
necticut affected Updike's characters.*

I would guess that this statement was delivered sometime in the
1970s, born of Mother's long-standing rejection of being considered a "regional writer." The 1950s *Kirkus Review* quoted at the beginning of this chapter typed Mother as a "regional novelist." In
Mother's view, as early as the 1940s, such a term automatically
limited the scope of her novels for readers. In those years I heard
Mother and Joe Howard and Dad, talking in our house, vehemently reject this typing of novels set in the West. In the early
1950s in college and in the late 1950s and 1960s at academic gatherings back east, I heard the term used often, usually dismissing in
part the accomplishment of a writer. The term seemed to be used
almost entirely for novels set in the West, less so for novels from a
region like the South. Since good reviews from back east were coveted by writers out west, always by Mother, this was a sore point.

Mildred Walker, the novelist, would have cheered a 1999 interview with William Kittredge on the subject of regionalism. Kittredge, a Montana writer whose work is read widely and who
admired Mother's writing, answers a question from Megan Mc-
Namer, another Montana writer, for the *Missoula Independent:*

> INDEPENDENT: *Do you think artists—or writers—
> should try to be regional?*
> KITTREDGE: *I don't think you can help but be regional.
> I really don't think we should try to be regional, but we
> shouldn't resist being regional either. Nobody can be more
> regional than Proust; nobody can be more regional than
> Tolstoy; nobody can be more regional than Virginia
> Woolf. They're specifically set in a whole emotional,
> physical setting of one kind or another—but at the same
> time I think that you want to reach out to the universal
> things, too, the things that really apply to everybody. . . .*

In other words, your concerns in Great Falls are the same
concerns, the fundamental concerns, that Chekhov had.
Or whoever. (October 14–21, 1999)

Mother understood this when she was writing her novels; it was the sting of the charge in reviews that made her want to deny being "just" a regional novelist.

The minor characters of *The Curlew's Cry* are more important to me now than when I first met them. At first, I thought they were too accurately based on people Mother knew, whom all of us knew. This thought shocked me into muteness on the subject of the novel when Mother brought it up in conversation. As a reader I wanted these characters not to be caricatures. In my mind Mother was mocking these characters, not only the prototypes but a good many of the people I had grown up with and learned from.

But after subsequent rereadings of the novel, I came to see these characters through Pamela Lacey's eyes. That was the thing to do, of course. Ruby and Slim, who have no last name in the novel, are the husband and wife who keep the ranch going for Charlie Lacey. Pamela has grown up with them and depends on their way of looking at life, depends on their affection for her:

> *No woman Pamela knew was like Ruby. "A broom with*
> *an apron and a shawl tied on her," Slim called her be-*
> *cause she was so thin and straight and her face and neck*
> *and hands and arms were the color of a wooden broom*
> *handle. Her hair was no color at all and brushed back in*
> *a tight knot. You never could remember the color of her*
> *eyes except when she was mad and then they were glaring*
> *light yellow and white. But you could count on Ruby; she*
> *didn't change from one side to the other the way Mama*
> *did. (47–48)*

The description of Ruby fits the Lottie who had worked for Mother at Beaverbank—too close for me. But the Ruby Pamela knows belongs to Pamela's affection for the ranch. Pamela doesn't feel that same affection for the town or for her mother. And in town Pamela's life is framed, in spite of herself, by her mother's.

Pamela's father feels the same as Pamela does about the ranch. In a scene that shifts to Charlie Lacey's point of view, he sits on the front porch of the Western Hotel smoking a cigar and not wanting to go to the house. The house in town seems to him to be Maybelle Lacey's, but, he thinks to himself, "the old place on the ranch was his":

> There wasn't a thing out there that wasn't meant for comfort. Nothing was ever missing because it had gone to be cleaned or reupholstered. Ruby wasn't too good a housekeeper, but he didn't mind an ashtray filled to overflowing and a smoked lamp-chimney or a little heap of dead moths on the oil-cloth covered table, nor a bed that was left as you crawled out of it. Ruby always had coffee on the stove and a good meal coming up, and you could take a drink without anyone to say, "Not too much, Charlie!" (67–68)

And Ruby's livable presence is a big part of Charlie's comfort.

Again and again it is a revelation to me to see my mother the novelist evoking a setting like that at the Lacey ranch and approving that setting in the eyes of her characters. My mother the doctor's wife, I knew from experience, could never tolerate such a setting for herself. In her house, rugs were removed to be cleaned and comfortable reading chairs were absent in order to be upholstered. And when she visited my various apartments or houses, she was gratified out of all proportion to see that there were no overflowing ashtrays or beds left unmade as the day went on. No, Ruby is not a caricature of the Lottie who worked for my mother. Mother was avidly, perhaps, aware of those she observed—how they peopled a place, how they lived their lives with particular idiosyncrasies, and how they could be important to her main character. I want to say that the less their outlook was Mother's, the more she invested in them as characters.

In *The Curlew's Cry* Pamela sees two minor women characters as unafraid of being themselves. There is Ruby the ranch cook, whom Pamela feels takes her seriously even if Ruby's seasoned advice often comes out as a rebuke. When Pamela returns to the ranch from living back east for only a few years with her husband, Ruby confronts Pamela:

> *"Did you leave him for good?" she asked, yellow-gray eyes almost crossed as she looked at the cigarette paper she was sealing with her tongue. . . .*
>
> *"I didn't ever really love him," Pamela said, her eyes on the slow movement of the river.*
>
> *"That's the worst thing a woman can do, Punk. It makes me ashamed of myself that I never taught you any better. It's worse than a lot of things people think is worse." (230)*

And there is the French milliner, Madame Guinard, a widow who has firm opinions. She has her own business and recognizes Pamela's yearning to be comfortable with herself in such a role—as a dude ranch operator. Madame is spirited, enthusiastic on Pamela's behalf:

> *"Here's to your ranch! May it make you plenty money and bring you great pleasure! It is very great pleasure to be independent and know you do it yourself." Confidence warmed Pamela as she sipped her wine, and a sense of excitement. She and Madame Guinard had something in common; they were both independent of other people. They made their own way without a husband. She hardly saw Madame Guinard's wrinkles or the gray close to the roots of her hair, only her bright eyes and gay laugh and quick interest that made it easy to talk to her. . . . "You will be pioneer in dude ranches!" Madame Guinard laughed. The word "dude" tickled her every time she said it. (303–04)*

The novel is divided into three parts. Each part specifies the years in which the events will take place. Part 1 covers three years, 1905 to 1907; part 2, half as long as part 1, covers eight years, 1912 to 1918; and part 3, with about the same number of pages as part 2, covers sixteen years, 1926 to 1941. I mention this construction of the novel because it stresses the importance of Pamela Lacey's early convictions of who she is and who she wants to be.

A quotation prefacing each part gives direction to the reader. Part 1 begins with a quotation from Edwin Arlington Robinson's "Cassandra": "We are young; / Oh, leave us now, and let us grow." In the first chapter the Brandon Rapids High School senior class is planning a float for Pioneer Day. The opening sentence of part 1 is in the mind of the teacher of the class: "The teacher was weary with Pioneer Day before it started," a foreshadowing of how Pamela comes to assess the pioneer myth and its nostalgic hold on the town's descendants of pioneers. She sees how a more modern business ethic outdates her cattle rancher father's beliefs. Her grasp of the conflict, and her disappointment in losing the young man she expected to marry, goad her into a marriage that takes her back east.

Part 2 is prefaced by an unattributed quotation: "Some people are molded by their admirations, some by their antagonisms." In the spring of 1912, five years after the end of part 1, Pamela returns to Brandon Rapids determined to end her brief marriage. Rose and Wrenn Morley have moved back to the town with their small son. During these eight years Pamela inwardly wars with her antagonisms toward the Morleys and other townspeople and with her panic at being unmarried and lonely in Brandon Rapids. At the same time she develops a loyalty to the country outside the town, namely, the part of the cattle ranch that is still her father's. The First World War sends the men of the town to the army; the influenza epidemic strikes the town, and Pamela nurses Rose Morley back to health; Wrenn Morley returns from the war, and Pam discovers that she doesn't love Wrenn, perhaps is incapable of loving anyone.

Part 3's opening quote is from Dylan Thomas's poem "Especially When the October Wind": "Shut, too, in a tower of words, I mark / On the horizon walking like the trees / The wordy shapes of women. . . ." Pamela Lacey, with her dismayed father looking on, turns the ranch into an adventure for paying guests from back east—"dudes." Chapter by chapter she makes a success of the business but increasingly is overcome by her loneliness. As in so many of Mother's novels, the tempo of events speeds up as the novel comes to a dramatic end.

I noticed only idly in my first readings of the novel that in each of the three parts some of the individual chapters are dated, sometimes including the month or the season as well as the year. Turning back to these chapters in my rereadings, I wondered what these intermittently dated chapters were meant to point out. For instance, in part 2, six of the twelve chapters are dated; they begin with chapter 1, "1912," and end with chapter 11, "Fall, 1918." The dated chapters that follow chapter 1 are clustered, 7, 8, and 9, and concentrated on the effects on the principal characters of both the war and the influenza epidemic. In parts 1 and 3, the dating of chapters is also intermittent. Why the author chose to do this puzzled me until I saw it as a device to underscore particular events or moments significant to Pamela Lacey's way of seeing her life.

On the other hand, the last chapter in part 2 appears without a date. It is one of the longest chapters in the novel, detailing the tragedy in the Morley household, Pamela's nursing of Rose, and Wrenn's return from the war. But these events of the chapter assume less importance than its last paragraphs of self-description Pamela allows herself in her exhaustion:

> *When she was beyond the houses, she turned across the open ground that always seemed to stretch way to the far line of mountains. . . . Burrs caught against her skirt as she walked, and milkweed rattled when she brushed against it. She picked off a pod, already emptied by the wind, and held it in her hand. It was a shell, not a sea shell, but a dry-land shell, that had once been filled and now was empty. She played with it, curving her fingers around the brittle husk, then she crushed it in her hand and threw it away. If she didn't have her love for Wrenn, then she didn't love anyone, anyone at all. (296–97)*

So I can't be sure of my explanation for why some chapters have dates and others haven't. When I turn back to her three earlier historical novels, I find that they, too, have an intermittent dating of chapters. A letter to Mother from Dan Wickenden, an editor at Harcourt, Brace, dated February 5, 1946, refers to her use of dates in her manuscript of *The Quarry*. After writing that "Lyman and Easy are characters as real as any you have created, and their relationship is beautifully handled and developed," and assuring her that she has "brought forth a full-size, mature, and moving novel," he adds:

> *I think it is a remarkable achievement to have been able to create a sense of growing time over so long a period without any feeling of strain in that direction. I found myself reading the dates at the head of each chapter, but not really paying much attention to them. The story, itself, gives the required back-ground in time.*

Still, Mother would use the device to show the passage of time, the relevance to Pamela of certain years in her life. *The Curlew's Cry* was the fourth of the historical novels she published, eight years after *The Quarry*.

A final supposition I'd like to make about *The Curlew's Cry:* Montana exerts such an effect on its characters, as it does in Mother's other Montana novels, that the country becomes a character itself. The country responds to Pamela's mood, even need, by its very nature in this passage toward the end of *The Curlew's Cry:*

> *She hadn't been lonely all the time, nor sad. There were good days, too. There was one day, in particular, when the world was crystal: so cold and clear and sharp-frozen that each blade of grass, each twig on the stilled aspen trees, each hair on the steers' hides seemed separate and distinct. There was no wind, only sun. She had bundled up in her warmest clothes and slid down the bank to the frozen river that wound ahead, a long smooth snow-covered highway.*

And Pamela's response as she walks up the frozen river:

> *A sense of exhilaration had possessed her that day. She had realized suddenly that she was happy . . . maybe con-*

tent was the word . . . but not because of anybody, nor for
any reason of herself or because of any happening. She
had gone back to the house in a kind of humble amaze-
ment. The feeling hadn't lasted, but if she had it once, it
would come again. That was something you might never
feel unless you were alone she told herself now as she
drove into town. (373–74)

If a Lion Could Talk, Mother's fourth novel with a Montana setting, was published in 1970, billed by Harcourt Brace Jovanovich as
"a tale about the Wilderness—not as Hawthorne's dark evil, nor as
Faulkner's lost birthright, but as non-communication and confusion of meaning." The publishers called it "an ironic and original
novel."

Twelve years after its publication, Mother prepared the following commentary for a Montana writers' conference held in Havre:

This novel was a long time growing in my mind. Al-
though it is set in the Wilderness of the Northwest in the
mid-eighteen fifties, the idea for it didn't begin with Place
but, as a novel always does for me, with characters at a
particular point in their lives. As newcomers to the State
[Montana] are apt to do sooner or later, I went to see Fort
Benton and looked at the pile of stones that is all that re-
mains of the old fort and tried to imagine how it must
have been. Then I saw a drawing of the fort when it was
occupied, standing there looking too small and defenseless
in all that wide country.

There were teepees clustered near it. Later, in the Histori-
cal Library of Montana, I stumbled on Volume X of
"Contributions to the Historical Society of Montana,"
which contained the Fort Benton Journal from 1854 to
1856. The daily entries were very brief, listing arrivals
and departures, or the amount of wood chopped or dobies
[clay bricks] made, but their very dailiness gave me a pic-
ture of what the life must have been like in that fort. In

> *the volume also were pictures of Major Culbertson, the*
> *head of the fort, and the Indian woman who was his wife,*
> *Natawista Iksana, the daughter of a Blood [Indian] chief.*
> *In the notes in the back, there were brief profiles of them.*
> *Also there was a reference to the first protestant mission-*
> *ary and his wife to come to the Northwest. They stayed*
> *with the Culbertsons at the fort, but only for four months*
> *before they returned to civilization. What had happened?*
> *Surely missionaries were made of sterner stuff. Here was a*
> *cast of four characters . . . if anybody wanted to write*
> *about them. I wrote an account of Natawista for the*
> Montana Historical Magazine *(1952) and tried to leave*
> *them there. But still they stayed in my mind for twenty*
> *years tantalizing me with their mystery. It wasn't until I*
> *retired from teaching that I came back to them.*

These four historical figures, so mysterious to Mother, became her characters in *If a Lion Could Talk:* Major Phillips and his wife, Eenis-skim, and the Baptist missionary Mark Ryegate and his wife, Harriet.

Her notebook for this novel indicates that she began work on it in the early 1960s. About this time she exclaimed indignantly to me that the poet May Swenson, who gave a reading at Wells while Mother was there, wrote, "There is no Wilderness in women / they do not look into the water rushing through the culvert." "Of course there is!" Mother said vigorously. She was teaching steadily at Wells College during these years, fresh from the triumph of her eleventh novel, *The Body of a Young Man* (1960), nominated for the National Book Award.

Her teaching included courses in the novel, as well as in creative writing. The notebook for *If a Lion Could Talk,* unlike Mother's earlier notebooks, quotes passages from one novelist after another whom Mother admired—Virginia Woolf, Henry James, Iris Murdoch, and others. The quotations are rarely for information she might need to depict the period, but instead are examples of how she might render a scene, portray a character's mood, or prepare for a flashback in a character's mind. How she could omit details of a character's getting from one place to another. How she could fuse memory with an immediate moment.

Mother makes notes about what Harriet Ryegate might be thinking as she looks out a window. Then she breaks off to quote from Woolf's *Jacob's Room,* prefacing the quote with "This way!":

> *A step or two beyond the window there was nothing at all except the enclosing buildings, chimneys upright, roofs horizontal; too much brick and building for a May night. And then before one's eyes would come the bare hills of Turkey—sharp lines, dry earth, colored flowers, and colours on the shoulders of the women, standing naked-legged in the stream to beat linen on the stones. The stream made loops of water round their ankles.*

Following this quote, Mother writes a trial passage for the novel in her notebook: "Looking out the window at the Dinwiddies' and the _____ and then seeing instead the pale grass on the rimrock and the crossed sticks at the top of the teepees. But the light was so different." Several incomplete passages in Mother's notebook put Harriet at the window of her Woollett, Massachusetts, home, looking down into the substantial houses of the street and seeing the Dinwiddie house. In the novel there are several scenes in which Harriet looks down from her window and imagines what Miss Dinwiddie must be thinking.

The novel's use of Virginia Woolf's technique—letting the mind of a character shift to a wholly different scene—is used extensively in part I, "The Return." Again and again, Harriet Ryegate makes the shift from where she sits or stands in her Massachusetts home to a moment she remembers in the fort. The shift is usually triggered by a color in front of Harriet or by a light in the room that lets her return to the Wilderness experience. She searches the recalled moments to understand them.

Throughout the notebook Mother defines the two separate ways that Mark and Harriet think of the Wilderness: Mark must change it, bring civilization to it; Harriet can observe it, even absorb it at times. Mother turns to a passage from Iris Murdoch to describe Harriet's response to the Wilderness:

> This is what I want to say about Harriet that doesn't happen to Mark—but how well Iris Murdoch does it: "There was also elsewhere, at what was by no means the lowest level; tho it was certainly the least articulate a consciousness of his surroundings, a participation, an extension of himself into nature."

One compelling scene in part 2, "Easter Sunday," relies on only a remembered description Harriet had heard at the fort in part 1:

> She went to the piano, playing chords, a little aimlessly. If she were at the Fort, would Mrs. Phillips be back by now? There must still be snow, but only in patches; most of the river would be running free again, wouldn't it? Along the bank where the sun was warm there would be clumps of those willows, leafless, but their bark would be gold colored. She dropped her hands in her lap. Why did she think of bright yellow willows against the riverbank? She had never seen them, only dry-leaved in the fall; yet she saw them now as clear as clear. (121)

Harriet is able to think of the bright yellow of the willows along the prairie riverbank because fifty pages earlier in the novel she had recorded in her journal this comment by the French-Indian interpreter, Pierre:

> I met Pierre as I was going to our room and he stood still and looked at me. "Madame," he said, "your hair is the color of them willows that grow along the riverbank. In the spring before they got any leaves on 'em the bark get like gold." I think he fancies himself a French gallant, but I don't see any of it in his treatment of his Indian wife! (73)

Harriet had just been baptized in the river and had unpinned her hair to let it dry. Her journal records that it was one of her few serene moments at the fort. Writing this I remember how Mother exclaimed one spring at the color of the bare willow bark as we walked together along the Missouri River at Beaverbank.

Mother quotes Emerson at length in the notebook as if she were looking for thoughts relevant to Mark Ryegate's attitude to Wilderness. In the opening pages of the novel, when Mark Ryegate sits alone in his dark study, the reader knows only that Mark and Harriet have returned to their house in Woollett, Massachusetts, with a sense of failure. Harriet has wearily gone to her bed and dreamed of herself in a nightmare at a fort where there are Indians. Before her troubled sleep she had stood on the front steps waiting for her husband to climb in a window. She had wondered what her neighbors would think and what the church would think about their returning so soon from the Wilderness in the middle of the night. As Mark broods in his study, the reader learns that he had gone as a missionary to the Wilderness. Mark finds a "scrap of paper folded under the inkwell—some quotation or idea he had scribbled down." The quotation is from Emerson: " 'What I must do is all that concerns me, not what the people think.' Emerson, of course. Emerson had said so many things he had taken unto himself." Mark continues to think how he came to take up with a missionary calling. He concludes in bitterness that "he had felt a powerful urge to go to the Wilderness, to preach to ignorant heathen who had never heard the Word. He had felt called of God. Or had he put it that way to himself? He was sick of questioning" (9).

The historian Bernard De Voto's important book, *Across the Wide Missouri,* informs Mother's knowledge of the period at several points. But one of De Voto's interpretations of Father De Smet, for many years a missionary with the Flathead and other Indian tribes in western Montana, has her thinking in terms of a direction she will take in her writing. In her notebook, she paraphrases De Voto, first saying:

> *De Voto has already said it but I can dramatize it—De Smet did not ask much of the Flathead except that they should assign his supernatural a more powerful medicine*

than their own & beyond that he liked them. The last
counted most: no Protestant missionary had ever tried lik-
ing his Indians.

The novel's early scene of Mark in his study does dramatize De
Voto's interpretation. Mark, remembering how ineffectual his attempts with the Blackfeet had been, hears again Pierre's remarks
about the Black Robe (the Catholic priest) who had visited the fort:

> *He thought of their departure. He had been as glad to*
> *leave the Fort as he had been eager to arrive there. The sa-*
> *lute from the cannon as they left belched in his ears with*
> *wry derision. He could never forget Aapaaki running*
> *along the shore as they pushed off, or the handful of Indi-*
> *ans who laughed and pointed at her. Even Mrs. Phillips*
> *laughed. Harriet kept her face turned away toward the*
> *other shore, he remembered. When the Black Robe left,*
> *Pierre had told him, the Indians, a hundred or more, fol-*
> *lowed him for three miles to get a last glimpse, and he had*
> *to stop and give them his blessing again.*
>
> *"He loved 'em like they were his children," Pierre had*
> *told him.*
>
> *When Marcus Ryegate left, he was followed by a single*
> *woman, an adulterous outcast with a cut nose. He had*
> *been relieved when she stood still; then he saw she was*
> *crying, and he had to wave to her. (20–21)*

But the failure Mark had felt most sharply was his inability to
speak with Eenisskim, who is Mrs. Phillips, the beautiful Indian
wife of the head of the fort. Mark knew that she understood English, was told that she spoke the language, but she would not do so
with Mark. In the midst of several entries in her notebook about
the thoughts that Harriet and Mark are separately struggling with
back in Massachusetts, Mother quotes unattributed: "He [Byron]
was a man who needed to think well of himself," and "so with
Mark. Effect on [Harriet] of feeling sorry for him."

Following these notes, Mother pauses to describe what she finds
to be the center of the novel: "This novel is about the inability to

communicate—the essence of that inability is symbolized in Ee-nisskim. She—it—comes between Mark and Harriet. The Wilderness for modern man IS isolation and non-communication." In the novel the Wilderness has affected Harriet and her husband, "two civilized persons who are accustomed to live in the world of words," Harriet thinks. The Ryegates had fled from the Wilderness as they encountered it in the Far West; Mark had fled from his sense of failure at not being able to convert the Blackfeet to Christianity. Once they have returned, Harriet has seen herself as an accomplice because Mark used her being with child as an excuse to leave the task he had set himself. But in the following days, Harriet becomes increasingly conscious of what the Baptist congregation thinks of their return and of how she finds it difficult to listen to the stiff pontificating of Mark's sermons and his lectures on the Wilderness. She worries about his obsession with his failure. All this happens in part 1, "The Return."

In this uneasy atmosphere, part 2, "Easter Sunday," begins. Mark Ryegate does not give the traditional Easter Sunday sermon on the women watching at the tomb and observing the risen Christ. Instead, he tells the waiting congregation:

> I decided . . . to try to come to a deeper realization of the joy of the resurrection of Christ by telling you of the abysmal darkness of death without it, as I witnessed this tragedy in the life of a human being. I am going to tell you of the death of a mother's son that took place not far off and long ago in Jerusalem, but last year in the Wilderness of our own country. (133)

Harriet, listening from her pew in the crowded church, wonders why Mark does this on Easter Sunday. "People didn't want to hear about an Indian woman and her son; they were tired of his talking about the Wilderness. Maybe she was, too."

Mark tells of his desire to comfort Eenisskim, the Major's Indian wife, when her son has drowned in the Missouri River, "in the treacherous river that connects that Wilderness world with civilization." Eenisskim had gone to a remote distance from the fort to grieve her son's loss by herself, but Mark describes his effort to console her by following her there. To Harriet's dismay his description of staying three days and two nights by Eenisskim's side is detailed and torturous. He continues, detailing how he crouched helplessly beside a woman who has disfigured herself, covered herself with river mud, who wails and moans unintelligibly; he speaks of his growing revulsion for her, then his pity, and finally:

> "[A] miracle happened" Mark said in a hushed voice, his eyes alight in his pale face. "I loved that wretched, dirty, sorrowing human being beside me. My repulsion and horror dropped away. I went to her, and put my arm around her, and called her by her Indian name. I understood, as never before, something of the love with which God must view our blind, suffering, grotesque humanity. I told her that God so loved her that He let his son be tortured and killed that her little son might live. . . . I felt that the love God had poured into my heart must reach her, but she was too lost in the depths of her pagan despair. . . . She didn't hear me. My words, the pressure of my arm around her, my eyes on hers never spoke to her."

Harriet has been listening intently but has also been aware of the church doors slamming as people in the congregation begin to leave. "Why hadn't he KNOWN the congregation would be shocked?" And when they discuss this at dinner, Harriet makes clear how she felt about Mark's confession to the congregation: "That was the trouble, Mark. They only saw you with Eenisskim—with your arm around her—and they were shocked." Mark replies that he doesn't care if the deacons ask him to resign.

An italicized conversation follows between two women of the congregation commenting on what the Reverend has said: "An insult and a disgrace to Christian people, that's what it was!" Early in her notebook Mother had written to herself that the congregation should be a kind of Greek chorus that spoke among themselves about the Ryegates, both the husband and the wife. And these comments become italicized sections in all three of the first parts of the novel. The device is also used for the opinions of the Church Sexton in part 3 who tells of seeing Mark praying by himself in the empty church and in part 4 by the reporter at the wedding, amazed by the spectacle of Eenisskim, and by the night clerk whose observations about the Ryegates end the novel.

Another use of italics toward the end of part 3, "The Wilderness," strikes hard as a painful illustration of the difficulty Mark and Harriet have in communicating with each other. Before, the italicized sections of a chapter have each time presented outside commentary on the Ryegates. This time the Ryegates are speaking to each other—from a distance—at dinner and about his leaving to speak for the Abolitionist movement:

> *"I quite understand your going out to Kansas, Mark."*
>
> *"I was afraid you would feel it was foolhardy. But it's the place where the issue of the freedom of the human soul is being fought out."*
>
> *"If you're working for the movement, of course, you want to be in the thick of it. I was interested, by the way, in a remark of Wendell Phillips's that I saw you had underlined in that article you left on the study table. 'If we never free a slave, we have at least freed ourselves in our effort'—wasn't that it?" (201)*

Mark objects to Harriet's taking the sentence out of context and quotes Phillip's whole passage, which ends, "to consecrate life to something worth living for!" Harriet retorts:

> *"You committed it to memory! I had thought your life was consecrated."*
>
> *"They need men out there desperately. . . . I feel I should go. . . . You must write me, Harriet!"*
>
> *"My letters will make such interesting reading: Marcia has gained. I believe her eyes are going to resemble yours. It has been warm today. Oh, yes, I trust that you are meeting with success in your chosen field."*
>
> *"I am concerned about your being alone so much, Harriet. I realize what I am asking. . . ."*

> *"So much so that you* volunteered *to go off to Kansas,
> but, of course, it's the next thing to the Wilderness you
> could find."*
>
> *"There is no need to worry about me. I shall keep
> busy. . . . If you'll excuse me, Harriet, I must look over my
> sermon for this evening." (201–02)*

The irony of communication—when it works and when it
doesn't—is set up early in the novel. And the lack of it between the
Ryegates becomes the real wilderness to Harriet. In the notebook
Mother writes: "They learn to speak a language of insincerity. Both
of them marvel at the ease & naturalness with which it comes to
their lips, yet they don't speak of it to each other." In the novel Harriet thinks these same words. But when she erupts and tells him all
her bitter thoughts about his having become obsessed, "be-
witched" by Eenisskim, Mark is not treated to a conversation between them. He says, "Harriet, when all the faith and understanding between two people have gone, there is no use trying to talk
with each other. They live in a wilderness of their own making. For
us the wilderness has shrunk to the space of this house—even
smaller than that, to ourselves" (209). For herself, early in the
notebook, Mother had written: "Novel should be centered on
woman trying to understand her husband (and so all women)."

In its announcement for *If a Lion Could Talk,* placed in the September 1970 *New York Times Book Review,* Harcourt Brace Jovanovich included A. B. Guthrie Jr.'s assessment of the direction of this
novel:

> *In* If a Lion Could Talk, Mildred Walker *after ten years
> of silence has come out with a novel that surpasses her
> others—which is no small thing to say of an author so
> skillful. With subtlety, with quiet and persuasive force,
> she has tackled an old but ever-abiding problem, one al-
> most too formidable for anything other than expository
> laments, and has brought it into the clear, where we feel it
> acutely and, feeling, wonder where are the answers.*

Mother's entries in the writing notebook consistently stress that dramatizing this "old but ever-abiding problem" is what she had wanted to do with the novel. Her two epigraphs for the novel, one of which provides the title, speak to the difficulty of communicating. The completed sentence from Ludwig Wittgenstein is the first quotation: "If a lion could talk, we could not understand him." And the second quotation describes the same concern, as expressed by Ralph Waldo Emerson: "In silence we must wrap much of our life, because it is too fine for speech, because also we cannot explain it to others, and because somewhat we cannot yet understand." Mother takes note of the problem of understanding in another respect, this time in her notebook when she quotes Proverbs 20:24: "Man's goings are of the Lord; how can a man then understand his own way?" The inadequacy of Mark's religion during his crisis is insisted upon throughout the novel.

The opening page of the writing notebook differs from that of all the other notebooks. It demonstrates that Mother had already thought through the sequence of the novel's parts before she began her entries. The first page reads as follows:

> Let the attitude of the world come in all through the novel in the voices of the church.
>
> Begin with their comments on Rev. Ryegate's going— then Mrs. Ryegate's.
>
> Then the return.
>
> Then the Easter Service.
>
> Seeing in his [Mark's] going to marry the Indian woman [to Major Phillips] the justification of his mission.
>
> Ironically he admits his failure. Like Strether he made her [the Indian woman, Eenisskim] into a part of his vision.

Again, unlike the earlier notebooks, there are many quotations from writers whose novels or studies speak to how Mother wants to portray a character or scene. She seems to be having a one-way dialogue with them, eagerly aware of techniques that will fit her purpose. Three-fourths of the way through the notebook, as she jots down possible dramatizations of events or attitudes between the Ryegates, she exclaims to herself: "Not going to think whether this speaks to anyone else—just going to lose myself in it."

Mother's exclamation suggests her excitement about the writing of this novel and her change of pace from that of the earlier novels. Both *If a Lion Could Talk* and *The Body of a Young Man,* her last two novels, were written while she was teaching the novels of writers whose techniques and complexities she admired. Her notebooks record new ways in which she wanted to write. She sped up the pace of events in these two novels. Eight of her earlier ten novels are divided into books or parts, and they renumber the chapters in each division, having the effect of coming to full stops. The two exceptions are *Unless the Wind Turns,* her fifth novel, covering rapid events in three days, and *The Southwest Corner,* her eighth novel, covering the spring, summer, and winter of one year. *The Body of a Young Man,* occurring in one summer, consists of consecutively numbered chapters without a separation into parts or books. *If a Lion Could Talk,* taking place in about one year, also has consecutively numbered chapters, although it is divided into four parts. This structural decision has the effect of a kind of enjambment, intensifying the occurrence of events and building toward the increasing tension between the principal characters.

In his introduction to the 1995 University of Nebraska Press edition of the novel, James Welch writes:

> Mildred Walker has chosen to tell this story of the young minister and his wife in an interesting style of flashbacks, letters, and diary entries, as well as straightforward narrative. The combination of such literary techniques is risky and can often lead to confusion, flatness, and unevenness in pace and tone. But Walker has given us a story that needed to be told about this period of clashing cultures and those individuals who are attracted to and repulsed by a people unlike themselves. And she writes in a consistently brilliant style, as only an author in control of her material can. (viii)

I would think Mother might have felt released from her chagrin over reviews she had considered unfavorable about her writing over the years if she could have read Welch's estimate. Her notes for this last novel show her confidence in gaining control of her material. Welch goes on to say, "In a denouement that combines all her stylistic gifts, she brings together the wilderness and civilization in a startling, but inevitable, manner" (xii).

In the denouement Welch refers to, Mark Ryegate is forced to acknowledge the powerlessness of his eloquence. His self-recognition overwhelms him more than the physical injury to his throat at the hands of the Missouri anti-abolitionists that renders him voiceless. He had been certain that his oratory for a just cause would prevail. As he stumbles down a dark road in the last chapter of the novel, defeated again, he thinks "[w]hat a posturing, yapping, humorless fool he had been, lost in the forest of his own trite verbiage. Trying to ape the great, sonorous phrases and images of the Bible."

A few years after the novel's publication, Mother told me how important her father's belief in his own eloquence had been and how aware of his conviction she had become as she grew up. "Why, he was convinced he could bring any man to see reason, settle any acrimonious dispute!" she said, shaking her head. But her admiration for the sermons he wrote to deliver each Sunday to a Baptist congregation stayed with her all her life. After her father's death in 1939, she saved the sermons in an old leather trunk that she kept with her wherever she lived. The sermons were in ink, handwritten in a flourishing script on thick white paper. When she lived in retirement in Grafton, I often saw one of these sermons open on her desk. "After he had written one," she told me, "he folded the sheets in a third and left it on his desk while he preached. He never needed to refer to it again." All of the sermons kept in the trunk were folded in exact thirds and dated. "You should read them sometime. They're very beautifully and powerfully written," she advised me. And then there was Mother's disclosure, as if talking to herself, that, yes, she had had her father in mind when she conceived the character of the minister Mark Ryegate. "Of course," she confided wryly, "I couldn't have him live in Vermont and I couldn't use Baptist."

Mother's mother was named Harriet, as is the heroine, but she was not the prototype for the wife in *If a Lion Could Talk*. It was a commonly used nineteen-century New England name for a woman, and Harriet Ryegate is given a complicated character that I think Mother never attributed to her own mother. But Harriet Ryegate's complexities were given short shrift in the early 1990s by two women consulting with Mother on writing a script for *If a Lion Could Talk*. They justified their story line to Mother by explaining that they saw Harriet Ryegate as a kind of cold, witchy New England woman, detrimental to her husband's state of mind; Mark Ryegate was the novel's protagonist, they insisted. Mother was adamantly opposed to their interpretation of the novel. "Can't they see that Harriet is as troubled and confused as Mark is by what happens to them, that she searches their predicament even more deeply than he does?" Fortunately for Mother, the prospective playwrights dropped the project.

In this novel's writing notebook Mother tries a passage that does not become Harriet's in the novel. Harriet is writing in a journal kept while she is living at the fort:

> *I've been happy in a strange way today. I wandered out all by myself. The day made it impossible to be afraid—or danger itself was golden. It was the first day since Mark came into my life that I didn't think of him all day. It was a relief not to be occupied with loving. Wood of the cottonwood tree where roots can always find water.*

This passage is followed by Mother's comment to herself: "Dammit—this novel is so good—things I know & can't use." Why can't she "use" them? I think it is because her intention in the writing of this novel is to move rapidly from one perilous thought to another that threatens Harriet's love for her husband. Things she "knows"—like how a cottonwood can be nourished—are not explored as metaphor; they are instead absorbed and in this way charge a character's intensity and daring of feeling. The psychological pace of her characters' lives had become Mother's tenet for her eleventh (*The Body of a Young Man*) and twelfth (*If a Lion Could Talk*) novels.

Mother had begun this last adult novel during her teaching years but finished it for publication in September 1970, the first two years of her retirement. Living in her old family home in Grafton, Vermont, she was put in touch with the well-known portrait photographer Clara E. Sipprell, who lived and had her studio in nearby Manchester, Vermont. Clara Sipprell took the photograph of Mother for the dust jacket of the Harcourt edition of *If a Lion Could Talk.* Another of Sipprell's photographs of Mother was used in the *New York Times* advertisement announcing the novel's publication. Both photographs, the latter which shows her wearing an open jacket, looking just off from the camera with a quizzical smile, and the former which also shows her wearing a sweater, leaning on her right elbow with her arm raised to the back of her head and looking down to her left with a slight smile. This second photograph is a favorite in my family because it shows her as we knew her when we had become adults. The few times that I happened to look at the photographs with her, Mother did not object to them as she had always done to other shots, but I thought she saw something of herself that she hadn't expected to be revealed.

Clara Sipprell became a close friend of Mother's in the following years. She borrowed a large three-paneled silk screen that Mother had had made during her Fulbright teaching fellowship in Kyoto, Japan, in 1962. Clara liked to use the screen as a backdrop for her indoor portraits. Whenever Mother spoke of Clara, it was with affection and admiration. Mother was proud of owning an autographed copy of Clara's photographic collection, *Moments of Light,* published by the John Day Company in 1966. The inscription to Mother is dated 1969, the year she took Mother's portrait for the new novel.

Among Mother's material and notes for *If a Lion Could Talk* is a tattered reprint of *Journal of Peter Koch, 1869–1870,* published in January 1929 in *Frontier, a Magazine of the Northwest* at the State University of Montana, Missoula. I am intrigued by the coincidence that Mother's last Montana-based novel is published in 1970, one hundred years after the journal kept at a Montana fort. But it is more than coincidence that she turned to mid-nineteenth-century Montana to explore the wilderness that came to exist in Mark and Harriet Ryegates' souls.

I know that Mother didn't think this novel would be her last major publication. But after its publication, she felt she had defined a part of the importance of Montana for her life and for her children's lives. Her dedication was "For Æquanimitas and the Tupa Tribe," referring both to the mountain goat head my father had mounted on our cabin wall above the door in 1937 to ensure a prevailing spirit of equanimity in the cabin, and to *tupa*, the Finnish word for a one-roomed cabin. By 1970, we had become what she chose to call a "tribe"—two sons and their wives, a daughter and her husband, and six grandchildren, with four more to come, all of whom returned regularly to the cabin. I think that my brothers and I were amazed to be included in her writing world by this dedication; I certainly was. And for the first time she had given us each our own copy of a novel, each copy inscribed. Mine is addressed to my husband, David Hansen, and me, "who entered into all my travail and had faith in the idea and me—all these ten years it's been in the making. With the hope that some wind in the Balm of Gilead trees and fragrance of the sage in the sun gets into these pages, beyond the words." Now, thirty-some years later, when I stand on the porch of the tupa and look into the Balm of Gilead trees (the regional name for the Black Poplar tree), I realize how much her twenty-two years of living in Montana had stayed with Mother, "beyond the words."

9
Teaching Years, Aurora, New York, 1955–1968

B arely two months after selling her home in Montana and moving east, Mother was settled in Aurora, New York, to begin her teaching career at Wells College. She had rented a small furnished house from a retired professor where she felt comfortable. And she began a new journal unlike those she had kept before. Her journal entry for October 6, 1955, reads:

> *To let desolation sweep up & fill you—not to hold back and try to save yourself; to stay open to life. There is a little strength this way, none the other way. To let myself cry out—Ferd—oh Ferd—*
>
> *Isn't this really what I craved—work to do and words and matter to think on? Why has my mind become so stolid when I read poetry?*

Two weeks later on October 18, she writes about her teaching: "I didn't do well today, trying to lay open the loveliness of the Ode to a Nightingale—dull, heavy literal mind. And I should be able to, who knows how joy and pain are ever mixed." Four days later she describes a dissatisfaction with her work that seems to overwhelm her: "The trouble with my writing, my teaching—me, is that I am not sound. I pretend to know—and here I am destined to go on doing just that. And where to start to begin to know. It is too late."

In the next days, Mother begins to write down passages from her reading for classes. Each seems important to her—Byron's *Don Juan*, Henry James's *The Ambassadors*, Thomas Mann's *A Weary Hour*. By November 12 at the end of an evening of reading, she turns to herself again:

Oh I must not fight loneliness nor try to fill an evening with something—I must take it in my stride—open the door to it, find it there in the house waiting for me when I come home—treat it as a friend. Perhaps there is a story in this. The only protection is busyness—a dog yapping & jumping and then the dog falls asleep. You look up and admit its presence. And the walls of the house and the roof make a place for you both to live in together.

A week later Mother records the first snowfall: "The first that Ferd has not seen—I tried to see it for him." She describes such a snowfall at Beaverbank, "so close that I had only to turn my eyes to the right to see it, but I didn't. I kept them straight ahead. And in the evening I had six guests for dinner—'tis the way."

This is how I remember Mother in the years to follow, teaching at Wells College. She grieved, she gained confidence in her teaching (often consulting David about characters and passages in novels), and she interspersed her quotations of the writers she was reading with questions to herself about a possible story subject. And always she entertained—in much the same ways she had done in Great Falls. I marveled, but I saw it as her reconstruction of a self, and a persona, that she could count on.

Back in Grafton, Vermont, in her old family home for the Christmas holiday of 1955, Mother has been reading Alfred Kazin's assessment of William Faulkner. She quotes several passages, then stops to comment on her own writing:

Years ago, in the summers here I determined to write and rushed off to the old swing in the barn loft or glued myself by my will to my room and "wrote." I don't know whether my motive was simply to be like Jo March in Little Women *or to do something to win some prominence or not. I hunted subjects so it wasn't that I had anything to say. Yet my urge has lasted all my life and I have written but not progressed very far. My books have not told "what people mean."—Can I now that I am alone as never before in my life—begin again?*

At first this journal seems intended to be a record of the progress of her feelings and discoveries of her teaching—not the kind of notebooks she had kept earlier. But by January 14, 1956, she questions herself about the "Congregational clergyman in Fort Peck, Montana," and concludes, "It is worthwhile as a theme I think." A week later, she records her sense that she will be able to write again: "I am excited for the first time in so long—a sense of life rises in me—the night is high and bright and cold. I can almost believe in my mind and think I shall write again. But differently—the essence—few details—Summer out of Winter. But I don't want to write about age." From this point on—the journal covers three years—Mother will use it as a writing notebook as well as a personal, often grieving, landscape.

Most of the early entries about her own writing concern what subject Mother might want to take on. This one occurs in April 1956:

> It is time for me to draw apart and contemplate my life though that is painful for I see how I hurried thru it and how my egoism got in the way. It is easier to contemplate life. To arrive at the old, old thoughts—of its brevity and constant change and beauty and terror. What should I write now that I want to write again? What have I to say that I never said before? Shall I write about—surely not love—I couldn't bear it.

In the next month she defines again what she wants: "I must have a short space of time—a quick sense of immediacy. It must begin with happiness and pass through suffering. What IS it I am trying to say? About a human relationship. Set it in a house—a professor's house?" In mid-May Mother goes to an Episcopal retreat with other women faculty for a few days. She writes about it extensively, aware that it is the first anniversary of my father's death:

> I have begun to feel my own mortality and to be able to imagine a time when I could leave the world in utter weariness with it—not screaming and holding on; once I couldn't have. I wish I could have understood this in time

> *to give Ferd more strength, not that he needed it, but he*
> *must have been so lonely. How brave he was and un-*
> *selfish! My stupidity & selfishness of thinking hurt me*
> *so—in a childlike way I feel my loneliness & sorrow now*
> *are penance. Ferd is saved this loneliness—the sense of*
> *the children's separateness, worry over them.*

I think Mother had no thought of how remote she seemed to her children in these years. She wanted always to have us understand how much she missed our father but seemed to have no interest in the ways that we missed him, too. Then, in conversation, she would change the subject to discuss the difficulty of teaching a particular poem or novel. David and I were both at Cornell University during Mother's first three years at Wells College—only thirty some miles away. Whenever she came to our apartment for dinner, she expressed her amazement that I could conduct a household she approved of. I was inordinately glad that she approved; before I married, I thought she would never approve of me. But I was always relieved when she had left because I felt more confident in my married and teaching world than I did sharing her world. If that caused the "separateness" that she felt, it could not be helped.

My brothers, both unmarried and living at some distance during those years, visited her at all the holidays. But her too often expressed "worry over them"—why they weren't doing or wearing this or that—was a cause of friction that possibly did distance them from her. Any disagreement with her view of what our lives should be caused her distress, but I think only momentarily. Mother demanded less from each of us, as to our personal lives, when she was writing steadily, I always thought.

By July 1956, she writes in her journal, "I believe I must write 'the burden' to get it out of my mind where it prevents anything else from growing." She mentions that I suggested writing it in terms of two writers. "I hadn't thought of that; like Joe and De Voto." She sets down a possible scenario. "Shall I do it thru wife's eyes? I think so." She concludes this section, "I won't publish it but I'll sharpen my claws on it." And she begins what she calls at first "the burden of friendship." It will become *The Body of a Young Man:*

She pinched off the dead blossoms of the scarlet Bird of Paradise so that her fear was hidden. The morning sun touched her cold hands briefly, not long enough to warm them. She knew just how Ben was sitting without looking at him because he had sat that way so much this year. He was staring at his hands, looking at them as though they were strange; not part of him. His face had that awful empty expression. His mind was beginning to change the color and texture of his skin. . . . She was always getting frightened and pretending that Ben was all right and chattering to him brightly, and it was no good; she didn't get to him. . . . It must all take place in one summer in Vermont. The tranquil greenness seems at first such a haven—then it becomes indifferent. Then the smallness and rigidity hold them there. A sort of colony & people coming up—good for Ben—but it wasn't.

The day after this entry, Mother questions whether at fifty-one she can live deeply within herself: "Walk around in my own mind and depend on no one? I try to write a 'talk' for Bread Loaf and it makes me aware of the shallowness of my own understanding of writing as an art. . . . It is pretentious for me to talk about the Writer's Life." A week later she paraphrases Elizabeth Drew about women writers: "Woman's problem always first of all her human environment. Wherever we find first-rate work among women novelists today—find it in a study of intimate personal problems. I suppose so—and of course, it is true of Woolf and Mansfield and Bowen and Cather, too."

A month later Mother is at the Bread Loaf Writers' Conference in Vermont as a lecturer. She writes in the journal, "The talk on characterization got across but why? because of that 'warm personality' or because of what it said? It was a great relief. 'Setting' not written yet. But I am glad to be here. This place is stimulating. . . . It puts the seal on my new mental life." Back in her Vermont home, the next entries occur sparsely for the time that she is returning to a new teaching year at Wells College. She notes that she has been recommended "to be associate professor—I doubt if I should be, but it is energizing." As she records her loss of Dad and her thoughts for the novel into December 1956, she seems more and more certain of continuing with the novel. After quoting from James's *Ambassadors,* she writes, "This is the kind of intensity I would like to concentrate in myself—'the long straight shaft sunk by a personal acuteness that life had seasoned to steel.'"

For New Year's Day 1957, she is in Grafton. She writes in her journal: "A second year without my darling—but for me to live—really live—is for Ferd to live, too. Then I must live with a different quality than I have been doing—and I shall bring a written work to completion." Later, back at Wells, she writes several pages for the novel. A last paragraph, after exchanges between her four characters, assesses her idea: "It would be merely dreary except that they are all 'fine people'—troubled by what seems beyond their ability to cope." By June 1957, with the summer before her, she sets down her resolve to "get back to a novel. Perhaps it will be the record of a failure—I promise myself nothing." A day later: "No title yet. A title would help." The day after that she writes, "Might do for a title. From *The Fall* by Camus—'I have learned to be satisfied with understanding. It is found more readily & besides it is not binding. Friendship is less simple.'—call it Less Simple."

Five days later, Mother walks up the hill from the village to Old Town Cemetery carrying her journal. She is where she had often sought refuge in her childhood: "Now there is the hoarse call of a crow. My back is against the old stone wall. Gnats crawl up my leg once in a while but the air is sweet, a little breeze stirs the maples. I can love the green again. I haven't written much but I don't feel that it's hopeless today. Shall I draw Josh & Olive from life?" Mother starts in. Josh and Olive have invited James (whom Mother first named Ben) and Phyllis to Vermont for the summer. The friendship between Josh and James, as seen by Phyllis, is at the heart of the novel:

> *Josh is bigger than James. He is impressive at once. His Boston intonation arrests attention. James is quicker witted—slighter—more nervous. Olive everything Phyllis admires. [Josh's] irritation with James for smoking. James is failure & uncertainty & age to him. There had always*

been a quality in them she could not touch—they didn't
seem to have to wonder & doubt & hear over again what
they had just said as she did. Was that what poise
meant?

When I described *The Body of a Young Man* in chapter 2 as being the
third of Mother's novels set in Vermont, I mentioned that I did not
find a writing notebook for this novel among her papers in the
American Heritage Archives. I see now that this is that notebook.
It must have seemed too personal an account for her to have included with her donated papers; her earlier notebooks had concentrated only on her writing.

Most of Mother's entries for the next month are quotations
from novelists whose comments interest her for her second summer of lecturing at Bread Loaf. But the quotations are interspersed
with possible scenes of the novel in progress and, often in this
summer, with the problems she finds in her approach to her own
writing. Early in August she writes:

> *The kingfisher fishing from the elm outside the window*
> *distracts me. Let me write it down because I can never*
> *seem to remember: intransigent, uncompromising, irrec-*
> *oncilable. Pride has been and is the controlling factor in*
> *my life—not even wholly conquered by Ferd's love. I see it*
> *with loathing. From here on—I can only beat it down. . . .*
> *Suppose I give Phyllis pride and let it complicate the sit-*
> *uation.*

A few pages later, she quotes a passage from Forester's *Aspects of the
Novel* describing Dostoevsky's characters: "Characters and situations always stand for more than themselves; infinity attends
them; . . . Every sentence he writes implies this extension and the
implication is the dominant aspect of his work." She relates this
analysis to her own work:

> *There is no implication of infinity in my novels—least of*
> *all in* Curlew's Cry. *But I think* Curlew's Cry *is a reflec-*
> *tion of my own limitations of soul. It showed that I feared*

for myself more than Ferd—feared loneliness & change.
Pamela cared only about herself. She had no vision & the
book had none. Do I have any now? In my new one—
what will the book mean when they find themselves not
equal to friendship? What if James realizes that no one
can help him and each of them sees him walking off by
himself feeling his personal failure?

At this point Mother may have felt close to the focus of her novel. She asks herself: Were the demands made by a friendship too much of a burden? Was Phyllis asking too much of James's long-time friends Josh and Lucy (formerly Olive)—that they help James recover from his guilt over his student's suicide?

Mother is still, however, concentrating on what new strengths her writing could have. A week later she records an evaluation of her writing sent to her by Helen Taylor, an editor with Viking who had also been a classmate of Mother's at Wells. Mother had saved the letter since receiving it in 1948, almost ten years earlier:

If you could sit down every day for six months & write
down what interested you, really, without any regard to
marketing it, you'd come closer to finding out what dissat-
isfies you about your output than anyone could tell you.
. . . You are not sweetness & light, by a long shot. You
have a quick, sardonic mind—you're quite capable of
looking at and examining closely the uglinesses of the
world. Yet you hardly ever touch upon the ugliness except
in terms of someone's sympathy, which is somehow false
and unrealistic. You are entirely capable of realism but it
never comes clear. . . . The other choice amounts to a
course in self-analysis, without which any serious writer
cannot do at least once or twice in his lifetime.

Mother replies to the letter in her journal: "Now that I've written this down maybe I can take it unto myself. I've had the interim of unproductivity which is the same as failure and I'm having the in-terim of self-analysis—but hard—forced on me." A second summer at Bread Loaf, Mother writes, "went well enough," and by September 8, 1957, she is back in Aurora. Her comments show that she is using the journal for her questions about the novel and the possible directions it could take while she writes the rough draft of the novel separately—as was her habit with her earlier novels.

Through the academic year of 1957–58, Mother's journal continues with quotes from the writers she is reading for her classes and scenes for her novel. She travels to Ann Arbor, Michigan, for a writers' conference in May 1958. In Ann Arbor she is able to meet with her writing professor from the 1930s, Roy Cowden. She has shown him a portion of her manuscript and talked with him about changes, and she writes in her journal, "I said there couldn't be much action in this book & he said—plenty of drama though."

In late June 1958, Mother and my brother Christopher started from Aurora to drive to Montana. They stopped in Minneapolis briefly to see my husband and me. Since we lived in a one-room apartment, they stayed at the Curtis Hotel and Mother recorded the moment in her journal: "Luxury to stay high up in the Curtis— full of thoughts of being there with Ferd, but not saddening ones; rather they spur me on."

We joined them for dinner at the Curtis Hotel, where Mother seemed in high spirits, regaling us with colorful stories of living in Aurora. My husband, David, was in the Ph.D. program at the university, and Mother asked him question after question about his interpretations of novels and poems that she would be teaching the following year. My brother and I were catching up on each others' lives: his work for his uncles in Detroit and my work at the university press in Minneapolis. When Mother turned her attention to us, she had more questions. It was familiar: she was perplexed by what we were accomplishing and why we were wearing what we were. We recognized that she saw us as her children needing guidance rather than as the adults we felt ourselves to be.

My brother left to drive back east, and I drove with Mother the rest of the way. She was exultant to be driving back through Montana: "Coming back to Montana was a greater joy than I ever dreamed it could be. . . . The sky, the prairie, emptiness of little villages—sage & meadowlark & kill deer—bareness—all these pushed back mental walls & released one's spirits." I went back to work in Minneapolis in the second week of July, Mother insisting that she wanted to live at the cabin for a month and get the novel finished. The focal point for her staying that month in Montana was the writers' conference she had agreed to attend in Missoula in late July.

Mother kept her journal each day as she had promised herself she would. She continued quoting from her reading, writing sections of conversation for the novel, and remembering moments at the cabin with Dad. She writes that she felt hampered by visits from old family friends but glad to see them. Twice she made trips to Great Falls, eighty miles away, to visit people there but was always grateful to get back to the cabin. At the Missoula conference she decided that she would not want to teach at the university ("too competitive and critical"). She describes her main interest in being there in her journal: "But I heard some good things and met Bernard Malamud whom I won't forget . . . with warm sad eyes & a smiling mouth. He wants to get into writing love of human beings. Made me feel I could get love into my novel." Leslie Fiedler also speaks at the conference, and Mother compares his conviction about writing to Malamud's: "Malamud believes negative reveals man but can't get over the wonder of man. . . . Fiedler believes literature should be comic—sees only future for novel in picaresque form." She comments in the journal, "But my novel can't be picaresque—can it have humor?"

On July 29 she is back at the cabin. She indicates that she is writing steadily in spite of interruptions: "I am thru breakfast & going to start in writing before anything happens or anyone comes. . . . I worked from breakfast time till two-thirty with fifteen minutes for lunch changing the first chapters so Josh's irritation (with James) doesn't come so soon." A week later Mother has apparently put down her manuscript to write in the journal: "Out here on the front steps in the sun I have a kind of happiness. I have been working on the novel and I find myself copying Ferd's gestures, the cigarette, the walk over to the stove to drop the match in, the cup of coffee, the meditative walk to the john. Easy to be close to him here." On the last page of the journal, her notes remember that she had sat on these same steps twenty years earlier, fearful of losing

Dad. The second sentence reads, "It must be a fundamental trait of some women & I mean to put it in Phyllis & let it be something Josh feels in her and attacks because it nibbles at his own security—but I must show it very subtly and slowly." She continues with a brief summary of each of her characters as they will appear in the finished novel.

Her final entry on the last few lines of the last page suggests that she feels she has arrived at a workable point during her summer stay back in Montana: "So ends this journal of three years. I miss Ferd no less but I have found ways to make life endurable—thru work & books and nature, like many another mortal." A month later in her first entry of a new journal, she describes herself at the beginning of a new academic year, her fourth, and hopes it will be "a much more mature and productive year than any of the others. At least, I have a novel really under way and MUST finish the rough draft by the new year; that should make it easier to write at the same time that I am teaching, should give my year a core."

Mother doesn't make that deadline for another eight months, but she is also making important decisions during these months. By October her journal shows that she is hoping to receive a Fulbright lecturer's grant to Japan for the following year. She hopes it will be "a door into a new kind of living. I am dissatisfied with what I am & the lack of serenity & beauty in the pattern of my life now." Her choice of Japan for a year was prompted by the invitation of a former Wells classmate, Mineo Takada. Mineo had attended Wells as a student from Japan, married a Japanese scholar of western philosophy, and at this time was a professor herself teaching at Doshisha College in Kyoto.

By December Mother is working out what the ending for her novel might be as she continues writing paragraphs of dialogue in her journal. "What do I want to show at the end?" and a few pages later: "Why is it I want to write this? As I put it down it seems to escape me. Is it anything? Because such a bitter, disillusioning experience must show people something." It is the last moments between the two women in the novel that Mother keeps working on in these trial paragraphs; the women are grateful the summer visit is ending, both thinking of the effect it has had on their husbands.

A few more paragraphs of dialogue and then Mother writes, "Let silence grow between them." A quotation from Virginia Woolf's *The Voyage Out* follows: "Helen & Rachel had become very silent. Having detected as she thought, a secret, & judging that Rachel meant to keep it from her, Mrs. Andrus respected it carefully; but from that cause, though unintentionally, a curious atmosphere of reserve grew between them." And Mother's response, "This is the way!" shows that she has again found a solution to a writing problem from her reading.

In February Mother notes, "Tomorrow I shall accept the Fulbright Grant to Japan and trust in God's strength not my own to be equal to it." And on her birthday, May 2, she writes: "I am lucky to have so different a new year to look forward to, but I feel older, more aware of the burden of flesh, less sure of my ability, but understanding a little better about the way one learns to accept life. . . . If I could only bring to Ferd my slightly deeper knowing! His went so very deep." I can see now, reading in the journals of 1955 to 1959, that Mother felt as if she had come through an ordeal with sufficient strength to recognize herself again. She has schooled herself to live with the pain of losing Dad, she has learned to teach successfully, and after five years, she is completing a novel. I think my brothers and I were awed by an air of renewed confidence that we felt in her. She only announced her decision to spend the following year in Japan to us in late spring of 1959.

A journal entry that summer while she is vacationing in Vermont states that she is "stuck at the moment—at p. 231. Both my women sound alike. Maybe the viewpoint is the trouble." At the same time she is thinking about the lectures she will give in Japan. She studies a commentary on the painter Morris Graves, who embraced Zen Buddhism and evoked the Oriental. Three full pages of quotes follow. Then she turns to Chase on the American Novel and a discussion of the significance of a tragedy caused by resistance to an offering of help. She writes:

> *In a way, tho' I had not thought of it before, my story parallels the experience of America in trying to give generously to troubled countries only to find that they cannot*

give what is really needed. But no one else would ever guess this parallel. Still—it makes for richer complexity of meaning in my sense of it.

In between more quotes from writers, Mother writes of her dissatisfaction with herself over the past year and concludes: "I would like to learn to listen to people talking to me and books and to the voice within me. I must find a different way of life." On August 9, she ends this part of the journal. She writes a last sentence with no accompanying comment: "Mark Twain's mother always warmed the water before she drowned kittens."

When Mother stopped writing in the large journal, she was preparing for the trip to Japan, and she began a smaller journal for her year there. It begins on September 18, 1959, the day her ship embarked. As she drove west with Christopher, she stopped two days in Minneapolis. She spoke apprehensively about the year to come and said quietly but urgently to me, "I don't know what my role should be." I felt at a loss to be helpful. It seemed a strange concern, but by then I dimly understood that she felt a role was essential if she was to triumph in a new situation.

Her new journal shows her willingness and eagerness to observe the people and customs of Japan. She enjoyed the days on the ship and was grateful for the introduction to the country received by the passengers on board who were Fulbright lecturers. She recorded the information in her journal extensively. Four days after sailing, she writes that she "was stupid in the Japanese class today" and, in the next breath, that she was "having trouble with the last chapters—not good to feel this at the end."

But by October 4, settled temporarily in the International House in Tokyo, Mother has finished the novel with some reservations:

I did make myself come to the end of the novel—only 200 pages. I managed to write 30 odd pages on the boat and that is better than I have done before for a long time. The end is not obvious but perhaps not clear. I don't know

now if Harcourt takes it how Meg and Roger will. I sup-
pose I will lose them forever. Yet I don't believe Ferd would
disapprove of the book.

In my earlier discussion of *The Body of a Young Man,* I was conjectur-
ing that the novel was autobiographical. And Mother's entries in
this journal confirm that: Josh and Lucy of the novel are based on
my parents' close friends Meg and Roger; James has my father's
ways; and Phyllis moves through her husband's crisis as my
mother did attempting to hold off my father's illness. That is one
explanation, too, of why the novel is dedicated simply "To F.R.S.,"
her husband.

In the next few days, traveling in Japan, Mother records her impressions of the people at work in the fields, villages devastated by
a typhoon, and her accommodations at a Japanese hotel in Yos-
hida: "At night a tatami is spread, covered with a futon. I have my
meals alone. The room opens onto a most beautiful garden. Everything invites meditation, rest, and work." She observes that having seen the home of her former college friend, Mineo Takada, she
will find it a difficult place for her to live "all year. . . . It seemed
cramped because of the terrible Western style furniture, dark
rooms." She completes these pages of October 9 entries with the
decision "to copy the ms. of the novel to send Mr. Cowden," and
continues with another possible scene for the novel:

> *Phyllis asks, "Is sorrow easier to bear one place than an-*
> *other, do you think, James?"*
> *"I'm thinking how the terrible things that happen*
> *never make a sound."*

Mother's observations of her surroundings and the Japanese
professors she meets, her preparations for lectures and her extensive quotations from English and American novels, fill the next
pages of the journal. On January 1, 1960, she writes:

> *Incredible! At midnight Mineo & Sabro [Mineo's hus-*
> *band] and I climbed a hundred high stone steps to a tem-*
> *ple where the priests were striking the great copper bell*

108 strokes. Where I had expected wild brazen clamor
only a merged & mellow sound, a single resonance in the
night. Stone lanterns gleamed out of the mist and dark-
ness, crowds moved in and out and past. No religious
sense—but a sense of epoch and time.

On the same page in the journal, Mother turns to a lecture she is preparing to give in Tokyo on Twentieth-Century Women Writers. She is working on her presentation of Willa Cather and quotes a George Kates on Cather's unfinished work: "Even if she surmised that her powers were failing, she may have wanted the companionship and solace of a piece of work in the making, as it always had been for her in the richer years of her own life. To work also was to pray." I think of Mother writing this down on the first day of 1960 in Kyoto and of how she could perhaps have remembered it twenty years later in Grafton. This characterization of Willa Cather's feeling for her writing, a writer Mother always admired, could describe Mother's persistence in her eighties in writing a novel she could not complete as she failed in health—"the solace of a piece of work in the making."

In Kyoto on January 8, 1960, Mother records the completion of her novel, and this time she gives the final title:

Sent off the ms. of my eleventh novel—only God's help got
me to the end of it. Maybe it works its theme too hard—
not subtle enough. Too much PROBLEM, *not enough life.*
Next one will be different. Sic semper! But it is a great lift
to have FINISHED *it—brought it to an end, after letting it*
lie so long in the drawer at home or here on the shelf. The
Body of a Young Man.

She continues to have more discoveries of Japan under the direction of the Takadas and to describe these in detail. And she has become observant of her students and their responses to her teaching. On March 30, enjoying a plane flight within the country, she writes in her journal, "Time now to think of new novel? No, better put my mind on Japan." At the end of the same day, however,

Mother proposes a plot for a novel that she will begin twenty years later.

In almost all the journal entries for April, Mother has kept her "mind on Japan." One entry late in April considers that knowing spring in a foreign land is to "love the essence of it rather than any provincial essence. The warmth of the sun—the tender green of tassels of the pines—the Ginko tree I saw shorn last fall fresh budded; the new freedom in people's movements—these things are spring." On her birthday, May 2, she begins by writing, "For once gratitude underlay my whole day." A week later she turns to her own writing:

> Have written very little this year and will regret it. The reason lies partly in having the novel around. A novel draws everything into itself. Mailed off the galleys today at high noon and shall not see it again until it is in book form, but for all the awkward places I think it is the best one I have written. I have a feeling that it "rings." I only hope it will seem to Meg and Roger to have gone beyond the personal. That I ever really got it written seems a miracle—to be correcting proof on my 55th birthday both lucky and I hope a "sign" for the future. But I must start a new one before I leave here.

Mother continues working on her Fulbright lectures to be given in May at academic centers around the country, and recording her impressions of street scenes and of the Japanese as a people: a Shinto funeral going on across the narrow street from her window; the constant gray weather as she accompanies the Takadas to museum exhibits and temple treasures; or "the artistic seriousness people bring to the smallest task like arranging a flower cart in the street." It is mid-May when she writes to herself, "Why is it the Japanese [who] are so aware of the relationships of green shapes in their gardens or of textures in their houses are so careless of the relationships between people?" Mother quotes extensively from the *Japan Times* about the present alarm of a communist takeover of Japan that would harm Japanese-American relations. By mid-June she notes her feeling that "time is moving almost too fast now" and that Wells College has already scheduled the Fulbright lecture for September 27.

By mid-July Mother is traveling by train on her last trip through Japan to take a ship to the United States. She writes, "Now the year seems so short." She is not sorry to be leaving in one moment but then sorry in the next. Her chief regret is for "what I have not learned or written or read." She travels by cargo boat and is "thankful" that she will have "time to savor the year & read & think." She records some of the reading she does and "gloats" in the days at sea ahead of her. On July 23 she remembers that it is her parents' anniversary: "Bless them. If it weren't for their spirit, energetic, active, invincible, I would never have gone to Japan."

At this point Mother's journal seems to cover her every thought, every apprehension, every hope. Suddenly she is writing on the cross-country train, traveling east from Los Angeles: "This luxury train offends me. . . . Japan grows on me as I get farther away." And to add to that feeling, she is reading and quoting from *The Ugly American*. In the journal, she barely notes the western landscape passing outside her roomette window, as she works on her Japanese lecture. She pauses to summarize the result of her year:

> *I don't mean to be dramatic & perhaps I am under the influence of a kind of nostalgia for Japan & the Ugly A., but I feel that something has happened in my life: the same things aren't going to matter. I'm more grateful than when I went away that I can live my life simply—quietly. I'm going to impose new standards of personal frugality out of taste. I think I have a new patience with unhappiness.*

I have followed Mother's thoughts so closely in these two journals—the first beginning in 1955 when she has begun her teaching, and the second kept during the academic year in Japan, 1958-59—because I have wanted to know how she willed herself to write again. As her entries show, especially at the time she sent off the printed galleys for *The Body of a Young Man*, she felt it was miraculous that she had accomplished it. But I sense, as well, that she felt it was an achievement she owed herself.

The novel's publication date is September 14, 1960, but Mother is so dismayed about the early reviews that she thinks of the book as "rejected." This is her journal entry for October 30, about two weeks later: "Haven't been able to write—mostly because of the rejection of the book on every hand. I hadn't expected that. What does it mean? For it has truth in it and life. So be it. I must take it and be patient and go on writing." Another mention of rejection occurs a week later: "Kennedy elected—but no change in the lake, nor the cold November air, yet an ominous sense of change in the weather. And Nixon—I know how he feels—little man that he is—rejected as THE BODY was. Have to take it, Mr. Nixon—nothing for it."

The *Library Journal* reviewer termed the novel "sensitive and well written but not compelling." The *Herald Tribune Book Review* concluded, "The writing is lean and polished but, mainly due to the nature of the plot, lacks the pace and glow of fictional persuasion." The *New York Times Book Review,* the review Mother always coveted, was perhaps the worst: "Her style seems pedestrian and her characters are too neatly tailored to their predicament—occasional dramatic impact." And in her disappointment, Mother probably dismissed this more favorable comment in the *New Yorker:* "The atmosphere is warm, tense, and sympathetic, and so is the writing." In spite of these reviews *The Body of a Young Man* was nominated for the National Book Award for 1960, but Mother makes no mention of that in her journal. Philip Roth's *Goodbye, Columbus* won the award for 1960.

Mother turns to writing a new novel, her twelfth, almost immediately. It is a subject she had already considered—the young missionary and his wife who return from the Wilderness to New England, defeated in their mission to Christianize the Blackfeet Indians and obsessed by the mystery of the beautiful Natawista. "The story of Natawista," she writes on December 12, 1960, "would say two things—that American men long for the wilderness but can never hold it. The little pretty woman with the soft hair & the violet eyes sat still in the one room of the railroad station. The wilderness came close. She realizes that she is having an experience most women did not have." Mother will work on this historical novel she calls "Stand Outside and Laugh" for the next ten years.

The journal ends as Mother is finishing the academic year of 1961. Each entry that describes her reading blue books soon expands to yet another possible scene for the new novel. Finally, the last pages are crammed with disparate quotations from writers and critics. No more mention is made of the novel just published nor of its critical reception.

Mother did not begin a new journal for two years. She took a winter sabbatical in a rented villa in Sicily during that time, but I have found no journal for those six months. I have a packet of letters she wrote from Sicily, usually when she was cold or uncomfortable or irritated about the small thefts the caretakers committed. Soon she would write again in triumph that she had contrived to have the items returned. She mentioned only briefly that she was working on "the Wilderness novel."

The next journal begins in October 1963, when Mother has returned to Aurora and moved into an apartment in the village fronting on Lake Cayuga. The journal entries are few until January 1964. On January 18 she writes:

> *The novel in its entirety sits here & I do not type & send it off. The role of the missionary seems . . . ? mawkish, unsophisticated, flat. I have been at lowest ebb about it today, and yet suddenly—the first time I have ever seen one, a deer came up from the lake across the lawn. A sign of the Wilderness? What else could it mean?*

By the end of February she writes:

> *Into my restlessness & frustration over the novel today comes a lift—a new patience and willingness to go on discovering my material . . . finding a way—meaning, seem more important than the relation to myself—M. Walker getting out a novel. May it last. I haven't really* LOOKED *at those scenes. Some of them are mere sketches of what I want. Why do I think I can just write it off? If only I can truly discover the way if I* AM *patient.*

Sometime in March, Mother must have sent the manuscript to Henry Volkening, her literary agent in New York. The last day in March she records the response in her journal:

> I got a letter from Volkening today telling me the novel is no good. I'm still stiff mentally from taking it in. What does it mean in terms of the future? Am I through? Pathetic to think I wasted all that time in Sicily on it. I haven't had anything turned down since Dr. N's Wife and Ferd gave me a sleeping tablet and I woke ashamed— and rewrote the novel, but I don't think I will this one. I'll let it go.

The next day she reiterates her feeling that she "has nothing ahead, nothing to look forward to." She thinks of how she must write back to Volkening, but she can't yet. "And there is nothing to say. Shall I give the novel up? Yes, no, yes, no—Yes!" Farther along in this day's entry, Mother exclaims about the lift she has from reading Iris Murdoch's *Severed Head* and calls it "such a brilliant novel":

> Ideas are generated so fast by this book of Iris Murdoch's I can hardly keep up with it—could I have the middle section of the novel in the present—some later incarnation of these two & reaction to past at the end? I can't leave S O & L. alone. It gets in my way when I'm working as no novel ever did. Suppose Mark gives up church & becomes Abolition speaker—living on sense of eloquence & power—thinking of free men in Wilderness—but asked to preach Easter sermon.

A page later, Mother outlines a new three-part structure for her novel. She seems to have accepted that she will rewrite the novel, and she intersperses passages from Lawrence's *St. Mawr* and from Ford Maddox Ford with her thinking about her novel: "Trouble with S O & L. (initials Mother uses for her working title, "Stand Outside and Laugh") is that I don't know what I'm saying—I need response of civilized to wildness," and later, "The wilderness of the heart is what I must write of, not the story of the West." As she ends her comments on this academic year at Wells, she includes several new paragraphs she might use for the rewritten novel.

Mother's summer of 1964, spent in the Vermont house, is recorded as a restorative time. She reads on the screened-in porch above the branch of the Saxtons River that runs below the house and comments on her pleasure in living there. Her reading, thoughts for the novel, and repairs to the house and garden are fully described. Her family, coming for visits and leaving, are barely mentioned. It is her encounters with people in the village or visits of house guests from college that are described in the most detail, sometimes prompting possible story ideas. One moment she quotes T. S. Eliot on "the progress of an artist" and the next describes the sight of a man in the field across the way: "Across the brook a man is cutting the thin hay; it is almost worthless and I feel that he hates cutting it just as I hate reworking the novel. Yet it has to be done if anything is to be salvaged and if a new crop can spring up." An idea for the novel is the last entry for the summer and one that will shape her sense of what she wants the novel to do. Mother told me later that the novel was about the lack of communication:

> *I never have seen clearly what my material said. Is it that the wild—larger than man—elemental forces laugh at man's puny effort to say something? But man must say something to one other person all the same? Howastena [the Indian woman] never speaks. Mary can never say to her mother how she hates Indian blood. Col. Phillips cannot say what holds him here. Honora learns to speak her love—and Mark.*

(The name of Howestena will later be changed to Eenisskim, and Honora to Harriet.)

Back in Aurora in September 1964, Mother writes of herself as the new academic year begins: "The year is started. Let it come then. Let me see what I can do; if I CAN hold to a routine and find the time for the extra writing better than last." A few days later, she quotes from a *New York Times* review of Saul Bellow's new novel.

She underlines a part of the following sentence: "[T]he book is structured with great subtlety, By The Whim of Mood & Memory." And continues quoting: "The other device is the letters, which crop up constantly by wholes and by fragments, & which are set in italic type." This account precipitates the following notes in the journal:

> *What about having Mark at time he has been asked to re-sign—sitting at desk deciding to go out of ministry. Or be-gin with his having had a nervous breakdown and church urging him to take a leave of absence—his countering with mission field. Honora looking at him and wonder-ing—not being able to understand why she isn't the an-swer. Do whole boat trip in Honora's journal.*

In the finished novel Mother does write the boat trip up the Missouri River in Honora's (Harriet's) journal and in italics. A month later she writes again about the needs she sees for the novel: "What a fool, what a fool I have been not to see that. I must have the beauty, seen in exact images, of the wilderness haunt & lure & confuse them both. . . . Could my way of giving larger meaning to lives of these two people be thru place? w symbol. Laughter." The "laughter" in the finished novel belongs to Eenisskim, the Blood Indian wife of Major Phillips. Harriet and Mark hear it as a mockery of their ways, especially in memory after they have returned to the East. Soon after the entry above, Mother writes that the novel will not be called "Stand Outside and Laugh." She does not explain, but it seems clear that the novel has changed direction for her. On the same pages of the journal, she quotes several passages from Lawrence's *Sons and Lovers,* interjecting, "And this to show my stupid mind how it's done." The passages describe how Paul Morel sees the fenlands and the sea beyond them in the wilds of Lincolnshire, "stark enough to rejoice his soul."

Well into February 1965, Mother continues to refer to Lawrence's descriptions of a character's response to the wildness surrounding him. Abruptly, and angrily, in the midst of her quotes she writes this passage about herself:

Sometimes my amazement & horror at the complacency
of my "literary" stance thru the loveliest years of my life
fill me. I didn't read—really read—Shakespeare. I never
read James or Lawrence or Joyce! & I was limited & smug
and my writing had truly only "warmth." The only im-
portant question is whether it is too late now. How much
I needed those novels for my own life! to share them with
Ferd—but I wonder if I could have read them then? At
least it is something along with the gray hair & the crepey
throat & the need for more sleep—all these things that I
loathe—to know that I understand a little more.

Mother's sudden outbursts of wrath at herself, when she spoke them aloud, always seemed to dissipate rapidly. Often that was bewildering for me.

On May 2, 1965, Mother turns sixty. She begins with a denial of any achievement—"I wonder that I've been let to live so long with such happiness when I've not written anything decent—really good—& failed in human relationships again & again." But in the next two paragraphs she veers with her usual dizzying speed to happiness: "Here I am at sixty where I was at twenty with the same heady sense of ecstatic suspense at life. The day of a piece with that other—the lake, the air, the bursting color in bud & tulip the same." She continues with a description of the birds she has seen outside her window, of the ducks "dipping in the lake as at Beaverbank," and concludes, "And I am reading *Mrs. Dalloway*—what more?"

The next entry finds her in Montana at the cabin in July. By then my husband, David Hansen, was teaching at Dartmouth College in New Hampshire, so I had driven from Vermont with her and my two young children. She notes that she is at the cabin "with Peg [my childhood name] and her children." Though Matthew and Melissa were her first grandchildren, she didn't always seem comfortable with their presence at the cabin. She writes:

I have a restless sense of waiting. I am learning a bit how
to be "the old doe"—wiser, sadder, more resigned. . . . I

have learned again that I am alone from here on out and must remember it. No need for self-pity—it is the human fate. . . . At last, I am growing up, perhaps. It has taken long enough, and it is not pleasant.

But I have a pleasant memory of Mother sitting up in her bunk wearing red flannel pajamas, holding Melissa in her red sleeper suit. They are both smiling sleepily. Melissa turned one year old in August, and Mother cut out a string of paper dolls to dance above the cabin door for the day. I know she and Melissa had some good hours together when Matthew and I were away horseback riding.

That was Mother's only entry for the summer. By mid-August she was back at the Curtis Hotel in Minneapolis on her way east:

It is a little relief to take up my life alone again—loneliness and all. The anxiety over [the children] is too soul and nerve wracking, since I really can do nothing to help. . . . Odd that after a summer of stalemate the urge to write begins once I am alone. This I can do. Ferd would know and understand my sense of lonely satisfaction or relief in picking up my own life again.

I had understood that my brothers and I, though grown and interested in what we were doing, would always be a burden or, perhaps, a source of unrest for Mother. But, sentimentally perhaps, I had thought she could take pleasure in our children. As the years went on, and she acquired ten grandchildren, she was a dutiful grandmother but seldom a captivated one.

By September 1965, Mother was back at Wells College, writing fairly regularly in the journal. The number of paragraphs mapping out the novel increase in early 1966, and by February Mother writes what will become the opening scene for the published novel. On February 13 she notes, "Father's birthday—and a great man—the Mark of my novel really." A page later in the journal she quotes from an introduction (unattributed) to Wallace Stevens's poetry and highlights: "One of the dilemmas of writing is the need to get the idea *written* and yet have the patience to wait to *see* it for what it is." Mother follows with the possibility this suggests to her: "Mark's secrecy and possessiveness about his vision. Harriet's silence about her fear. Could I parallel similar experiences in time?" The next passages she quotes are from Conrad's *Heart of Darkness.* "Reading *Heart of Darkness*—thinking all the time about my novel. This is the way to do the river." She quotes again: "And outside, the silent wilderness surrounding this cleared speck on the earth struck me as something great & invincible, like evil or truth, waiting patiently for the passing away of this fantastic invasion." She also quotes from a biography of Eva Le Gallienne in which the writer (unnamed) refers to Fenelon's *Oeuvres Spirituelles:* "He was ag[ainst] the danger of constant self-reproach, of over-scrupulous introspection."

By early May Mother writes her last entry for the academic year of 1965–66: "Suddenly I find myself anxious to stop teaching here. How amazing the way the desire is there! If there should not be very much time I don't want to use it here—doing less than well. Yet I am committed to the next year." Arriving in Grafton for the summer, she writes, "One could be very free if she could handle the solitude." The first month of the summer is spent preparing her lectures for the writers' conference in Colorado. As she finishes her preparation, she writes, "I shall not keep reworking, for Tues. at latest I am starting novel."

It is a year later, August 19, 1967, when Mother begins a new journal. It is a smaller notebook, what she terms "a proper notebook to help myself creep or crawl back in." She opens by writing, "Let me begin a journal again with this quotation from James's journal—notebook rather, and mine is too." And this notebook holds steadily to quotations about writing and new ideas for stories she might write until an entry on August 27 describing her feelings about returning to teach at Wells:

> *Tomorrow and for the last time I drive back to Aurora to*
> *begin a new term. On the way down I shall examine my*
> *feelings about it, testing out how I shall feel next year*

when I don't go. . . . . Foolish to make such a thing out of
last times as I just started to—why shouldn't the next ex-
perience be as absorbing?

The notebook continues as before with impersonal entries until October 30: "When life spread out all ahead I was so STUPID—why did I not want to share Donne with Father?—KNOW how Mother Schemm felt with all her sons married." This will be Mother's only reference to the recent events that had touched her life: In June, her younger son, Christopher, married; in October, her elder son, George, married. I was very happy for my brothers because they married wonderful women. Both weddings took place out west, and as Mother arrived for each, she expressed her misgivings for her sons to me. Even though I knew that mothers had been said to feel this way about their sons marrying, I was shocked to find her unwilling to share my brothers' happiness in beginning their new lives. Perhaps their happiness was one of the reasons she felt more alone than before.

By January 1, 1968, Mother records a good feeling about her life:

A wintry day—I talked with all the children and felt
"good" about them. In the afternoon I walked two miles
up Dublin Hill for the free joy of walking on a country
road in winter, turning often to rest and see the band of
sun lying on the lake. I felt exhilarated & stronger than I
have in ages.

For the rest of the academic year, she writes in the journal only about three times a month, again quoting passages from *Jacob's Room* and Leonard Woolf's *A Writer's Diary* as well as Kierkegaard, Jane Austen, and senior theses. She writes down possibilities for her novel and records her personal feelings. And on January 30 she allows herself to think of a year beyond teaching:

This day—a Sunday—I have left my curtains drawn to
suggest I wish solitude, as indeed I do. I shall plan in this
day the syllabus for my novel course—turning over books,
reading, thinking. And it is pleasant. But how much plea-

santer it would be to have the day free to write? Reading
when I needed to for inspiration. I can't believe the day
wouldn't be as rich.

Later she quotes Kierkegaard again, calling the long quote on serving God, "Kierkegaard and Mark." She continues quoting from Heidegger and Buber as well as Kierkegaard until about two weeks later she notes, "Suddenly ideas start coming."

In April, Lawrence's *St. Mawr* interests Mother again. She quotes a passage and then enters her comment: "I would be doing something like L. does in *St. Mawr*—but isn't it that Harriet will help Mark find the life he denied in the Wilderness? No time to think about it now, but later—later in the 'generous patient mornings.'" She sketches another novel possibility, then quotes from Langer's *Feeling and Form* about memory as "the great organizer of consciousness" and "the real maker of history." The last entry in the notebook for the academic year of 1967–68 touches also on history—this time from Sir Philip Sydney:

> *For an historiographer discourseth of affairs orderly as*
> *they were done accounting as well as the times as the ac-*
> *tions, but a poet* thrusteth into the midst, *even where it*
> *most concerneth him, and there recoursing to the things*
> *forepaste & divining of things to come, maketh a pleasing*
> *analysis of all.*

Mother has underlined "thrusteth into the midst," a device she has written about before for restructuring her historical novel. These last entries for the academic year seem directed ahead to a time in which she will have more time to write. She expresses no regrets in her journal about her departure from Wells College or about ending her thirteen years of teaching.

10
Back in Grafton, Vermont, 1968–1986

I n Mother's first summer of retirement, living in the Grafton house where she had first begun writing, family descended on her. George and his wife, Janet, who was soon to give birth to their first child, were on their way to make a new home in Philadelphia; my father's brother and his wife came from Detroit; Mother's sister and her husband came from their retirement in Bradenton, Florida, to stay two months; and my two young children and I had come east for a month to help Mother with her move from Aurora back to Grafton. Such times of having a full household would happen to her often in the years ahead.

This first summer of 1968, though, Mother seemed to have accepted all of us as a moment in transition. Her first journal entry is for August 3, 1968, and it notes that all of us have left or are leaving soon:

> Now I shall begin to make my own life here—on this summer day of Sunday afternoon stillness. . . . For me one day can follow the next—no school to brace myself for—no other residences to move to & take on a different role. What will give my life form and meaning? What routine shall I impose? The routine of light & dark and changing seasons is one. . . . Sitting at my desk writing shall be the major fact of my existence no matter what the result. I've got to go deeper. I've lived largely at surface level this summer.

In the next weeks there are more visitors. She describes them briefly, noting that she has "a craving to be at work." In describing these moments, she questions her tendency "to ward off" friendships and adds, "It is no good to be afraid of entanglements. Because I relaxed ever so little in my stiffness, it meant something to me. . . . I can LIVE only if I reach down into a deeper level of relationship. It is my timidity that cheats me."

Mother's entries begin again in October, following the familiar pattern of quoting passages from her reading and proposing story ideas to herself. She has been reading Kay Boyle and seems brought up short by this passage she quotes in her journal: "I began again trying by writing to transform the image of what I knew I had become, but so flagrant the failure that I did not have the will to put a stamp on it & send it off for those I believed in to hold up to the light." Mother responds: "So applicable—I have become lazy, uncertain—dull and whether I can transform my image I honestly don't know. It will be only by steady, persistent sitting at this desk as the weather changes and writing. I don't believe I dare even wait for 'the splendid idea.'" After three more journal pages of penciled two- and three-line story ideas, on November 3 Mother writes:

> *Almost futile to copy down quotations, and perhaps I shall cut this out and glue it to the center cupboard of my desk. It is from the* Diary of a Country Priest *by Georges Bernanos: "To doubt oneself is not to be humble. I even think that sometimes it is the most hysterical form of pride, a pride almost delirious, a kind of jealous ferocity which makes an unhappy man twist and read himself. That must be the real truth of hell."*

Mother then writes in pencil, which has its own kind of ferocity:

> *Two things I swear I will do—I will reread all the novels I have written—whether I suffer or not. And I shall start out to write my own biography until I find something I want to write about. There is something I am not facing. And to hell with Henry [Volkening] and his LITTLE faith in me and short stories.*

By mid-November Mother refers to starting on her self-analysis, recommended by Helen Taylor twenty years earlier, but she doesn't say what form it takes. "It's not pretty," she writes. "I have always been an egoist—self-centered. My inability to be selfless with other people may have made it impossible to be selfless with writing—to care more about it than my own indolent comfort of mind as well as body."

The pages that follow are taken up with long quotes: from a review of a biography of Edward Hopper and from an essay on a novel by Elizabeth Hardwick. Mother underlines a number of statements with which she agrees. In the midst of these quotes she makes this entry on November 21: "As I look at this journal Mark and Harriet [the main characters in what becomes *If a Lion Could Talk*] are still all thru it so there is no earthly use not writing the novel." She is well into the early months of 1969 when she makes notes about western country ("sage brush—tumbleweed & bunch grass grew out across the prairie") and then an isolated entry: "As though Emily Dickinson had married her young minister & gone to the Wilderness with him. Must read Emily tonight." It is early May 1969, when Mother is "Hunting subjects for Easter Sermon." She quotes several passages from the Bible. Two weeks later she is quoting long passages from Flannery O'Connor's essay on her own writing. The quotations Mother copies describe the value for O'Connor of using violence:

> *"I have found that violence is strangely capable of returning my characters to reality and preparing them to accept their moment of grace.—almost nothing else will do the work. This idea that reality is something to which we must be returned at considerable cost is one which is seldom understood by the casual reader, but it is one which is implicit in the Christian view of the world.*
>
> *(Some writers) always assumed that violence is a bad thing and meant to be an end in itself. With serious writers violence is never an end in itself. It is the extreme situation that best reveals what we are essentially and I believe there are times when writers are more interested in what we are essentially than in the tenor of our daily lives."*

In this journal, Mother fills nine pages with quotations from O'Connor's essay. At one point she underlines, "[N]othing in this world lends itself to quick evaporation so much as religious concern."

My hunch is that in spending this amount of time with O'Connor's use of violence and religion in her novels, Mother had found a way of managing what had seemed insoluble in her own novel. The next journal entry, a month later, is Harriet's bitter response to the Easter sermon Mark has given. It will have the same wording in the finished novel. Three days later, at the end of June, she quotes from Deuteronomy: "Then we turned, & took our journey into the Wilderness." It is as if Mother could turn to her novel at this point and complete it.

Mother does not write in the journal for the next five months, and then it is to record that she had sent off the manuscript the week before (October 25, 1969) to her editor, Dan Wickenden. She goes on to describe her state of mind while she is waiting to hear:

> There have been so many times when I despaired of finishing it, the actual typed manuscript is a triumph, for all its weaknesses. I think it is original in the vehicle used to explore the difficulty of communication—and absorbing once you start. Could they turn it down? Will the Church interludes stop them? I am in limbo waiting—but still it is something at 64 to be waiting to hear about a novel. I hope they take it. But I dread going out to the mailbox for the letter that I think will come this week.

The journal continues for the next seven days with brief daily entries, each recording that there has been "no word yet." Her comments on the novel while she waits go from "fear of total dismissal" to "what can the delay mean?" At one point, after describing the day as "dreary" and filled with her "feckless" activities around the house, she writes: "I keep dipping into the ms. for reassurance but do not know that I can judge. Still it is no ordinary tale." On November 10 she does receive word and records it:

> But the letter came—from Dan and they are taking the ms. What a relief. I hardly breathed as I opened it. He

finds it "fascinating & original" . . . and thinks Mark the "most impressive feat of characterization really, the most complex & subtle"—at the end he calls it "a good book."—I should be content—at least, I am grateful. It changes the whole color of my living and gives me justification for my retirement & leisure. Life is good to me.

In these later years when Mother talked about her writing with my brothers and me, I became used to her reception of such good news. It always ranged from elation to dissatisfaction. If we expressed our delight for her, she was quick to respond glumly that it had only been called "a good book."

In December, Mother complains in the journal that she hasn't heard anything more about the novel for a month. She records that she gave a sherry party and enjoyed "the door opening & closing to friends & the house full of candlelight & talk." Toward the end of December, after describing a few story ideas that have occurred to her and quoting from reviews of new books in the *New York Times,* she writes that she feels "the first urge toward writing I have felt since I sent the ms. off; the blessed bubbling of the incorrigible spring." It is early February 1970 when she writes: "Got the revised version off yesterday. A bad time. Got frantic before I was through. I must systematically work at learning to work differently—calmly keeping an inner quietude of mind." Often in these years I was disheartened by Mother's angry distaste for her way of working or for the difficulty she felt she had in accomplishing something. At first I suffered for her each time she complained about her inadequacies, but gradually I listened to her with a kind of indifference. Didn't I have to struggle with the way I managed to accomplish something? Didn't others? Why should she be exempt? It was ungracious of me, but I came to feel it was not necessary for me to anguish for her each time—partly because she would seem to recover so quickly.

By March 1970, Mother has seven months to wait for the publication of *If a Lion Could Talk.* The next entries in the journal for three pages describe her activities—giving a dinner, delighting in the spring season, and regretting her "confused inefficiency." She says of herself: "Came on a quotation, I think from Sir Thomas Browne, that Ferd copied out. His small neat handwriting makes my heart leap. 'Study then the Dominion of thyself and quiet *thine own commotions.*'" She has underlined Browne's last three words, and adds later of herself, "And that I shall labor to do." She mentions that she sent off her version of "the jacket blurb—certainly more interesting than Dan's. I wonder what he really thinks of me either as a writer or a person. And whether he will use my blurb."

In these same months Mother refers to a speech she has been writing, saying to herself that she "must type it on cards & run thru it every day till I go." By May 4 she notes that she is back at Wells College to give the speech, "and it is more thrilling than I had expected . . . and I reach back to 1955 when I first learned how to live alone. My spirit lifted this morning and embraced this beautiful village and the lake. In a way I had pushed it from me." She continues in the next paragraph to describe her story idea, which will become her thirteenth novel, *A Piece of the World,* published two years later:

> And with the rise in spirits comes the repetition in my mind, though more strongly, of an idea for a child's story—about Serpentine Rock. A boy coming to visit his grandmother tries to remember something from his last visit (when he was taken to a picnic by the rock), can't quite remember, only the feeling—yet some sense of secrecy held him from asking about it. Something odd—desire to protect it.

But the next day she writes that she didn't give her speech because the convocation was canceled; the students called a strike to protest the college president going to Cambodia. She reads the speech later in the evening to a group of her former colleagues and declares it a *"terrific anticlimax. . . .* I think I mind that students who supposedly wanted me to speak didn't care enough to put off the strike till the next day. . . . And maybe I cared too much about the personal triumph it would have been for me and better that I didn't have it." She concludes that she "was happy to leave the next morning. Suddenly I wanted no more of Aurora. . . . Put the speech away with all the others and forget it—enjoy the irony—and get to work."

Back in Grafton, Mother makes another note in the journal for the story she now calls "The Rock": "Have the girl meet a geologist who tells her it was dropped by the glacier and a strange woman who is sitting there being the rock. Each contact sets off a discovery. Out of it comes her own strength." But by July Mother is uncomfortable with the domestic arrangement she calls "the confines of this threesome—I have claustrophobia and am tempted to take off for the Tupa." She is referring to her summer visits from her sister and brother-in-law. She continues:

> *Perhaps my state of desperation is due to getting off the page proofs yesterday and feeling let down—instead of thankful that the idea ever got that far. The only surcease is to hie myself out to this ice house & write—even though what I write is nothing. Maybe something will come out of it. Managed a couple of pages on The Rock.*

The ice house is the small one-room building set apart from the main house where blocks of ice were once stored. My grandfather had opened the back of it with a large window so it was filled with the sound of the Saxtons River running directly below it. Everyone in the family thought of it as Mother's writing place, her refuge.

However, by September 1 she notes that she "got thru all that without too much irritation showing and have come away to the Tupa after all, because George & Janet really seemed to want me to come." She enjoyed the time there with my brother and his wife, she writes in the journal. The journal shows quotations from her reading and one entry for "The Rock." By mid-September she writes again from Grafton:

> *Tense as a cat waiting for the novel to come out. Tonight it seems too religious to be interesting—a sick flat sense lies at the back of my mind. How could I feel triumphant about it and then so hopeless? . . . V. Woolf didn't go thru any worse tortures than I do. Yet I hope I am wrong.*

She turns to noting who she saw and talked with, describes her friend coming to help her clean the house, then writes, "The days go over my head without shape or any work done . . . yet I think the concept of the novel *is* beautiful whatever the details." September 30, 1970, is the announced publication date. Mother describes it in this way:

> And then the date of the novel's official appearance marked by the listing in the New York Times *in the way I mind—Event in life of a missionary to Indians of Upper Missouri—and in the evening I took Helen & the Piels to Windham Hill. But it is published whatever. Now let me see if I can as H. James says—"live in the world of creation—to get into it & stay in it—to frequent it and haunt it—to think intently & fruitfully . . . this is the only thing."*

A week later Mother has what she calls "a listless, apologetic note" from Dan Wickenden, "sorry he forgot the date the novel 'came out,'" promising an ad toward the end of the month, and informing her that "3,003 copies sold by that date." She also quotes Wickenden saying, "Not too bad for a recessive year." After several journal pages paraphrasing an article on western civilization, she writes on October 29, "DAMNING & PATRONIZING descriptions of novel in both PW [*Publisher's Weekly*] & *Kirkus Review*. And NO reviews." She notes "a few people . . . find it good"—Bud Guthrie, Helen Taylor, and my brother George and I. It must have been especially important to her to have Helen Taylor's approval.

In mid-November, Mother is in Philadelphia where George and his wife are living. Her entry in the journal is very like the long-distance phone calls I used to have with her in those days:

> On a gray Philadelphia afternoon I sit in George & Janet's house in the blessed interval when the children are sleeping. This is a long week. I am getting better at it, but what if I had to make my living doing this! or had to live in any of the children's homes, warm & pleasant as they are! Yet the children are very bright & appealing and I am learn-

ing to forget my dreadful & limiting self-absorption oc-
casionally so that I see them. Perhaps it is as good as
any place to be in this horrible aftermath of the novel. It
seems clear that it is going to be a failure in every way but
some small triumph of my own in completing & publish-
ing it. It has met with a complete blank.

Back in Grafton, Mother records that her "delicate balance has been righted again—I don't know why or how. I must have some unusually strong WILL to survive so that I can't sink utterly into despair. The answer of course & always—work."

Long quotes from Enid Bagnold's *Chalk Garden* follow, and midway in them, as Bagnold describes minutely her husband's moment of dying, Mother has copied a passage that will engage her for the next long novel she is thinking about: "But I can't belittle the inventions of life even if one of them is death. It's hard to surpass this brilliance we live in." When Mother told me, perhaps five years later, that she thought of naming her new novel "The Inventions of Life," I was intrigued. But her idea of the novel moved away from that possibility to "The Orange Tree," a novel that remains unpublished. Still, she was in a working state of mind, and she wrote on New Year's Day of 1971:

12:10—a new year. I've talked to all the children & drunk
to Ferd, my very beloved. . . . And tomorrow I must at
least attempt to write again. Every sign shows me I am
too old yet, yet—to be worth my salt I must keep to a stern
schedule of work for work's sake. After being up so late &
so much sherry I may write drivel but still—. A new
year's beginning is a precious thing. My love to life! How
schmaltzy can you be? No matter.

The next day Mother writes in the journal that she "took up the story of Serpentine Rock, still not knowing where I am going with it, but wrote 300 words on it and shall hold myself to it every day, now until it is finished or I have to abandon it." Most of the few entries for January are quotes from a writer named Wechsberg. She underlines one statement: "Writers have to be tough & resilient to function. They cannot afford self-pity." By the end of the month, she reacts fiercely to what she sees as having been a lack of interest in *If a Lion Could Talk:*

> *The debacle of the novel is complete. In my worst night-mares I never thought of anything so bad. . . . But I am in danger of letting the reception of it turn to bitterness & self-pity. . . . My only hope is to work. This story of ser-pentine is too small a thing, but I must at least finish it. I could so easily stop writing altogether.*

She seems to have been reading reviews of other novels just out, one of which she has read and not found "remarkable" in spite of its favorable reception. At the end of this entry she reminds herself of Wechsberg's comment on self-pity.

Among the quotations that fill the next pages of the journal are several from Thomas Mann on his own difficulties in writing. "Without work," he writes, "I wouldn't know how to live." Following this quotation Mother writes: "How universal is the experience of writing from the great ones like Tho. Mann & H. James & Woolf to my own. Once committed to writing—writing is one's life—but it makes for desperation just now when nothing goes ahead." Her work on "this story of serpentine rock" must have been going ahead in the next month, however, because by early March she calls it "The Erratic Boulder," but notes that it "folded on me today."

> *I have not accomplished a sentence or anything else all day. Only tonight I set down a few incidents to try to get going again. Tomorrow . . . I will tackle the first as an as-signment and not stop until it is done—then the next—and* believe *that something will emerge from it. But it is hard hard going.*

Mother's journal entries continue, noting "feckless" days in which she accomplishes no writing, and sleepless nights, one in which she is "up to roam in the moonlit house between four &

five." In another entry she responds to a quotation from Marianne Moore about the writer needing to objectify "what is indispensable to one's happiness to express." Mother writes: "And in a sense that is true about this child's story of Serpentine. Its *thereness*—its alien origin, its secrecy now *are* in my mind." This journal ends in early April 1971 with Mother considering whether or not to accept an offer to teach at nearby Castleton College in Vermont for the following academic year. She is afraid that she would regret passing it up but questions whether her health can sustain her in such an increase of work. She will be sixty-six on her approaching birthday.

Mother begins a new journal a week later, on April 15, with a quotation from Loren Eiseley's *Unexpected Universe.* It is her only entry until the following October, when she explains her long silence: "I had no urge to write from April thru the time at the Tupa with all the family, and the month of August with Peg & Homer here—until now in October." All of us had gathered at the cabin in Montana for a family reunion that summer of 1971—for Mother's pleasure, we thought. But the small clearing was clamorous with so many of us—my two brothers and their wives, my husband and I, and six children ranging in age from one to ten years. We came and went in the two months that Mother was there, but she had us all at once for almost a week. We young parents thought Mother would enjoy her grandchildren about her immensely, but we saw that trying to keep us all orderly wore on her.

She had brought with her to the cabin a finished version of her juvenile novel of the Serpentine Rock, which she had apparently not sent yet to her publisher. She gave it to my ten-year-old son, Matthew, to read. I remember him lying in his uncle's hammock on a summer afternoon reading the manuscript pages. He was completely absorbed in it as the other children, his sister and four girl cousins, swarmed around him, and that pleased Mother.

Back in Grafton in the fall, Mother makes her first written mention of having a grandchild: "There is now a Paul Christopher Schemm in the world to carry on the sturdy and beloved name— and six others to carry on the strengths and weaknesses in their personalities—all of Ferd's branch and mine." Coming upon this passage in Mother's journal, I was startled, as I have been all my life, to discover what was important to her. Her priority struck me as archaic, or baronial! Her first grandchild "in the world," my son, had not merited such a written welcome because his last name was not the family name? Was this why there had been no mention in her journals of the later arrivals of her first five granddaughters whom she assumed would take other names? But after a little fuming, I realized that I was being absurd. The following spring, she recorded the birth of "George and Janet's third child—Joanna Morgan Schemm." And added, to my relief, "I am rich with eight grandchildren." Perhaps it was this realization which prompted her dedication of the juvenile novel published as *A Piece of the World:* "For my eight grands, especially Matthew," because Matthew had been the first youngster to read the story. I know that we as Mother's grown children were happy about the dedication, but a little surprised.

By October, waiting to hear from the children's editor, Margaret K. McElderry, at Atheneum Press, Mother writes in her journal in a familiar pattern: thoughts about where she is in her life; quotations from Lionel Trilling's criticism; and possible beginnings for "the new novel." On October 25, she writes:

> *Forty-four years ago was my wedding day! Always I walk about with a sense of wonder & richness & great thanksgiving that Ferd loved me. It has made all the difference in the world. Suddenly I wonder if I should try to write about that—of how marriage* CAN *make over a woman. Though I wasn't going to write about married people again. A coming of age thru marriage & love as I did? or at least came a ways.*

She has made no mention of having begun the teaching year at Castleton College, but she begins the next important entry on November 17, 1971, from that context: "In the study with all the preparation for tomorrow still ahead of me, but I must record a prayer answered—Margaret McElderry at Atheneum took my Erratic Boulder—(but wants to change the title). And now my mind is free to move in writing patterns. Hallelujah!"

The next journal pages continue as before with no mention of the upcoming publication of her novel. In mid-December her reading of Marya Mannes prompts a personal comment. "[She] speaks of giving up her weekly program on the radio network for the exact reason I am giving up Castleton," and Mother quotes Mannes: "I had found that the weekly program had become a daily absorption at the expense of thinking & writing." Aside from the time teaching is taking, Mother is feeling distressed about not doing any writing. She writes, "When I have no novel in mind I am aimless."

In January 1972, Mother is discussing illustrations for *A Piece of the World* with a Vermont artist, Christine Price, a woman who will become Mother's friend in a reserved Vermont way. Mother writes of Price's acceptance:

> *She showed, I thought, a muted kind of enthusiasm. This was a hunch to mention her—really don't know how well she can draw these children—most of her work has been illustrating folk tales, but one has to accept a "leading." One thing she said shocked me—she has never drawn Vt. before!! How could you live here & not?*

Later, Mother writes that she has sent Price "a piece of the rock & pictures of it before the trees grew up to hide it—and a poem of Kathleen Raines. I hope they will excite her a bit—that she'll do something great and really suggest the mystery of the rock hidden in the woods."

The journal fills in the next few months with Mother's thoughts veering from writing another children's book to a collection of short stories, each story based on one of the seven deadly sins. Again she is also quoting from book reviews. After quoting Joyce Carol Oates's review of a book by Alvarez on the attraction of suicide for intellectuals, Mother stops to comment, "Suicide has never occurred to me. Does that imply shallowness?" She has not been feeling well, but by April she is vacationing with my father's brother and his wife on the island of Little Cumberland in Georgia and recovering her spirits. She writes: "It is a cloudy sultry day but birds chirp & twitter in the lovely stillness. The gray beard moss blows softly. It is very green, very soft & peaceful. I have recovered my health, and the flu is finally gone. I am grateful to be & feel well." On her last day of the spring vacation, she thinks of her stay as "lovely & unique . . . coming out on the beach—those endless stretches of hard white sand—even cutting my toe on an oyster bed while hunting for clams—so different from anything I've ever done—a new dimension."

Back in Grafton, near the end of April, Mother's entries in the journal are enthusiastic about what she next proposes to write:

> Let me write quickly, exuberantly, while my mind feels alive. I have a whole idea for a book—a collection of short sketches—stories—that will tie together because they are all about the same village & I think it is viable because in it ideas I have vaguely entertained all winter come together. Possession is the underlying & central theme. About houses in a village such as this & their owners. Quick, while I feel it fresh within me.

One after another she sketches seven possible stories. At the end of these sketches, she notes to herself, "At least I have a theme & an assignment for a summer of work ready." In the next years she would complete these stories, try them separately with her agent, but have no luck in getting them printed. The finished collection, "Houses," remains with her papers.

Mother records that on May 2 she turned sixty-seven and "neglected to make an entry" because my brother Christopher and his family had come to celebrate with her. She adds, "No time now to think about it—just live the day & love it. Live with enough intensity to make excitement for oneself. And always a sense of the incredible goodness of life to me—far beyond my deserts." I quote her at this moment because we children rarely saw her reveal these high moods of self-confidence. Two weeks later in the journal, she describes her state of "deterioration" because she is not getting to work at her writing. And it was usually this discouraged state Mother would describe to me when she called on the phone.

Mother continues to include quotations in the journal: from James Agee, Eleanor Roosevelt, her friend Janet Schroeder's commonplace book, John Gardner on Updike. Then she describes the funeral of her distant cousin Amy Davis, who "had spent all her 89 years in Grafton! . . . She looked noble up there with the flowers where she had so often arranged maidenhair & flowers herself. Some faint echoes of her tart voice lingered." Amy Davis was a person of the village Mother had characterized in an essay she had written when she, Mother, was "20 or so"—as hurrying along at dusk with gathered flowers in her arms.

On July 20, 1972, Mother writes that "the first copy of *A Piece of the World* is here and it is a handsome little book with Christine's drawings. I hope so that it does creditably for McElderry's list—AND for me. I could do with a bit of success in the book line." It will be September 8, 1972, when she next mentions the novel: "The day *A Piece of the World* was officially published. My chief feeling is gratitude that it got itself written & was published. A kind of miracle after the debacle of The Lion novel." Mother's entry continues, describing a dinner she had that evening with one of her closest Grafton friends, Helen Evans. A retired professor from Sarah Lawrence College, Miss Evans was a devoted fan of Mother's novels, and this evening she listened with such interest to Mother's ideas for the short stories she planned next that, Mother writes, "I caught fire again myself . . . and Helen did it—Oh people—wonderful, wonderful people." Christine Price is of importance to Mother, too, at this time. Miss Price comes for a visit which Mother describes with great pleasure, saying they walked to the Serpentine Rock and picnicked there: "It must have been remarkable for Christine to see how exact her drawings of the rock were. I felt the presence of the rock acutely." The next day they walk to another favorite spot of Mother's in the narrow Vermont valley, and Mother's description of Miss Price continues: "She is so creative, so attuned to nature she refreshed my mind whereas most guests leave me weary. Perhaps the best return of *A Piece of the World* is coming to know Christine, who is such a rare spirit."

For the next two months Mother writes intermittently in the journal about books she is reading and about the first snowstorm with a tone of contentment. But the first week of November 1972, she records her disappointment at the critical reception of *A Piece of the World:*

> *And now the news is in & this book, too, has failed. The* PW *calls the divorce, which precipitates Calder's [the book's main character] coming to Vt. in the first place, "irrelevant," says the children are frustrated by the engineer who splits the rock, and pronounces both writing & illustrations pedestrian. It could hardly have been more thoroughly tunked. Today's Children's book section of the* Times *ignores it completely. All this in my 68th year should stop me, but it doesn't quite.*

There was a written notice in the Grafton newspaper on the day of the book's publication. And with it a photograph of Mother smiling broadly. The brief article describes Mother's literary achievements and then lists her connections to the area as "a descendant of the Walker family of Windham County for which 'Walker Bridge' was named . . . and Walker School, one of the original little red schoolhouses of the Grafton Village." Although Mother does not mention it in her journal, this connection endeared her book to the local schoolteacher, who had her students read it. Mother honored the children's request that she take them to Serpentine Rock, and the photographs she saved show her surrounded by the children in front of the school and then climbing down from the Rock.

The next entries in the journal veer between fears Mother is experiencing about dizziness, crises like putting on a dinner for six when the electrical power goes out, and her need to take down more quotations. She is particularly interested in John Updike's newly published short stories. "Makes me itch to write some of my own—phrases dart into my mind," Mother writes. The next journal pages alternate between describing one of her possible characters in a setting and quoting lines of Updike's she calls "provocative." On a chapter of Virginia Woolf's biography, Mother comments: "Reading her Journal makes me more willing to accept (how pompous that sounds) one's own life exactly as it is. . . . She speaks of being visited by the spirit of delight & that I know, too." Mother gives her own examples: "A flock of yellow grosbeaks in the road when I was taking my bath—the thunderous sky but at the same time lemon yellow light—waking from a nap & seeing a streak of light on Ferd's face in his photograph."

In the next pages of this journal Mother will quote from Milton, Zen Buddhist teachings, letters from friends and former students. She will question her way of accomplishing little in her writing: "I am always copying these things about craftsmanship & working, then I work at half intensity or don't work, and the result is as might be expected." She turns down invitations to vacation spots because she wants to "stay put and write." The journal takes her through the end of 1972, all of 1973, and to May of 1974 without any further mention of *A Piece of the World.* She was already concentrating on the collection of short stories with the working title of "Houses."

In *A Piece of the World,* Calder's summer visit to her grandmother in Vermont is precipitated by her parents' divorce. I knew that Mother's major feeling about divorce was one of distaste—not in a novel but in her family. When David Hansen and I divorced in 1974, Mother was shocked mainly because, she said, I hadn't confided in her first. But in the months ahead, she was supportive of me, deciding that she had seen it coming.

My husband and I had been teaching literature at the University of California at Riverside. I left California in 1973 and returned to Montana with my two children. Matthew was twelve, and Melissa was nine. Because they had spent summers at the cabin since they were very young, they were glad to make their new home in Montana. I began teaching part time at the University of Montana in Missoula in the fall of 1973. There were old friendships to renew with people in the English Department whom I had known when I taught there in 1954 and 1955. The children became comfortable in the house we found and in their schools, slowly reconciling themselves to their father's absence.

In 1972, George had returned to Montana to practice neurosurgery in Great Falls, 165 miles over the mountains from Missoula.

That gave my children close family living nearby. After that, Mother made yearly visits to both our homes, frequently surprised I think to find two of her three children and their families living back in Montana.

In the summer of 1974, I married the poet Richard Hugo, director of the creative writing program at the University of Montana—with my children's enthusiastic approval. He became a good friend to them and was proud of having stepchildren. My brothers and their families became his good friends, too, and we had memorable gatherings in the next years. Mother responded to Dick gradually at first and then came to accept him warmly. She was pleased and intrigued that he was nationally known for his poetry, but there was a moment when she said to me in a mystified tone of voice, "Why would you write poems when you could write novels?"

For the next twelve years Mother continued living in Grafton. She wrote two versions of a short novel about her dog being stolen and held by a ring of dog thieves in New York State while she was teaching there. These versions were turned down because the editor at Atheneum felt it was an adult story rather than a children's book. She went on to finish the collection of short stories, "Houses." After that, the novel she had thought about for a good number of years, "The Orange Tree," became her chief interest. "The Orange Tree" remains in several versions, unpublished.

Mother continues writing in her later journals in these years, often leaving them unfinished and starting a new one after a stretch of several months, sometimes several years. In October 1975, she has been reading and quoting from *The Well of Loneliness*, thinking about "The Orange Tree": "Somebody says to heroine of *The Well of Loneliness*—'You're not working and yet work's your only weapon.' And the same I can say to myself—against age." Aging haunts Mother, chiefly because she feels it is detracting from her energy to write. And while she is "making overtures" to a new agent, she writes this assessment of her worth: "However, at 70 I can't seem a promising property to anyone. And all this when I'm not getting ahead with my novel!" By December she has a new agent in David Stewart Hall, and she notes, "I actually feel stimulated to work rather than merely desperate."

In late January 1976, Mother writes: "Finished Transcendental Meditation course yesterday—don't know that I ever 'transcend' but I'm glad to have taken it. Amazing to think I shall meditate twice a day for the rest of my life." The journal reveals that she tries to write steadily but is not always pleased with the two or three pages she manages in a day. In late May she writes:

> *I have no faith in myself any longer because of my procrastination and self-indulgence and pure laziness. . . . Tonight I wrote a couple of pages. I am unsure of it—even of the idea, but the only way to decide whether it is worth doing is to* DO *it—to get it down. But I must stay with it* DAILY *to keep my mind working on it.*

The summer ahead is busy with family and visitors, and the journal contains only one comment. She is musing about the young woman character in "The Orange Tree": "Does the girl—Olive— get a job? What kind of a job can she get?—could it be in a museum? Is my trouble that I feel a need to know too much about the details of a character's life?" But four months later Mother mentions that she is working on "the last section of my novel" and by the following March that she has "brought the novel of Paulo and Tiresa to an end." She notes that she has sent it to Helen Taylor "to have her professional judgment on it. . . . I feel a lack in it—of style, of radiance, and BEAUTY. Last night I was utterly discouraged. . . . Still it is good to have that 360-page opus that has been on my mind for two years." The novel was turned down by Atheneum in August and by Little, Brown and Company in November. But Mother writes, "Yet still I believe it will find a place." It is a year later when Mother turns to her journal again. As she describes putting away the novel in her study, she adds, "Except for the waste of time and hope and energy and loss of faith of everyone in my ever publishing another I almost don't care that they didn't take it." She has returned to the short stories that she sees as a collection called "Houses," a series linked by a realtor who observes his buyers and their reasons for choosing to live in old houses in a small village—like Grafton. In November 1980, Mother observes, "I'm writing for my life now."

Mother's journal ended with that comment, only a third of the journal written in. She began keeping a commonplace journal in early May 1981 when she had turned seventy-six. These were quotations from writers, reviews, and early letters from her mentors that she wanted to remember. A good number covered discussions of aging and ways of regarding it. There were no notes on any writing that she might have been doing. The last quotation is from Robert Frost: "What to make of a diminished thing."

At this time in my own life I had two terrible losses. My husband, Richard Hugo, became ill with leukemia in September 1982 and died a month later. He was vigorously pursing his work that fall: judging the Yale Series of Younger Poets for the sixth year, planning his Collected Poems at W. W. Norton, and beginning the teaching year at the university. He was about to turn fifty-eight. The children and I kept wondering how this would be, living without him after eight wonderful years. Melissa determined to finish her last year of high school "for Dick's sake." Matthew, just graduated from the university, completed his work in oral histories for the Montana Historical Society and traveled in Europe for four months as Dick and I had encouraged him to do for a graduation present. I found a job teaching composition and literature at Northern Montana College in Havre for the fall of 1983.

We might have made it except for the unbearable loss that occurred next. Matthew became ill, and in November 1983 he was diagnosed with Burkett's lymphoma. After six months of treatment at the University of Washington hospital in Seattle, we were told that nothing more could be done. Matthew came home to die in April 1984. He had just turned twenty-three and felt a wrenching disbelief that he couldn't continue with all he had planned to do in his life. Melissa felt betrayed by the life she saw before her without her brother.

I include these sorrows in this book that belongs to Mother because they inform all my years since. I think this was an inconceivable situation that she could not quite touch in her mind. But I was consumed with bitterness and couldn't bear her refrain of "How do you stand it?" I survived by working on the books Dick and Matthew hadn't been able to finish and on the projects they had cared about. I wanted Mother to think of them in these terms, but she didn't express any interest in doing so. She pitied me, I know, but I would see in her next years that she had to concentrate on trying to write and staying well enough to maintain a style of living that she had perfected.

Mother's health failed rapidly in 1986, and she suffered a stroke in May of that year. But she soon began a good recovery. I went east then and persuaded her to move out to Montana; she admitted that she didn't feel up to keeping the Grafton house going. Her reluctance to make the move gave way to the adventure she would make of the move. That included choosing an apartment a mile from my house in Missoula, Montana, and then having all her treasured pieces of furniture moved to Montana. When she had moved in, she seemed herself again; she went to work to change things in the apartment that dissatisfied her until she reproduced on a smaller scale the look of her Vermont house. She takes up her journal in September 1986:

> *So—I'm settled in. It's very comfortable. I'm learning to look above the garages at the well-grazed hill out the end window. Now can I get back to writing here? and not let the days go by in feckless frittering. Time will tell. And can I keep this journal? I'm trying it again. It used to be so easy.*

Two days later Mother writes that she has a new possible title for "my revised novel," and adds, "Anyway, it's a stirring of the imagination."

A friend had sent her an article, "Late Great Works," from which she quotes: "Late work of major creative artists is often unprecedented, problematic, and, above all, fearless." She follows this quote with one of Kenneth Clark's, also on the subject of "very old artists," and responds from her own point of view: "I'm not a 'major artist,' Heaven knows, but perhaps I still have something, have learned a little, experienced something that I can give if I only work hard enough. Exhilarating to read the article anyway as I begin a new life here." On the same journal page she quotes from an advertisement for a new play, *Roza:* "What will survive of us is love." From this she turns to the main character of the novel that she wants to revise: "That's what is true of Tiresa so that her plotting, conniving, using another life are dwarfed by her love. Which is not to justify but to understand, for in her effort she also sacrifices herself." This description seems at the heart of the unfinished novel, "The Orange Tree," in each of its three versions that I have read.

The considerable writing community in Missoula welcomed her, many of them having read *Winter Wheat.* She was startled by this, at first, but then mingled with these younger writers easily at parties and readings. A year following her arrival, she was invited to give a reading in Helena. In January 1988, she read from *The Body of a Young Man* for a weekly reading series put on by the University of Montana graduate writing program. She writes that she enjoyed doing it when she "got going," but didn't know "how it really went." Her usual complaint was that she "felt flat" afterward. I wasn't in town for that reading to give her the reassurance that she said she needed.

During the years that Mother lived in Missoula, Melissa was in her early twenties and often visited Mother with me. She thought "Gran was stylish, not grandmotherly." Melissa had a clear memory of an afternoon when Mother brought a package of singly wrapped slices of processed cheese from the kitchen and dropped it in my lap. She didn't want it, she said; I should take it. She knew it would be useful at my house. I said no, thank you, but I preferred cheese in a block, and I passed it back to her. Mother slapped the package down in front of me. I slipped out a slice and tossed it in her direction. When Melissa gasped, Mother turned to her and said, "Shocking behavior, isn't it?" Then she tossed the remaining slices around the room with "a wicked smile," Melissa said. We were all shocked into helpless laughter. Mother declared to Melissa that she thought she had given a splendid performance.

In the winter of 1988, Mother writes that she "actually did a little work on the opus": "The first person won't work for this novel.

It's too limiting and there is too much conversation. It seems artificial. Now I'll chuck the twenty odd pages I've changed into the first person and go back to the third person, but use Tiresa as the 'central consciousness' as H. James calls it." In March she alternates between working, wishing spring would come, and feeling fatigued too often. "I feel useless," she writes. By April she feels she has accomplished little, "but life's been pleasant." And then she adds, "Ferd encouraged me. And now I feel great need of him as I try to write." I drove Mother to the cabin in May for her birthday. She writes that it was cold with lots of snow "but with a fire in the stove it was snug." In the morning—her eighty-fourth birthday—she notes "the sound of rain falling on the roof like a blessing."

Mother's next year was one of extremes. She flew to Florida to see her sister in a nursing home and was devastated by her condition, continued her trip to Wells College to see her former colleagues but was saddened by it, and finally visited Grafton: "I marvel that I lived there so long. Have to think about it a while to know how I felt. . . . Grafton doesn't belong to me anymore I feel and that is right enough." Her first journal entry on her return expressed her gladness to be back in her apartment in Montana, where she felt relaxed. "Now to order my life and do over that novel—if I only can," she wrote, but she had trouble doing that because she began to have bad spells of extended weakness and confusion.

In May 1990, Mother and I went again to the cabin for her birthday. She recorded it in the journal, the last entry she would write:

> *A whole year later—a year in which Peg [her older sister] died and is blessedly free from loneliness and limitation and suffering & I have known real threatening illness myself & at first an intimidating perspective—and now we are back at this beloved tupa, not long before my* EIGHTY-FIFTH *birthday. I am full of gratitude for all this place has witnessed—all it means to all of us. I shall take a new lease on life here.*

But in late May Mother had more difficulties, and her physician in Missoula advised my brothers and me that Mother would be safer living in a retirement home. We found it very difficult to ask her about this. She was adamant that she didn't want to live in one of our homes and that she wanted her own surroundings. I think we each understood that she did care about us; it was just that she felt she would be freer to write and to learn to live with her increasing difficulties without their being observed.

By the end of the summer of 1990 we were able to convince Mother that George and Janet could find a pleasant place near them in Oregon for her to live. And they did—a retirement center ten minutes from their home. She chose a one-room apartment with bath into which she fitted the essential pieces of her furniture in muted red upholstery and dark cherry woods—the same colors we had always known in her homes. She had her desk by a window that looked out on a garden, the bed she had had since her marriage to my father, her chest of drawers, two bookcases, her cherished dodecagon table topped with a large brass lamp, a small winged chair we had known since our childhood, and finally her tall gray metal filing cabinet with her manuscripts. Janet worked tenaciously with her to bring this about until a moment came when Mother felt herself in charge of her life again.

What amazed us was that Mother slowly decided she had a role in the retirement center. She decided which of the other residents were interesting to know and talk with and which of the staff were helpful to befriend. I think she felt obliged to maintain a position she had always embraced: She dressed meticulously, handsomely at first, and befriended her contemporaries whom she saw weakening. The staff saw her as a gracious, warm woman. She came to make the most of her situation, although she often wryly expressed her sense of confinement to us. Her main dissatisfaction with the retirement center was that she wasn't able to get any writing done because she didn't feel well enough to write.

During the six years that Mother lived in the retirement center, she was made a part of all George and Janet's family gatherings and the comings and goings of their four grown daughters. She went on excursions with them, commented on her granddaughters' ways of dressing—in a maddeningly familiar way to all of us— and exacted assistance from one or the other of the family on exhausting shopping trips. I know that she felt comforted by being able to express her health concerns to George when he came by the center in the afternoon from the hospital where he worked. They would have a glass of sherry together, and she would speak proudly of her doctor son afterward at her group dining table, then again proudly disclose that her youngest son was a doctor, too.

Because the reprinting of Mother's novels by the University of Nebraska Press had begun in 1992, a new interest in reading her work grew rapidly soon after she had settled in Oregon. George and Janet took her to readings held in Portland bookstores, one where her presence was acknowledged by the writer William Kittredge, who gave the reading. He had met Mother in Missoula when she and I attended readings and parties, and he spoke of her as an important novelist, especially valued for her writing in Montana. This moment must have pleased her. But, as was her way, she lightly disparaged the honor.

In 1994, Molly Gloss, author of *Jump Off Creek,* requested an interview with Mother for *The Burnside Reader,* published by Powell's City of Books in Portland, Oregon. Janet Schemm arranged this meeting and especially enjoyed Gloss's opening paragraph when the interview was published in the spring of 1995:

> *Mildred Walker had dressed to meet me, in a trim suit of Black Watch plaid, a chambray shirt, navy hose and shoes, bright green scarf and earrings. Later, when she strips off the earrings—"I believe I've dazzled you long enough with my finery"—the long lobes of her ears are bright pink where they've been crimped. Her white hair is pinned softly at the top of her head and escapes the pins in a wispy corona. She is slender, a little stooped, and I imagine that she must be fragile—she is 89—so her handshake is unexpected and reassuring, a grasp as firm, as forceful, as a man's. Maples standing beyond the windows are flame red, and she tells me that she misses the fall palette of Montana, the vivid clear yellow of willows and aspens. Her voice is strong and clear. (41)*

This was certainly how our family saw Mother. One of a new generation of Mother's readers of the Nebraska reprints that were being published in the 1990s, Gloss describes what appeals to her:

> *One of the great strengths of her writing is in the careful detail, not only of place and scene but of feeling. These are books so minutely observed, so wise and watchful, so attentive to the small motions of the moment, that we are wholly drawn into the imagining, and we recognize and understand the familiar in what has been unknown, uncommon. (45)*

I'm sure that Mother was pleased with this description of her writing, but it remained a sore point with her that her novels hadn't gained her a wider literary reputation. When we were talking on the cabin porch a few years earlier, she had said suddenly, "Well, at least I can say that I published the same number of novels as Jane Austen."

Visiting in Portland in 1995, I felt a desolate emptiness in Mother because she could no longer write. I think she kept willing herself to overcome the series of small strokes that she had endured. But in that same year, Oliver, the grandson who had imagined a rousing story on Mother's behalf, told me of a long visit he had had with her at the retirement center. As they spoke, he said, "Her whole life seemed to be happening at the same time." He felt "her memories were keeping her company." He enjoyed remembering her anticipation of his taking her to have lunch with him, saying she just "hopped up" into his Bronco.

Mother died four years later in 1998 of a massive stroke just past her ninety-third birthday and was buried beside my father in the Schemm family plot in Saginaw, Michigan. We held a memorial service for her in Missoula, where she had become good friends with the Episcopal minister Steve Oreskovich and his wife. Mother's family members were present, including her three children, three of her grandchildren, and her one-year-old great-granddaughter. Friends she had made in Missoula in the four years she had lived there were also present.

Those last years when Mother couldn't manage to do the one thing that had informed her whole life, couldn't bring about the steady push to write that she described again and again in her journals, I felt her anguish and frustration painfully. But she wasn't willing to give up. The last time I talked to her in her apartment at the center, she made her way to her desk, sat down, and turned to me with a smile of shy triumph. She reached her hand to the keys of the familiar Smith-Corona typewriter on her desk and said, "You see, I'm teaching myself to type again."

Bibliographical Note

All quotations from Mildred Walker's works and their page numbers refer to the University of Nebraska Press Bison Books editions.

The principal materials referred to in this memoir, *Writing for Her Life: The Novelist Mildred Walker,* are located in the permanent collection of the American Heritage Center at the University of Wyoming in Laramie. They are listed under the name Mildred Walker Schemm.

From 1971 to 1981 Walker sent a manuscript or galley proof version of each of her thirteen novels and a hardcover edition of each to the American Heritage Center. She accompanied these with her handwritten notebooks for most of the novels, correspondence, original reviews, news clippings, and copies of translations into nine foreign languages.

In 1998, after Walker's death, her family found more materials she had packed away, including personal journals written from 1955 to 1989. These were added to her archival collection at the American Heritage Center in 2001, and papers and letters found more recently were added in 2003. Remaining in her daughter Ripley Hugo's possession are Walker's unpublished last novel and two unpublished collections of her short stories.

Index

Numbers in italics refer to photographic inserts; the first number is that of the text page preceding the insert, the second that of the illustration number of the insert.

journals (1968–1986) (*cont.*)
ill health, 267–68; on move to
Montana in 1986, 264; on retirement, 245; short stories mentioned in, 257, 258, 259, 260,
261; on sixty-seventh birthday,
258; on writing, 246–47, 254,
257, 258, 260–61, 262–63, 265–
67. *See also* diaries; journals;
journals (1955–1968)
Julius Caesar (Shakespeare), 130
Jump Off Creek (Gloss), 269
Junior League Magazine, 126, 136

Kates, George, 231
Kazin, Alfred, 218
Kelsey, W. K., 89
Kern, Dennis, 105
Kerr, Chester B., 90
Kierkegaard, Søren, 242, 243
Kirkus Review, 185, 194, 252
Kittredge, William, 194–95, 269
"The Knife" (Walker), 126–28, 131
Korn, Michael, 118

Ladies' Home Journal, 148
"Lasca" (Desprez), 117–18
Lawrence, D. H., 239
Le Gallienne, Eva, xxii, 24, 114, 115,
187, 241
Library Journal, 234
The Life of Sir William Osler, 49, 55
Light from Arcturus (Walker): ambitions of protagonist in, 63–64,
69, 70–71, 72–74; ending in 1933,
64; and feminist readers, 72–74;
first published, xxv; introduction by Mary Swander, 73; lives
and incidents based on, 63, 68–
69, 73; reprinted, 73; woman's
selfhood in, 73–74; writing device in, 72
Literary Guild of America: and *Dr.
Norton's Wife*, xxii, 49, 77, 84;

and *Winter Wheat*, xxii, 140,
149
*A Literary History of the American
West* (Lyon, ed.), 167–68
Little, Brown and Company, 263
Little Cumberland GA, 257–58
Liveright & Co., 48
Lojacano, Marie, 68, 69, 73
Lojacano, Salvatore, 68–69
London, 177–78
The Loon Feather (Fuller), 114, 115
Lottie. *See* Barton, Lottie
Loy, Myrna, 169

Major's Lady: Natawista (Walker),
178–79
Malamud, Bernard, 226
Mann, Thomas, 254
Mannes, Marya, 257
Manske, Winfried, 181, 183
Marquette MI, 68
Maurer, Alfred, 105
McElderry, Margaret, 40, 256, 259
McNamer, Deirdre, 27, 94, 133, 148,
167–68
McNamer, Megan, 194
McReynolds, Jean, 111, 112
Medical Meeting (Walker): and *Dr.
Norton's Wife*, 170; dust jacket
appraisal, 170; and Ferd's re-
search, 165–66; first published,
xxv; medical research in, 79, 80,
81–82, 82–83; notebook for, 166;
relationship between husband
and wife in, 164; translations of,
xxii, 175
The Merchant of Venice (Shake-
speare), 5
Merrifield, Harriet. *See* Walker, Harriet Merrifield (mother)
Merrifield, Oscar, 11
Michigan: novels set in, xxii–xxiv,
63. See also *The Brewers' Big
Horses*; *Dr. Norton's Wife*; *Fireweed*; *Light from Arcturus*